ADORNO ON NATURE

ADORNO ON NATURE

DEBORAH COOK

ACUMEN

First published in 2011 by Acumen

Acumen Publishing Limited
4 Saddler Street
Durham
DH1 3NP
www.acumenpublishing.co.uk

ISBN: 978-1-84465-255-6 (hardcover)
ISBN: 978-1-84465-262-4 (paperback)

British Library Cataloguing-in-Publication Data
A catalogue record for this book is available
from the British Library.

Printed in the UK by the MPG Books Group.

CONTENTS

ACKNOWLEDGEMENTS

The first four chapters of this book originated as pilot essays that were subsequently expanded and extensively revised. Chapter 1 appeared under the title "Adorno's Critical Materialism" in *Philosophy and Social Criticism* **32**(6) (2006), 719–37. The pilot essay for Chapter 2, "Nature, Red in Tooth and Claw", was published in *Continental Philosophy Review* **40**(1) (March 2007), 49–72. A shorter version of Chapter 3, "Thought Thinking Itself", appeared in the *Journal of the British Society for Phenomenology* **38**(3) (2007), 229–47. "Adorno's Endgame", on which Chapter 4 is based, was published in *Philosophy Today* **52**(2) (2008), 173–87. I am grateful to the anonymous reviewers of these essays for their critical commentary.

Parts of *Adorno on Nature* were presented at York University in Toronto, the Academy of Sciences in Prague, Princeton University, Dartmouth College and the Rome campus of Loyola University. A year after reading a very early version of Chapter 1 at the University of Liverpool in 2005, I delivered a revised version of this chapter at Warwick University. I learned much from participants at these two seminars and would like to thank Gerard Delanty and Ralf Rogowski for their kind invitations. I received equally insightful comments on earlier versions of the manuscript from Alison Stone (Lancaster University), John Abromeit (State University of New York at Buffalo), Michael Palamarek (York University), Eric Nelson (University of Massachusetts at Lowell), and Samir Gandesha (Simon Fraser University). I would like to extend my gratitude to Alison, John, Michael, Eric and Samir for their critical support.

My colleague Jeffrey Noonan read versions of most of the chapters and obliged me to think more critically about Adorno's views on political praxis. I continue to defend these views but, by opposing them, Jeffrey prompted me to find better arguments in their defence. Two of my students, Jeffrey Renaud and Michael Walschots, deserve special mention for their comments on the manuscript at various stages of its development. In the face of the setbacks, extensive revisions and surprising metamorphoses that accompanied the writing of this book, Jeffrey and Michael's unwavering enthusiasm was a constant source of encouragement.

A Humanities Research Group Fellowship at the University of Windsor allowed me to work uninterruptedly on the last chapter of this book during the winter semester of 2009. Affording me the irreplaceable luxury of time for reflection, the fellowship also gave me the opportunity to present to students, professors and the wider public a distillation of some of the central ideas in this book. The lively discussion that followed my presentation only confirmed my view that Adorno remains relevant for understanding our current predicament. Finally, a sabbatical leave made it possible for me to bring *Adorno on Nature* to completion.

I dedicate this book to my former thesis supervisor, the Adorno scholar and editor at 10/18, Olivier Revault d'Allonnes. An unrepentant *soixante-huitard*, he spoke out courageously against oppression and exploitation, while actively supporting those who work for social change. May his example survive him in the environmental movement and beyond.

ABBREVIATIONS

AT   *Aesthetic Theory* (1997).

DE   *Dialectic of Enlightenment* (tr. Cummings, 1972)/*Dialectic of Enlightenment: Philosophical Fragments* (tr. Jephcott, 2002).

HF   *History and Freedom: Lectures 1964–1965* (2006).

KCPR   *Kant's "Critique of Pure Reason"* (2001).

MCP   *Metaphysics: Concept and Problems* (2001).

MM   *Minima Moralia: Reflections from Damaged Life* (1974).

MTP   "Marginalia to Theory and Praxis" (1998).

ND   *Negative Dialectics* (1973).

P   "Progress" (1998).

PMP   *Problems of Moral Philosophy* (2000).

PT2   *Philosophische Terminologie zur Einleitung* [Introduction to philosophical terminology], vol. 2 (1974).

RCT   "Reflections on Class Theory" (2003).

SO   "On Subject and Object" (1998).

INTRODUCTION

[I]t would be up to thought to see all nature, and whatever would install itself as such, as history, and all history as nature.
                                                    Theodor W. Adorno (*ND* 359)

Decades before the environmental movement emerged in the 1960s, Theodor W. Adorno criticized our destructive and self-destructive relation to nature with the ultimate aim of reshaping that relationship in more mutually beneficial ways. His criticisms originally appeared in a 1932 essay, "The Idea of Natural-History", where he advanced the project of showing that human history is always also natural history and that non-human nature is entwined with history. This project informs all Adorno's work, including *Negative Dialectics* and the unfinished, posthumously published *Aesthetic Theory*.[1] The idea of natural history provides the template for interpretive practice in philosophy: philosophical interpretation "means reading nature from history and history from nature" (*HF* 134). Philosophy is tasked with demonstrating that human history is linked inextricably to both our own internal, instinctual, nature and non-human nature. But philosophy also shows that nature is historical, not just because nature evolves and constantly changes, but because it has been profoundly – often negatively – affected by human history. Adorno's idea of natural history reveals the dynamic, and potentially catastrophic, interaction between nature and history.

When philosophy reads nature from history, the idea of natural history becomes "the canon of interpretation for philosophers of history" (*ND* 359; see also *HF* 125).[2] Adorno also made this point in *Dialectic of Enlightenment*, where he and his co-author, Max Horkheimer, denied that the history of our species could be traced in the development of concepts like freedom and justice. Instead, a serious history of the human race would reveal that all our "ideas, prohibitions, religions, and political creeds" are

1

tied to conditions that serve either to increase or decrease "the natural survival prospects of the human species on the earth or within the universe" (*DE* C:222–3, J:184–5).[3] For millennia, we have sought to dominate nature – to predict, control, manipulate and exploit it – in order to improve these prospects. Our history can be interpreted as natural history because its trajectory can be traced in the vicissitudes of our instinctually driven domination of nature. Human history "remains under the spell of blind nature" in the form of the unbridled instinct for self-preservation (*HF* 124).

Conversely, when history is read from nature, nature "appears as a sign for history" (2006b: 264). Nature's historical character is evident in the growth, maturation and decline of natural things, but history also leaves its mark on nature when we treat natural things instrumentally and reduce them to their exchange value in the capitalist marketplace. Exchange relations damage human beings as well by expunging differences between them in order to make "nonidentical individuals and performances become commensurable and identical" (*ND* 146). This damage has only been exacerbated by the forced renunciation of our internal nature in the form of needs and drives. On this point, Adorno largely agrees with Sigmund Freud: our history can be read in the increasingly aggressive behaviours to which civilization gives rise when it demands that we constantly "exercise rational control over ourselves and over external nature". More critical than Freud, however, Adorno goes on to observe that "the balance sheet which forms the foundation of this entire calculus of the renunciation of instinct and the domination of nature can never be presented because if it were presented, the irrational aspect of that rationality would become inescapably visible" (*PMP* 139).

A thoroughly "*critical* concept" (*HF* 116), the idea of natural history makes visible the damage that has been inflicted on both human and non-human nature by our compulsive attempts to dominate nature to satisfy survival imperatives. To shed greater light on this concept, Chapter 1 opens with a discussion of Adorno's thesis concerning the preponderance of the object. This thesis postulates the primacy of both internal and external nature in human life, while emphasizing at the same time the preponderance of society, in the guise of exchange value, over individuals. In fact, the idea of natural history complements Adorno's thesis about the "weightiness" of the objective world because it affirms the preponderance of "first" and "second" nature over individuals as it explores their unending entwinement (*ND* 358).

The preponderant objective world is not a mere reflection of mind or spirit. Instead, nature and history are resoundingly real; they are powerful material forces. Chapter 1 also describes the central features of Adorno's materialism, taking its point of departure from Brian O'Connor who compares John Searle's account of the non-dualistic and non-reductive relation between the brain and consciousness to Adorno's account of the relation between subject and object. However, I also take issue with O'Connor when I argue that Adorno grounds this epistemological relation in his idea of natural history. Adopting Karl Marx's ideas about the metabolism between our species and non-human nature, Adorno speculates that human consciousness first emerged in the struggle for survival. His account of the emergence of consciousness helps to explain why the affinity between nature and history authorizes neither the reduction of nature to history nor the reduction of human history to nature. In fact, Chapter 1 ends with the claim – developed in subsequent chapters – that Adorno's non-reductive and non-dualistic idea of natural history may help to solve Kant's antinomy of causality and freedom.

Chapter 2 explores some of the implications of the preponderance of the objective world for our knowledge of nature. On the one hand, we can apprehend natural things only because we have an affinity with them as thingly creatures ourselves. Even the concepts we use to understand nature derive their meaning from our material encounters with it. On the other hand, Adorno agrees with Kant that there is an obstacle or block to knowledge. Nature cannot be known as it is in itself; it can never be grasped fully in concepts. Yet Chapter 2 will argue that our knowledge of nature is problematic, not simply because it involves conceptual mediation, but because we have taken an adversarial stance towards nature as a fearsome Other that threatens our prospects for survival. This antagonistic relation to nature manifests itself in our subordination of natural things under abstract concepts and exchange relations. Since we have masked nature's diversity and thwarted its internal development, I also ask what "nature" might signify when I assess two attempts to make sense of this concept.

If preponderant external nature always lies beyond our conceptual grasp, preponderant internal nature eludes our attempts to repress it. Today, the renunciation of instinct issues in blind aggression towards everything deemed merely natural. By no means an orthodox Freudian, Adorno nonetheless endorses Freud's theory of instincts, agreeing that instincts have both somatic and psychological components. In keeping with his idea of natural history, however, Adorno adds that instincts are thoroughly historical because they are invariably shaped by prevailing socioeconomic conditions. Discussing Adorno's appropriation of Freud's instinct theory in the second section of Chapter 2, I also review Joel Whitebook's claim that Adorno follows Freud's injunction to displace the ego with respect to the id to promote greater autonomy. Where Whitebook thinks that Adorno needs (and surreptitiously uses) a concept of sublimation to achieve this goal, Adorno contends that individuals should become more fully conscious of themselves as embodied and instinctual creatures. Critical self-reflection – reflection on nature in the self – is the hallmark of a more enlightened form of reason and the harbinger of freedom.

According to Adorno, the entire programme of Western philosophy has consisted in thinking about thought. Chapter 3 explains how Adorno tries to advance this programme with his critique of the prevailing form of thought: identity thinking. Shaped by socioeconomic conditions and driven by survival instincts, identity thinking reinforces domination in conceptual form when it compulsively identifies particular things with universal concepts. Chapter 3 begins with a brief account of the historical trajectory of Western reason as an organ of adaptation to the natural world, placing special emphasis on the development of its subsumptive, identitarian employment of concepts. Since modern science wields concepts and mathematical formulae in a similar fashion, Chapter 3 includes a discussion of Adorno's critique of science and the concept of causality, rehearsing his objections to the reduction of reason to quantification and calculation.

Following this account of Western reason and modern science, Chapter 3 explores Adorno's alternative cognitive paradigm: non-identity thinking. Here I examine J. M. Bernstein's important gloss on this paradigm while offering a more dialectical reading of it. In contrast to identity thinking, which ignores the particularity of natural things when it substitutes unity for diversity, identity for difference, non-identity thinking deploys concepts to break through concepts with the aim of apprehending non-conceptual particulars, even as it acknowledges the lack of identity between universal and particular. Bernstein is certainly right to say that non-identity thinking tries to circumvent the abstract universality of concepts by turning back to the material particulars that spawn concepts. However, non-identity thinking also has a speculative, proleptic dimension that is reached by means of determinate negation. Adorno calls determinate negation a methodological principle (2008: 28),[4] which, by negating the damage we inflict on nature, offers an indirect glimpse of undamaged life. Deployed in a constellation of concepts, the emphatic ideas derived from determinate negation point to less instrumental and exploitative relationships with nature in a freer and more rational society.

Chapter 4 focuses on the preponderance of society over individuals. It begins by remarking on the isomorphism between identity thinking and exchange relations. Just as identity thinking treats natural things (including human beings) as mere instances of more general kinds with a view to manipulating and controlling them, exchange relations serve survival imperatives when they turn individual people and things into commensurable units of value. Both identity thinking and exchange relate "all phenomena, everything we encounter, to a unified reference point" when they subsume individual people and things "under a self-identical, rigid unity, and thereby remove them from their dynamic context" (*KCPR* 114, trans. mod.). Indeed, Adorno claims that identity thinking and exchange relations are isomorphic because thought mirrors the prevailing mode of exchange in a given society.

Chapter 4 also examines Adorno's critique of the process of individuation under the monopoly conditions that characterize late capitalism. On Adorno's admittedly bleak view, since late capitalist society obliges us to focus exclusively on our own individual survival, it arrests individuation and places nature as a whole in jeopardy. Like Samuel Beckett in *Endgame*, Adorno foresaw the catastrophic annihilation of all life on this planet when he warned that society's "principle of particular private interest" might well lead to "the death of all" (*ND* 298). At the same time, Adorno explored the prospects for transforming socioeconomic conditions with the aim of avoiding that fate. Highly critical of existing forms of collective action, he claimed that those individuals who have developed their capacity for self-reflection can play an important role in initiating the transformations needed to avert catastrophe because they are able to look critically at the conditions that shape their own thought and behaviour. Critics of our current predicament have the task of analysing the obstacles to social solidarity and the emergence of a global subject, using determinate negation to generate new ideas about solidarity, exchange relations, self-preservation and freedom.

In contrast to the first four chapters, which outline Adorno's philosophy of nature, the fifth chapter compares and contrasts his ideas with those of three prominent representatives of radical ecology: Arne Naess, Murray Bookchin, and Carolyn Merchant. Like Adorno, these ecologists stress the urgent need to alter our interaction with nature in ways that will benefit both non-human nature and ourselves. Insisting that we become conscious of nature in ourselves, they also echo Adorno when they denounce the current emphasis under capitalism on economic growth for its own sake while advocating substantive changes in society and championing new forms of ecological sustainability that give due weight to both the flourishing of the natural world and the satisfaction of human needs.

Adorno also speaks to issues in environmental philosophy such as anthropomorphism, the intrinsic value of nature, speciesism, the origin of our domination of nature, the idea of "good" nature, the feminization of nature and the naturalization of women, and the emancipatory potential of technology. However, one of the more important points to emerge from this comparison between Adorno and radical ecology concerns the efficacy of collective action today. If radical ecology is to improve our prospects for survival on this planet, the tendencies and trends that often make environmental activism ineffective must be better understood. To bring about the changes that radical ecologists rightly insist are needed, we must first acquire a better understanding of the natural and historical forces that now undermine all types of activism. Since Adorno devoted a great deal of his theoretical and empirical work to studying the impediments to effective praxis under monopoly conditions, Chapter 5 argues that he has much to contribute to the environmental movement.

Another, related, point emerges from this comparative study: radical ecologists are grappling with the perennial philosophical problem of unity in diversity. This problem should concern environmental activists to the extent that activism itself presupposes the unity – in the form of solidarity – of diverse individuals, but it affects our relation to non-human nature as well. Among the pressing questions that Adorno raises are: how can solidarity be achieved such that individuals with divergent viewpoints and concerns can work together effectively to bring about the changes necessary to ensure our survival? And, how might we relate to non-human nature so that it can thrive in all its remarkable diversity? I do not pretend that Adorno definitively answered these questions, but I do claim that they are among the more vexing and important issues he addressed. Radical ecology, and the environmental movement generally, can learn from Adorno's concerted attempts to find new ways to articulate the relationship between unity and diversity, the One and the Many.

CHAPTER ONE
CRITICAL MATERIALISM

Adorno's work has been variously described as Nietzschean, Weberian, Hegelian, idealist, Marxist and materialist.[1] With equal frequency, commentators have excluded Adorno from one or the other of these camps. So, for example, Stephen Bronner argues that Adorno's work has nothing to do with materialism "unless that concept is configured in the most abstract terms" (1996: 186–7). Some Italian Marxists were even more critical than Bronner, excoriating Adorno as a romantic idealist. This is certainly true of Lucio Colletti, who, as Perry Anderson observes, soundly denounced Adorno (and others as well) for his allegedly Hegelian rejection of materialism (1976: 70). This charge reappears in a different form in Sebastiano Timpanaro's influential *On Materialism* (1975). Among other things, Timpanaro objects that the Frankfurt School as a whole has an "antimaterialist, anti-Enlightenment, anti-jacobin orientation". All the school's theorists are pessimistic thinkers who "end up in, or at least tend towards, more or less explicitly religious positions" (*ibid.*: 19).

These barbed criticisms contradict Adorno's own description of his work as materialist in orientation. Although he would reject Timpanaro's claim that a materialist would never reduce experience to a "reciprocal implication of subject and object", Adorno advances a version of materialism that agrees in part with Timpanaro's view that materialism involves "above all acknowledgement of the priority of nature over 'mind'" (*ibid.*: 34). Furthermore, both Timpanaro and Adorno acknowledge their debts to Marx. In *Negative Dialectics*, Adorno cites the same passage from the preface to *Capital* that Timpanaro endorses in his discussion of materialism. On Timpanaro's interpretation, this passage shows that the later Marx was a materialist because he gave priority to physical and biological nature. The passage reads:

> My standpoint, from which the development of the economic formation of society is viewed as a process of natural history [*als ein naturgeschichtlichen Prozeß²*], can less than any other make the individual responsible for relations whose creature he remains, socially speaking, however much he may subjectively raise himself above them.
>
> (Marx 1976a: 92; cited in part in Timpanaro 1975: 41)

Yet Adorno's gloss on this passage differs significantly from that of Timpanaro, who neglects to cite the second part of the sentence ("can less than any other ..."). Adorno not only cites the entire sentence, but also (albeit elliptically) the five sentences that precede it, and interprets Marx's reference to natural history as a reference to second – rather than to "first", or physical and biological – nature. To bolster this interpretation, Adorno cites a later passage from *Capital* where Marx declared that "'the law of capitalist accumulation ... has been mystified into a law of nature'" (*ND* 354).³ In fact, Adorno agrees with Marx: capitalism now appears in the guise of second nature because it seems to be governed by natural, immutable laws. Owing to this mystification, anything that might be deemed first nature has been masked or concealed. For bourgeois consciousness, "nothing appears to exist outside any more; in a certain sense there actually is nothing outside any more, nothing unaffected by mediation, which is total". As a result, the distance between human history and nature only continues to grow (*ND* 357–8).

Adopting Marx's critique of capitalism as second nature, Adorno also shares his interest in exploring the role of first nature in human history. Here, too, his reading of Marx differs significantly from Timpanaro's. For Adorno would contest Timpanaro's claim that "Marxism, especially in its first phase (up to and including *The German Ideology*), is not materialism proper" because the early Marx believed that first nature constitutes "more a prehistorical antecedent to human history than a reality which still limits and conditions human beings" (Timpanaro 1975: 40–41, trans. mod.). Citing a passage from *The German Ideology*, Adorno declares that the early Marx emphasized the unending entwinement of nature and history "with an extremist vigor bound to irritate dogmatic materialists" (*ND* 358). According to Marx:

> We know only a single science, the science of history. History can be conceived from two sides, divided into the history of nature and the history of humankind. Yet there is no separating the two sides; as long as human beings exist, natural and human history will qualify each other. (Marx & Engels 1976: 28)

8

Adorno follows this quotation with the assertion that the traditional antith-esis between nature and history is true in one respect and false in another. The antithesis is "true insofar as it expresses what happened to the natural element" – namely that first nature has been occluded to such a degree that what now appears to be natural is actually social in character. However, the antithesis is false to the extent that "it apologetically repeats the concealment of history's natural growth by history itself" (*ND* 358).

Since history has masked its own entwinement with nature, our under-standing of ourselves is seriously flawed. Adorno wants to correct this flawed self-understanding by employing negative dialectics "to break through the fallacy [*Trug*] of constitutive subjectivity" (*ND* xx), or the illusory view (which takes different forms) that mind, or spirit, constitutes nature. In set-ting himself this task, Adorno again follows Marx. For once Marx drew "the line between historical materialism and the popular metaphysical kind", his-torical materialism became "the critique of idealism in its entirety, and of the reality for which idealism opts by distorting it" (*ND* 197). A critique of the fallacy of constitutive subjectivity would show that the mind is not primary. Indeed, on Adorno's reading, Hegel himself derived self-conscious mind from matter. Hypostatizing the mind, Hegel was nonetheless barely able to conceal the origin of the "I" in the "Not-I". Even for Hegel, mind (*Geist*) ultimately originates "in the real life process, in the law of the survival of the species, of providing it with nutrients" (*ND* 198). Moreover, these sur-vival imperatives, which shape our relationships with organic and inorganic nature, are in turn embedded in, and shaped by, the capitalist mode of pro-duction with its instrumental and exploitative relation to nature.

These ideas will be explored here. Chapter 1 begins by exploring Adorno's thesis about the primacy (*Vorrang*), or preponderance, of the object. This discussion of the preponderance of nature and society, of first and second nature, over individuals will provide the philosophical frame-work for understanding Adorno's idea of natural history. If, as Marx insists in *The German Ideology*, it is not possible to separate nature from history or history from nature, the following section of this chapter will show that the idea of natural history supplements Adorno's thesis about the prepon-derance of first and second nature over human life by emphasizing their dynamic interaction. After examining Adorno's account of the imbrication of nature and history, the chapter will end by exploring the salient features of Adorno's materialism. Among other things, I shall argue that Adorno's unique version of materialism can accommodate his unwavering commit-ment to emancipation and freedom.

PASSAGE TO MATERIALISM

In a section of *Negative Dialectics* called "Passage to Materialism", Adorno asserts: "It is by passing to the object's preponderance that dialectics is rendered materialistic" (*ND* 192). Borrowing a phrase from Peter Strawson, Ståle Finke believes that Adorno's thesis about the preponderance of the object refers to "the weighty sense of an object of experience – and its extra-conceptual status" (2004: 127 n.17).[4] Finke's interpretation is correct as far as it goes, but Adorno's thesis does not simply mean that objects are extra-conceptual. Specifically, objects are weighty owing to their materiality; the preponderance of the object implies that matter (*Stoff, Materie*) preponderates over mind. This preponderance can be grasped subjectively by reflecting on our experience (*ND* 185), but Adorno also complains that, when a thing becomes an object of cognition, "its physical side is spiritualized [*vergeistigt*] from the outset by translation into epistemology" (*ND* 192). Rejecting such spiritualization, Adorno wants to do justice to things by disclosing those aspects of them that are not identical with concepts. These non-identical aspects "show up as matter, or as inseparably fused with material things" (*ND* 193).

Frustratingly, perhaps, Adorno never provides a full-blown account of matter. In his own defence, however, he contends that it is not possible to provide such an account because matter is always also mediated by mind, material objects by concepts. As he explains in his lectures on metaphysics, the "peculiarity of the concept of ὕλη, or matter, is that we are here using a concept … which, by its meaning, refers to something which is not a concept or a principle". Warning against hypostatizing the concepts that refer to matter, Adorno concedes that we invariably find ourselves captive "in the prison of language". Yet he also insists that we can at least "recognize it as a prison" (2001b: 67–8 *passim*). His thesis about the preponderance of the object elucidates this prison metaphor because it entails that material objects are distinct from, and not fully accessible to, the concepts (and practical activities) we use to apprehend them.

Adorno makes a related point when he criticizes Kant's concepts of form and content. The mediation of form by content and of content by form must be differently weighted because the forms (concepts and categories) of thought are "*essentially* mediated by contents and cannot be conceived at all in their absence", whereas the content always contains "a reference to something that is not fully coextensive with form and cannot be fully reduced to it" (*KCPR* 233).[5] Accordingly, the object's preponderance further entails that concepts themselves are "infiltrated" with a material, or natural element. Concepts not only refer to non-conceptual, material particulars (*ND*

11), but also emerge in historically situated and conditioned encounters with them. Concepts are "entwined with a nonconceptual whole" because what survives in them by dint of their meaning (*Bedeutung*) is their non-conceptual conveyance or transmission (*Vermitteltsein*) under specific historical conditions.[6] In turn, this historically generated meaning "establishes the conceptuality of concepts", including our concept of nature. But, while concepts always require "nonconceptual, deictic elements", they often pass themselves off as constitutive of things. To counter the mistaken idea that concepts constitute objects, Adorno urges us to recognize "the constitutive character of the nonconceptual in the concept". This recognition would have the salutary effect of stemming "the compulsive identification which the concept effects unless halted by such reflection" (*ND* 12).

On this point, however, it is important to avoid misunderstanding. For Adorno does recognize that nature will always be socially constructed (to use a contentious phrase, the corrective to which lies in Ian Hacking's [1999] question: the social construction of *what*?). Indeed, Adorno does not seek to forego mediation, as some critics, including Jürgen Habermas (1984: 382ff.), have mistakenly charged. What concerns Adorno is not the mere fact that nature is socially mediated, but rather the ways in which nature has historically been mediated. In his critique of the fallacy of constitutive subjectivity, Adorno objects to the prevailing form of conceptual mediation – the blind and compulsive subsumption of particular objects under universal concepts – because this identitarian use of concepts indicates only what nature "falls under, what it exemplifies or represents, and what, accordingly, it is not itself" (*ND* 149).

The preponderance of the object also implies that the cognizing subject is itself a material object. It is not necessarily "part of the meaning of objectivity to be a subject", but it is part of the meaning of subjectivity to be an object. Concept formation presupposes material particulars, and there is a decidedly material, objective dimension to the subjects who wield concepts as well (*ND* 183). Experience involves the encounter of a corporeal subject with equally material, physical things. Indeed, experience would not be possible if the subject did not belong "*a priori* to the same sphere as the given thing" (*ND* 196). The cognizing subject can experience things only because it is not radically other than them. Another reason why Adorno rejects the "supremacy of thinking over its otherness" – or the fallacy of constitutive subjectivity – is because mind is always "otherness already, within itself" (*ND* 201). As Adorno argues in "On Subject and Object", "No matter how the subject is defined, existent being [*Seiendes*] cannot be conjured away from it". Objects are not "so thoroughly dependent upon subject as subject is dependent upon objectivity" (SO 249–50).[7]

11

By emphasizing the materiality of the subject and the material ground of its concepts, Adorno underscores the resemblance between subject and object. He elaborates on this idea of the fundamental resemblance or likeness between subject and object *qua* material, physical, when he remarks, in his discussion of the concept of causality, on the affinity (*Affinität*) between them (*ND* 270). Here he asserts that causality is "nothing but the natural growth [*Naturwüchsigkeit*] of individuals, which they continue as control of nature" (*ND* 269). Our use of this concept to apprehend the natural world makes manifest our own natural growth because it has been driven by instinct.[8] A related point was made earlier: when we impose the concept of causality upon a material content, we are driven by a compulsion to identify objects with our causal conceptions of them. As Chapter 3 will explain in more detail, our use of concepts such as causality reveals our own affinity with nature because it has been driven by survival imperatives (*ND* 234).

Bernstein contends that Adorno's idea of affinity "represents the indeterminate idea of our immersion in and being parts of nature". He also notes that Adorno employs the word as though affinity were at one and the same time already established and yet to be achieved. Adorno expresses himself in this way in order to "halt an identitarian employment of our relation to nature", or to suggest that our affinity with nature has not yet been fully instantiated (2001: 291). Despite our *de facto* affinity with nature, we are largely unaware of this affinity because we have historically regarded ourselves as radically distinct from nature. We neither fully experience nor understand ourselves as natural – material, physical – because, among other things, we have not yet taken the full measure of the extent to which our behaviour and activity – both practical and theoretical – have been, and continue to be, instinctually driven. We therefore fail to respect the heterogeneous character of nature, including our own.

It may appear contradictory to refer to the heterogeneous character of nature in the context of discussing our affinity with the natural world. But to acknowledge our affinity with nature by no means implies that we are fully identical with it. "To be a mind at all", Adorno argues, the thinking subject "must know that what it touches upon does not exhaust it, that the finiteness that is its like does not exhaust it" (*ND* 392). Concepts too are heterogeneous with respect to objects. Emerging in our material encounters with non-conceptual things, concepts are subjective constructs rather than objective entities; abstract determinations, not concrete properties; universal, not particular. Abstract universality, which allows concepts to designate a class or category of non-conceptual particulars, is obviously a distinctive feature of concepts.

Although a particular thing is not "definable without the universal that identifies it", it cannot be subsumed without remainder under the universal. Adorno stresses this point when he remarks that the concept of particularity itself "cuts short what the particular is and what nonetheless cannot be directly named" (*ND* 173 *passim*). Owing to its universal character, this concept has "no power over the particular which [it] means in abstracting" (*ND* 174). In fact, the non-identity of concept and object could be described as the motor of Adorno's entire philosophical enterprise: "dialectics says no more, to begin with, than that objects do not go into concepts without leaving a remainder, that they come to contradict the traditional norm of adequacy" (*ND* 5).

Consequently, the affinity between subject and object, mind and nature, should not be posited as positive, that is, as though it authorized a foundational conception of nature, matter or the objective world (*ND* 270). Human beings are not wholly material, physical, because the human mind partially extricated itself from the material world in its attempts to dominate it: the mind's partial disengagement from matter means that mind is no more reducible to matter than matter is reducible to mind. However, if consciousness has succeeded, to a limited extent, in dissociating itself from the material world, it nonetheless remains "a ramification of the energy of drives; it is part impulse itself, and also a moment of that in which it intervenes" (*ND* 265). In the final section of this chapter, I shall take up these ideas about the emergence of consciousness again when I examine Adorno's non-reductive and non-dualistic account of subject and object, mind and matter.

While nature continues to preponderate, we persist in thinking of ourselves as completely other than, and separate from, nature. This misconception has an ideological dimension. Through it, the subject "announces its claim to domination", while "forgetting how much it is object itself" (SO 246). By contesting this ideologically freighted view of ourselves, Adorno's thesis about the object's preponderance is meant to serve as a stark reminder of the subject's own embeddedness in nature. At the same time, however, the preponderance of the object entails more than the claim that nature preponderates over individuals because the objectivity that weighs upon individuals is not just natural, but social and historical. Insisting on the preponderance of the material, natural world, Adorno also emphasizes the preponderance or weightiness of society – the "real objectivity of exchange" (*ND* 190) – over individuals.[9]

Adorno maintains that this twofold understanding of material objectivity has characterized materialism throughout its history. At the start of a lengthy discussion of the history of materialism, he states that there are two types of materialism: a social type, which focuses on society and its preponderance over individuals, and a scientific one, which focuses on the preponderance of nature. These two versions of materialism converge in their opposition to the lie perpetrated by the mind when it repudiates its own natural growth (*PT2* 171–2). They effectively target the fallacy of constitutive subjectivity by locating "the origin of mind – even its most extreme sublimations – in material scarcity [*Lebensnot*]" (*PT2* 173). In fact, Adorno tries to accommodate both types of materialism in his work, adding that individuals generally ignore the ways in which these aspects of the objective world preponderate over their thought and behaviour.

Adorno thought that society's influence on our thought and behaviour had become so far-reaching that it could plausibly be described as totalitarian. Referring to society as the "universal", he stressed its virtually irresistible power over individuals. But other philosophers have acknowledged society's preponderance as well, albeit often implicitly. For example, Hegel called this totalitarian objectivity "world spirit", and even Kant recognized the preponderance of society with his idea of the transcendental subject. According to Adorno, the transcendental subject "faithfully discloses the precedence of the abstract, rational relations that are abstracted from individuals and their conditions and for which exchange is the model" (*SO* 248).[10] Here again, Adorno followed Marx: society preponderates in the "law of value that comes into force without people being aware of it". Informing social institutions, agencies, relations and practices, the law of value is the "real objectivity" to which individuals must submit (*ND* 300–301). Today, "the standard structure of society is the exchange form". The rationality that underlies exchange "constitutes people: what they are for themselves, what they think they are, is secondary" (*SO* 248).

In his account of the preponderance of exchange relations over individuals, Adorno maintains that the "real total movement of society" – in the form of economic forces and tendencies – has become independent of the individuals who created it and continue to sustain it. These forces and tendencies now operate over their "heads and through their heads", and are thus "antagonistic from the outset" (*ND* 304). Observing in his 1942 essay "Reflections on Class Theory" that Marx had predicted the emergence of monopoly capital, Adorno also remarks that the concentration of capital has "reached such a size, acquired such a critical mass" that capital now appears to be "an institution, an expression of society as a whole".[11] Today, the fetish character of commodities, which makes relations between people appear as relations between things, ends in the socially totalitarian appearance of capital (RCT 99).

Late capitalist societies reduce individuals to "mere executors, mere partners in social wealth and social struggle" (*ND* 304). As so many instances of

14

exchange value, individuals today "are not just character masks, agents of exchange in a supposedly separate economic sphere". For commodification and reification have become so widespread, affecting so many aspects of human life that, even where individuals "think they have escaped the primacy of economics – all the way into their psychology, the *maison tolérée* of uncomprehended individuality – they react under the compulsion of the universal" (*ND* 311). Earlier, in *Minima Moralia*, Adorno remarked that life can reproduce itself under existing relations of production only when "the metamorphosis of labour-power into a commodity has permeated individuals through and through and objectified each of their impulses as formally commensurable variations of the exchange relationship" (*MM* 229).[12]

In *Aesthetic Theory*, Adorno asserts (with no little irony) that exchange relations have become the measure of all things (*AT* 310). The fetish character of commodities casts such a powerful spell over individuals that exchange relations now appear to be both immutable and necessary (*ND* 346). On Adorno's view, Hegel endorsed a similarly mystifying idea of society in the *Philosophy of Right* when he proposed that a state's constitution be depicted, not as the product of human history, but as something "'divine and enduring and above the sphere of that which is produced'". By making the historical appear to be natural, Hegel "absolutized domination and projected it on to Being itself, which is said to be spirit". As a result, history "acquires the quality of the unhistoric" (*ND* 356–7). It is to this idea of human history as second nature that I shall now turn in order to contrast it with Adorno's idea of natural history.

THE UNENDING ENTWINEMENT OF NATURE AND HISTORY

The objective world is both social and natural. Today, however, it is the social world – governed by exchange relations under the monopoly conditions characteristic of late capitalism – that appears to be natural. To return to Adorno's interpretation of the preface to the first volume of *Capital*, the so-called law of nature in Marx is the law that governs capitalist society (*ND* 354). Adopting Marx's idea that society's law of motion now appears as second nature, Adorno also observes that this second nature "is the negation of any nature that might be conceived as the first" (*ND* 357). In an illuminating gloss on this observation, Alison Stone states that the natural appearance of social relations "suggests to individuals … that 'first' nature, the material environment, gives rise to social relations ('second' nature), and that first nature must prefigure second in character" (2006: 238). Since social relations appear to be natural, individuals experience nature "as intrinsically prefiguring, and so referring to, particular social institutions and processes" (*ibid.*: 239).[13]

On the one hand, then, the social world seems to have evolved naturally. As a result, social relations appear to be inalterable. But, of course, this semblance of static immutability is illusory, false. Like Marx, Adorno believes that the ostensibly natural laws of capitalism are ultimately revocable; for it is "only in a sardonic sense that the natural growth of exchange society is a law of nature" (*ND* 190). That the laws governing capitalism are not immutable is "confirmed by the strongest motive behind all Marxist theory: that those laws can be abolished" (*ND* 355). Yet Adorno goes further than simply invoking the possibility of abolishing these laws when he denies that materialism implies an entirely affirmative view of the preponderance of matter and the material conditions of human life over individuals. Rather than straightforwardly condoning this preponderance, Adorno seeks to mitigate it.

Adorno also contends that Marx wanted to attenuate the preponderance of the object. On his reading of Marx:

> the telos, the idea behind Marxist materialism is the abolition of materialism, which means bringing about a situation in which the blind compulsion of material conditions over human beings is broken, and the question of freedom will at last be truly meaningful. (*PT2* 198)[14]

This idea reappears in a more nuanced form in *Negative Dialectics*, where Adorno argues that the "perspective vanishing point of historical materialism would be its self-sublimation, the spirit's liberation from the primacy of material needs in their state of fulfillment" (*ND* 207). The preponderance of the material world will diminish only when society satisfies the material needs of all the living, thereby enabling individuals to engage in activities that are not devoted primarily to ensuring their survival.

On the other hand, organic and inorganic nature are negated under capitalism. Nature has been negated precisely because society now assumes the mystified form of something natural, while the natural world is idealistically conceived as a mere prefigurement of social relations, institutions and practices. Owing to our distorted ideas of both external and internal nature, our experience of nature has been immeasurably impoverished, diminished. In our ceaseless attempts to dominate nature, we have turned nature into something to be controlled and manipulated exclusively for our own benefit by reducing nature to our concepts of it on the theoretical level and by equating nature with its exchange value in the capitalist marketplace.

Our largely instrumental relation to nature does not allow nature to flourish independently of human ends. In fact, Adorno remarks that nature has a purposiveness that is "other than that posited by humanity": a purposiveness that "was undermined by the rise of natural science" (*AT* 288).[15] As Stone also argues, our domination of natural things prevents them "from developing or behaving as they spontaneously would" (2006: 236). Failing to accommodate nature's own ends, we invariably violate it.

We now inhabit an inverted world where nature has been socialized and the sociohistorical world has been naturalized, turned into second nature. Nevertheless, there is a far less illusory sense in which human history is natural, and nature historical. The separation of history from nature is deceptive because, throughout our history, we have engaged with the natural world in productive and reproductive activities for the purpose of self-preservation. Conversely, nature is historical because it constantly develops and changes, both ontogenetically and phylogenetically. Moreover, nature is always also bound up with the historically and socially conditioned concepts and practices that we use to grasp and manipulate it. This idea already appeared in Marx's critique of Ludwig Feuerbach: our productive activity – "this unceasing labour and creation" – is "the basis of the whole sensuous world as it now exists". A nature that lies outside the ambit of human history no longer exists anywhere (Marx & Engels 1970: 63).

Bernstein claims that, with his idea of natural history, Adorno endorses Hegel's famous speculative proposition in the *Phenomenology of Spirit*: "Everything that is subject must be shown to be as much (historical) substance, and what is regarded as substance must be shown to be also subject" (Bernstein 2004: 20).[16] However, Adorno categorically rejects Hegel's claim that nature and history are ultimately one or identical, even as he agrees with Marx that nature and history are "not two separate things" (Marx & Engels 1932: 58).[17] Citing "The Idea of Natural-History" more than three decades after he delivered it as a lecture to the Kant Society in Frankfurt, Adorno declares that the task of thought is "'to grasp historic being in its utmost definition, in the place where it is most historic, as natural being, or to grasp nature, in the place where it seems most deeply, inertly natural, as historic being'" (*ND* 359).

Nature and history are unendingly entwined, not because they are one and the same, but because they converge. Adorno takes this idea about the convergence of nature and history from his colleague Walter Benjamin, who maintains that nature and history intersect in the moment of transience (*Vergängnis*) (*ND* 359). In *The Origin of German Tragic Drama*, Benjamin noted with approval that poets of the baroque age conceived of nature as eternal transience. At the same time, these poets wrote the word "history" "on the countenance of nature in the characters of transience" (1977: 177; cited in *HF* 125). Commenting on Benjamin's claims about the convergence of nature and history, Adorno observes that nature and history are present in each other: nature is "present as transience", and history is present in nature "as something that has evolved and is transient" (*HF* 135).

Susan Buck-Morss points out that Adorno tried to sublate the traditional antithesis of nature and history in this "moment of transitoriness, this 'one-time-ness' (*Einmaligkeit*)" (1977: 57).[18] But Adorno also stressed the critical import of the idea of natural history when he stated that, for "radical natural-historical thought, everything that exists transforms itself into ruins and fragments" (2006b: 265, trans. mod.).[19] The idea of natural history discloses the damage inflicted on natural things and processes owing to their entwinement with history, their subordination to ends extrinsic to them. Later, in his lectures on history and freedom, Adorno again describes natural history as a critical concept. This concept not only casts light on the damage we have done to nature, but makes visible the unfreedom of individuals whenever they are led blindly and compulsively by instinct. If everything natural must be seen as historical, it is also the case that "everything historical has to be regarded as nature because, thanks to its own violent origins, it remains under the spell of blind nature" (*HF* 124).

Both external nature and our own internal nature have been pulled into the orbit of history. For its part, however, human history is natural history because it can be traced in the displacement, distortion and repression of our instincts and passions (*DE* C:231, J:192). Adorno adopts a Freudian perspective on this dimension of history, agreeing with Freud in *Civilization and its Discontents* that "it is impossible to overlook the extent to which civilization is built up upon a renunciation of instinct, how much it presupposes precisely the non-satisfaction (by suppression, repression, or some other means?) of powerful instincts" (Freud 1975a: 34). Like Freud, Adorno sees human history as the history of renunciation (*DE* C:55, J:43). Throughout our history, we have renounced and repressed our instincts "for the sake of mastery over nonhuman nature and over other human beings" (*DE* C:54, J:42). If renunciation was necessary to preserve society as a whole, human beings rarely benefited from it, since "there is no real equivalence between renunciation of instincts in the present and compensation in the future". Society has been organized irrationally because "the equivalent reward it always promises never arrives" (*PMP* 139).

Although human history consists, in part, in the renunciation of instinct, one instinct has been allowed to "run wild" (*ND* 289). From its earliest beginnings (as even Plato implicitly acknowledged when he observed that society originated to satisfy needs), society has been impelled by the "principle of unreflected self-preservation" (*ND* 283). In fact, Adorno complains that the persistent degradation of human beings to a mere means of their *sese conservare* is the "law of doom [*Verhängnis*] thus far obeyed by history" (*ND* 167). Commenting on this aspect of Adorno's idea of natural history, Espen Hammer observes that reason and language have been fundamentally "shaped by the overall purpose of securing the individual's survival". Even scientific attempts to understand and explain the natural world fulfil survival imperatives because they are geared to "identifying, controlling, and organizing a hostile and potentially dangerous environment" (Hammer 2006: 45). As a result, science too remains bound to nature.

Late capitalist society is also bound to nature. Under capitalism, virtually all objects and activities have been commodified. The secret of the commodity form, which Marx described in the first chapter of *Capital*, is equivalence: the equivalence of one object or activity with a heterogeneous other. Equating unequal or non-identical things, exchange is the social model for what Adorno called identity thinking: a form of concept fetishism in which objects are summarily identified with concepts. Moreover, the emergence of identitarian exchange relations has its own natural history because it too was impelled by survival instincts (*ND* 146). Indeed, the exchange of equivalents is said to be beneficial to society because it ensures society's continued survival. As political economists such as Adam Smith have argued, when commodity producers, who are oriented towards private success in the form of profit-making, exchange their products on the market, they unintentionally promote the material reproduction of society as a whole. Exchange is therefore considered to be (and has historically been justified in this way) the most effective means of preserving both society and its individual members.

In *Dialectic of Enlightenment*, Horkheimer and Adorno insist that a truly "philosophical interpretation of world history would have to show how, despite all the detours and resistances, the systematic domination over nature has been asserted more and more decisively, and has integrated all internal human characteristics". More controversially, they claim that this interpretation of history, which sees it as driven by survival instincts that continue to pit us antagonistically against the environing natural world, provides an explanatory framework for "[e]conomic, political, and cultural forms" (*DE* C:223, J:185). Of course, this claim is controversial because it seems to be completely reductive; it turns instinct into a "base" on which the societal superstructure is built. But if *Dialectic of Enlightenment* appears at times to equate human history with the vicissitudes of our instinctual life, Adorno's independent account of natural history neither reduces one to the other nor posits them as completely distinct realms of being. Just as he refuses to reduce objects to concepts when he criticizes the fallacy of constitutive subjectivity, Adorno will not reduce mind to matter, human history to instinct.

History cannot be reduced to the vicissitudes of our instinctual life because our instincts are themselves shaped and conditioned by history. Despite their ostensibly reductive claims, in *Dialectic of Enlightenment* Horkheimer and Adorno briefly suggest some of the ways in which instinct is bound up with history when they outline the historical trajectory of self-preservation. In the early stages of nomadic life, "members of the tribe … took an individual part in the process of influencing the course of nature". To ensure their survival, they employed magical practices that, while submitting to nature, also determined the form that submission should take (when, for example, they draped themselves in the hides of their quarry while stalking it). However, this period in history, when all tribal members were deemed capable of using magic to capture their prey, was followed by one where "intercourse with spirits and subjection were assigned to different classes: power is on the one side, and obedience on the other" (*DE* C:21, J:15). At this historical juncture, a division of labour was introduced. As Marx observed in *The German Ideology*, this division occurred when mental labour became the dominant force within a given social order (Marx & Engels 1970: 51–2).[20]

Thus, as James Schmidt also notes, the transition from magic to myth involves both the "centralization of power and the development of a division between mental and manual labour" (1998: 830). Echoing Marx, Horkheimer and Adorno contend that this nascent division of labour, "through which power manifests itself socially", was meant to serve as the primary means for preserving society (*DE* C:22, J:16). But Schmidt comments on the psychological dimension of this transition as well when he adds that myth, in its concerted attempts to identify origins, already required the separation of ideas from reality, which was first achieved "by the reality adjusted ego". According to Schmidt, then, ego formation, which gave rise to the process of individuation, originates "on this side of the line between magic and mythology" (1998: 829–30).[21]

Exchanging "the invocations of the magician and the tribe" for "the carefully graduated sacrifice and the labor of enslaved men mediated by command", myths also replaced local spirits and demons with "heaven and hierarchy". Over time, the gods of myth were "separated from material elements" such as the sky, the sun, the weather and so on. On the basis of this separation, in which the gods were thought to control elements of nature rather than being directly identified with them, a single distinction developed between the *logos* and "the mass of all things and creatures" outside it.

In turn, this distinction would lead to a further distinction between human beings and the rest of the natural world which eventually made the world "subject to human beings" (*DE* C:8, J:5). However, the dissociation of the *logos* from nature was double-edged: for even as nature was turned into an object, human beings themselves began to be treated as objects of manipulation and control. As "the illusion of magic vanishes", repetition, "in the guise of regularity", imprisons human beings "in the cycle now objectified in the laws of nature, to which they believe they owe their own security as free subjects" (*DE* C:12, J:8).

Although Greek myth depicted Zeus as ruling over all living beings, the Judaeo-Christian tradition claimed that its god accorded dominion over living creatures to human beings. Later still, with the advent of enlightenment, which advanced the general trend of demythologization in the West (*KCPR* 65), the distinction between the divine and the human faded. As human beings superseded God, myth turned "into enlightenment, and nature into mere objectivity" (*DE* C:9, J:5–6). Still, enlightenment carried forwards the legacy that it inherited from myth when it supplanted the "manifold affinities between existing things ... by the single relationship between the subject who confers meaning and the meaningless object, between rational significance and its accidental bearer" (*DE* C:10–11, J:7). Ostensibly rejecting the mythic concept of fate, enlightenment's primary instrument – abstraction – nonetheless liquidates its objects as thoroughly as myth did by subsuming all natural entities under laws. Abstracting from the singularity of objects, it brought "nature" to heel in order to satisfy survival imperatives.

Here too, Adorno agrees with Freud: civilization primarily consists in the attempts of human beings to make "the earth serviceable to them", and to protect them "against the violence of the forces of nature" (Freud 1975a: 27). A nation is deemed civilized when it effectively ensures both the "exploitation of the earth" and "protection against the forces of nature" (*ibid*.: 28). Unlike Freud, however, Adorno tends to stress the compulsive character of self-preservation, arguing that, in our stubborn attempts to "break the compulsion of nature by breaking nature", we simply succumb more deeply to that compulsion (*DE* C:13, J:9). As a result, he rejects Freud's claim that some of the activities that have contributed to the preservation of our species – particularly scientific endeavours – markedly "distinguish our lives from those of our animal ancestors" (Freud 1975a: 26). Where Freud praised science as a mature attempt to master the narcissistic belief in the omnipotence of thought (Whitebook 1995: 94–5),[22] Adorno underscores its instinctual character. Science exhibits the concept fetishism that characterizes the fallacy of constitutive subjectivity when it persists in the delusion

21

that thought is omnipotent by subordinating objects under abstract mathematical and conceptual schema. On Adorno's view, then, the distinction between human beings and other animals is far less clear-cut than Freud thought.

It is not just the instinct for self-preservation that manifests itself in different ways in human history; all human instincts are historically conditioned to the point where they may even be radically transformed by history (*HF* 236). Bernstein makes this point as well when he remarks that Adorno refused to reduce internal and external nature to an "atemporal system of lawful regularities". Instead, he thought that even our "biologically given attributes are continually being formed, determined, and elaborated through cultural practice" (2001: 189). Consequently, there is "no pristine inner nature awaiting release from repression". We cannot make good on what we have lost in the course of history by ceasing to repress inner nature and ending our domination of external nature because "who we are and how we understand and comport ourselves in the world are formed through this process of renunciation and domination" (*ibid.*: 200). Neither inner nor outer nature subsists in a latent form untouched by history, which may one day be recuperated in its original, prelapsarian state.

Adorno did not describe the historical trajectory of other instincts, but he did stress their historical character in his 1942 essay on needs, "Thesen über Bedürfnis". This essay begins with the strong claim that need is a social category. Although nature, in the form of instinct (*Trieb*), is contained within need, it is not possible "to separate the social dimension of need, as something secondary, from the natural aspect of need as something primary". Instincts are so socially mediated that whatever might be deemed natural in them only appears as "something produced by society" (1972d: 392). Later in the essay, Adorno admitted that the impossibility of distinguishing between good and bad, genuine and artificial, true and false needs, makes it difficult to develop a theory of needs. On the one hand, a theory of needs that acknowledges their social character must regard the satisfaction of all needs as legitimate.[23] On the other hand, theory must recognize that, since "existing needs are themselves the product of class society", there are no needs in which a clear distinction can be made between "humanity and the consequences of repression" (*ibid.*: 393).

Just as instincts are shaped by history, organic and inorganic nature constantly change. To return to Bernstein's reading of Adorno, air "*becomes* polluted; animal species *become* extinct (on their own and through our intervention); mineral resources *become* depleted; new natural kinds are intentionally developed" (Bernstein 2001: 189). Changes in external nature can be traced to the impact of other natural forces (such as the climate changes that led to the Ice Age, and tectonic shifts). But (as Chapter 4 will show in greater detail), many such changes are linked to human intervention, whether intentional or not. In fact, Adorno complains that our current idea of progress has been "deformed by utilitarianism", and does "violence to the surface of the earth" (AT 64). Justice will be done to nature only when we recognize and redress the damage that we have inflicted on it by treating it instrumentally, as something that exists solely for our own benefit.

With his critical concept of natural history, Adorno tries to capture the important senses in which nature is always also historical and history always also natural. But this concept can easily be misunderstood. As Lambert Zuidervaart argues, it is important to recognize that Adorno's emphasis on natural history does not mean that he adopts Marx's early goal "of 'naturalizing' human beings and 'humanizing' nature". Rather, Adorno thinks that "human beings already are natural, all too natural, and nature is unavoidably human, all too human". Human beings are all too natural because they "carry out domination as if they were beasts of prey", while remaining largely oblivious of the fact that their behaviour is largely impulsive and instinctive. Conversely, nature has been thoroughly humanized; it has been subsumed without remainder under concepts, and transformed into "a mere object of human control" (1991: 165).[24]

To be sure, Adorno wants us to acknowledge both that we are parts of nature and that nature is always also caught up in human history. But it can equally well be said that he aims to dehumanize nature and denaturalize humanity. Stressing humanity's own natural history and criticizing its "humanization" of nature, Adorno's goal is to encourage the partial transcendence of nature by human beings, and of human beings by nature. Even as we come to terms with our affinity with nature, this affinity should not blind us to the non-identity of nature and human history. In the final analysis, then, Adorno hopes to foster a more dialectical relationship between human beings and the environing natural world.

To say that nature is always also historical, or that nature has been marked, not just by the impact of other forces and phenomena, but by our interaction with it, does not authorize the reduction of nature to history because nature cannot be identified entirely with its mediated forms (just as objects cannot be identified with concepts, or matter with mind). Conversely, history cannot be reduced to nature. Our history has been influenced by natural forces both within and without, but it is not reducible to nature because, among other things, our cognitive development enables us to distinguish ourselves from nature through reflection and self-reflection – if only, as yet, to a limited degree. In fact, Adorno's former student, Alfred Schmidt, believes that Marx had a similar conception of the relationship between nature and history. Although Schmidt seems to ignore Marx's early claim that society's goal is "the true resurrection of nature – the naturalism of man and the humanism of nature both brought to fulfillment" (1964: 137), he accurately captures Adorno's view of this relationship when he remarks that "[n]atural and human history together constitute … a differentiated history". Since they form an internally differentiated unity, "human history is not merged in pure natural history; natural history is not merged in human history" (A. Schmidt 1971: 45). In the next section of this chapter, I shall discuss some of the more important philosophical implications of this relationship between nature and history.

THE ANTINOMY OF FREEDOM AND CAUSALITY

Adorno's materialism is distinctive: it aims to show that history and nature are indissolubly entwined. But while Adorno agrees with Marx on many key issues, the degree to which his version of materialism remains faithful to Marx is moot. For it is certainly the case that many Marxists reduce the material dimension of human existence to socioeconomic determinants. As a result, they frequently ignore the interaction between society and the natural world. Kate Soper argues that this means Timpanaro "is right to pose the question of the extent to which Marxism either inherently or in its contemporary 'distortions' supports a false reduction of natural to social determinants". Rejecting the idea of nature as "a mere backdrop to a *deus ex machina* of social relations which really has all the action", Soper also agrees with Timpanaro's view that Marx is partly to blame for this "false reduction". Unlike Timpanaro, however, she believes that Marx's lack of clarity about the relationship between the social and the natural worlds extends to his later work as well (Soper 1979: 72).

For his part, Adorno maintains that Marx never fully reconciled the two sides of materialism: the positivistic, social scientific version and the natural scientific version. In terms of his own self-understanding, Marx thought that he was in agreement with positive social science (*PT2* 172). For Adorno, however, this agreement is problematic to the extent that it risks positing a single origin or foundation to which everything is reduced. As Simon Jarvis explains, Adorno thought that each version of materialism, taken separately, simply offered "some unexamined and quite abstract category such as 'matter' or 'nature' or 'history' or 'society' as though it represented an immediate given, a point at which theoretical inquiry simply had to stop" (1998: 16). By contrast, Adorno's materialism refutes the idea of an unspoiled basic stratum (*ND* 368) because it stresses the constant interaction between nature and history, even as it acknowledges their heterogeneity.

In *Marx's Ecology*, however, John Foster rejects the claim that Marx failed to reconcile the two types of materialism. He believes that Marx devoted all his work to developing a dialectical account of the relationship between nature and history. "As a form of realism", Foster writes, Marx's approach constantly emphasized the "perpetual and close connection between natural science and social science, between a conception of the material/natural world and the world of society" (2000: 7). Unfortunately, Foster bases his view of Marx's realism on Marx's comments about natural history in the preface to the first edition of *Capital* (*ibid.*: 258 n.18). Interestingly, he misinterprets Marx in the same way that Timpanaro did: he too fails to see that Marx was referring to capitalism as second nature. In the rest of the book, however, Foster finds better grounds for his claim about the centrality of the idea of natural history in Marx when he focuses on Marx's assertion that there is a "metabolic relation between human beings and nature". According to Foster, Marx later developed this idea in such a way that he was able to give "a more solid and scientific expression of this fundamental relationship, depicting the complex, dynamic interchange between human beings and nature resulting from human labor" (*ibid.*: 158).

Ironically, perhaps, Foster's defence of Marx as a consistently dialectical thinker who devoted much of his work to examining the relationship between nature and history seems to ally Marx much more closely with Adorno than even Adorno thinks. For in his interpretation of Marx's idea of the metabolic relationship between human beings and nature – and especially in his insistence on Marx's non-reductionist, non-dualistic and non-mechanistic conception of this relationship – Foster describes important aspects in Adorno's ideas about this relationship as well. Adorno's thoroughly dialectical view of natural history puts paid to Foster's contentious and largely unsupported claim that Western Marxists, including Adorno, "increasingly rejected realism and materialism, adopting the view that the social world was constructed in the entirety of its relations by human practice" (*ibid.*: 7). In fact, Foster simply puts a marginally different spin on Adorno's reading of Marx's ideas about the relationship between nature and history, beginning with *The German Ideology*, where, as Foster remarks, nature is neither reducible to human history, nor "easily divorced from human history, and the sensuous activity of human beings as it develops with a given division of labor, involving specific relations to nature" (*ibid.*: 116). In other words, nature and history co-evolve owing to their metabolic interaction.

Adorno recognizes that the concept of metabolism (*Stoffwechsel*) plays an important role in Marx's work, where production is necessarily connected to nature. Yet he also observes that Marx's concept of nature, "in which productivity is consummated, remains … undeveloped, as does the famous expression 'metabolism with nature' [*Stoffwechsel mit der Natur*]". In fact, Adorno thinks that Marx had philosophically sound reasons for leaving unfilled these lacunae in his theory: he wanted to suggest that nature is not reducible to what the subject makes of it. In other words, Marx "did not want to incorporate nature once again into identity-thinking" (*PT2* 268). This point was also made by Alfred Schmidt. Contrasting Marx's account of mediation with Hegel's, Schmidt observed that, in Marx, "it is nonidentity which is victorious in the last instance" because Marx rejected "the idealist interpretation of the mediacy of everything immediate" when he argued that mediating subjects are an integral part of "the reality of [the] things mediated through them". Mediated, or socially stamped, by individuals, nature "does not prove to be a vanishing appearance" because it "retains its genetic priority over individuals and their consciousness" (A. Schmidt 1971: 28–9, trans. mod.).[25]

One of the more striking features in Adorno's account of natural history is the pervasive influence on it of Freud's theory of instincts. Bernstein tries to account for this influence when he claims that "Adorno was interested, precisely, in psychoanalysis's conception of the transformation of the natural (drive theory) into the social and the recurrent interplay between these two levels" (2001: 245 n.11). However, Whitebook would qualify this interpretation of Adorno's interest in Freud's instinct theory for reasons Bernstein later seems to appreciate himself when he writes that instincts can be "neither somatic nor mental in character if the mystery of how pure reason can be practical is to be resolved" (*ibid.*: 256). Here Bernstein agrees with Whitebook's reading of Freud: instincts transgress the boundary between soma and psyche. In "Instincts and their Vicissitudes", Freud described instinct as "the psychical representative of the stimuli originating from within the organism and reaching the mind, as a measure of the demand made upon the mind for work in consequence of its connection with the body" (Whitebook 1995: 186, quoting Freud 1975b: 122).

In part, what recommends Freud to Adorno is his recognition of the interaction between nature and history. In "Die Revidierte Psychoanalyse", a lecture given to the Psychoanalytic Society in San Francisco in 1946, Adorno made this point in a somewhat different way when he defended Freud's approach against that of revisionists such as Karen Horney. Freud was "not content to leave reason and socially determined behaviour unexplained". Instead, he attempted "to derive even complex mental behaviours from the drive for self-preservation and pleasure". In works such as *Civilization and its Discontents*, Freud saw human history as natural history. Conversely, even though Freud mistakenly taught that the unconscious was ahistorical, he never denied "that the concrete manifestation of instincts might undergo the most sweeping variations and modifications" (Adorno 1972c: 22).[26] What Adorno draws from Freud's theory of instincts, then, enables him to elaborate from a psychological perspective on Marx's claims about the relationship between nature and history.

This "marriage" of Marx and Freud is not without its problems. Yet Buck-Morss correctly observes that, despite criticizing Freud for ignoring the dependence of unconscious phenomena on "'the material world, namely, society'", Adorno also praised Freud in his first *Habilitationschrift* for recognizing that "'[t]he motive of human society is in the last analysis an economic one'" (1977: 19, 206 n.176; see also Adorno 1973a: 433). And, if Freud acknowledged the economic basis of society, Schmidt contends that Marx understood the importance of instinct in human life when he described human beings as a totality of socially conditioned and historically variable needs and drives.[27] For his part, of course, Adorno placed particular emphasis on the drive for self-preservation. For thousands of years, human beings have largely sought to subjugate nature in the interest of their own survival, damaging (sometimes irremediably) both non-human nature and their own inner nature in the process. Hence, the trenchant distinction between nature and history "deceives us about the fact that heteronomous history perpetuates the blind growth of nature" (*ND* 141).

Adorno himself suggests that Marx recognized the role of instinct in human history. On Adorno's reading, the "truth content" in Marx's idea of natural history, its "critical content", consists in his recognition that human history, which takes the form of the progressive mastery of nature, merely "continues the unconscious history of nature, of devouring and being devoured" (*ND* 355). It is in this context that Adorno cites *The German Ideology*, where Marx describes the imbrication of nature and history. But Marx criticized humanity's rapacious relation to nature in later work as well when he observed that nature had become "'purely an object for human beings, something merely useful, and is no longer recognized as a power working for itself'". Even our cognition of nature's laws "'appears only as the cunning by which human beings subject nature to the requirements of their needs, either as an item of consumption or a means of production'".[28] Arguably, then, one of the few differences between Adorno's view of natural history and Marx's is that Adorno speculates that our antagonistic relation to nature may have originated by accident, whereas Marx thought this relationship was the necessary outcome of the trajectory of human history (*ND* 321).

If Adorno is right to suggest that Marx offered a rudimentary account of humanity's natural history, he makes a far more contentious claim when he states that there is a sense in which nature can rightly be described as dialectical. Flatly denying that dialectics can be extended to nature as "a universal principle of explication", Adorno nonetheless argues that it is just as wrong to say that nature is undialectical and society dialectical. There are not two truths: "a dialectical one within society and one indifferent to society". In fact, the trenchant distinction between history and nature, which fails to acknowledge their entwinement, only reflects the deceptive division of labour between the social and natural sciences (*ND* 141).

This division of labour is deceptive because both the natural and social sciences have a social character; their procedures, practices and concepts have developed within specific social contexts. For example, the prevailing scientific concepts of first nature – of biological, chemical and physical nature – developed over thousands of years of Western history in response to specific problems and projects that arose at particular times. Furthermore, as we have seen, the natural and social sciences retain a "natural" character because they are impelled by instinct to control and dominate nature. Somewhat hyperbolically, self-preservation is described in *Dialectic of Enlightenment* as the "constitutive principle of science, the soul of the table of categories" (*DE* C:86, J:68). With its instrumental orientation towards objects, science adjusts "the world for the ends of self-preservation"; it "recognizes no function other than the preparation of the object from mere sensory material in order to make it the material of subjugation" (*DE* C:83–4, J:65).

Since human beings are inextricably part of the natural world, with which they must constantly interact to survive, nature can be said to be dialectical. Adorno expresses this idea in a striking way when he declares: "Dialectics lies in things, but it could not exist without the consciousness that reflects it – no more than it can evaporate into that consciousness" (*ND* 205). Indeed, given Adorno's pervasive influence on *The Concept of Nature in Marx*, it is probably not surprising that Schmidt's interpretation of Marx as a dialectical materialist should describe Adorno's view as well. For both, "[n]ature becomes dialectical by producing men as transforming, consciously acting Subjects confronting nature itself as forces of nature" (A. Schmidt 1971: 61). Importantly, Schmidt adds that Marx did not deny that "matter has its own laws and its own movement". Instead, the properly "*dialectical* element of Marx's materialism" consists in its "understanding that matter's laws of motion can only be recognized and appropriately applied … through the agency of mediating practice" (*ibid.*: 97).

On this latter point, Marx and Adorno may also be contrasted. For while Adorno accepts that nature has its own movement and laws, he thinks that our understanding of them has been limited and distorted owing to the prevalence of identity thinking. As noted earlier, Schmidt portrays Marx as a non-identity thinker when he alleges that Marx always rejected the "equation of humanism and naturalism" – or the humanization of nature and the naturalization of human history (*ibid.*: 137). Schmidt tends to obscure the differences between Adorno's and Marx's versions of materialism because Adorno undoubtedly made far more concerted attempts to reveal the non-identity of nature and history, matter and mind, object and concept. Although Adorno recognizes that Marx wanted to avoid reducing nature to history, he criticizes Marx for underwriting "something as archbourgeois as the program of an absolute control of nature", and for trying to make things that are unlike the subject "like the subject – the real model of the principle of identity, which dialectical materialism disavows as such" (*ND* 244). In fact, Chapter 3 will show that Adorno's refusal to identify subject and object also led him to take a markedly more critical stance towards science than Marx did.

When he denies that human history can be reduced to nature, or nature to history, Adorno criticizes orthodox Marxism. He rejects its vulgar or mechanical materialism, its attempts to explain all events – including thought and human action – exclusively in terms of natural laws. In *Philosophische Terminologie*, he dismisses reductive accounts like these on moral grounds when he observes that "the idea of the materiality [*Stoffhaftigkeit*] of human beings can be extremely repressive" to the extent that it debases human beings to "pure objects of domination" (*PT2* 187). Orthodox Marxists effectively deny the very possibility of freedom when they reject a more dialectical understanding of natural history, of the mutual implication of subject and object. Although materialists such as Timpanaro claim to recognize the limits of mechanistic materialism, they never challenge its central premise, namely that human beings are identical with nature, and can be reduced to natural objects. Against such reductive accounts, Adorno insisted that materialist theory became untrue when it tried to reduce consciousness to matter because "[i]f matter were total, undifferentiated, and flatly singular, there would be no dialectics in it" (*ND* 205).

In his own defence, Timpanaro explained that by "passivity" he meant only that "there exists in knowledge – even in its most elementary form, sensation – *an* element of passivity, irreducible to the activity of the subject" because cognition requires "a stimulus coming from the external world which is precisely the 'given'" (1975: 55). On this point, Adorno would agree to the extent that he claims there is no sensation without a somatic moment. That a material, somatic moment can be found in sensation affects "not only the basic relation of subject and object, but the dignity of the corporeal" because it implies that corporeality "emerges as the ontical pole of cognition, as the core of that cognition" (*ND* 193–4). Nevertheless, in a remark whose implications will be explored further later, Adorno cautioned against emphasizing the passivity of experience: if "passive reactions were all there is, all would … be receptivity; there could be no thinking" (*ND* 217).

Adorno also charges that conceptions of matter as undifferentiated and monolithic exclude epistemology by fiat. By turning the human subject into a passive mirror of the objective world, the undifferentiated idea of matter also fails to do justice to the object, which (as I shall explain in the next two chapters) "only opens itself to the subjective surplus in the thought" (*ND* 205). This reductive view of consciousness also has an ideological function. In the former Soviet Union, for example, it was used as a justification for fettering "human consciousness instead of comprehending it and changing it" (*ND* 204). "If the subject is bound to mulishly mirror the object", Adorno contends, "the result is the unpeaceful spiritual silence of integral administration" (*ND* 205).

Along with his rejection of reductionism, Adorno rejects dualism, arguing that dualism agrees with *prima philosophia* because both posit an absolute "first" in relation to which everything else is deemed inferior (*ND* 138). When O'Connor compares Adorno's account of the relationship between subject and object to Searle's views in *The Rediscovery of the Mind* (1992) about the relationship between the brain and consciousness,[29] he rightly observes that both Searle and Adorno deny that the irreducibility of consciousness to matter gives rise to dualism even as they undermine "structures that have given rise to reductionism". In contrast to Searle, however, who blames "our 'definitional practices'" for the "problematic distinction between 'objective physical reality' and 'subjective appearance'", Adorno's reasons for rejecting dualism are supposedly epistemological in character. Rather than asking "*what kind of thing* the subject is", O'Connor alleges that Adorno is more interested in the "critical question of *what it does*". To distinguish the subject's activity "from the activity of material objects" does not perpetuate dualism because experience always involves "the interdetermination of subject and object" (O'Connor 2004: 97).

O'Connor claims that Adorno ultimately rejects dualism on the grounds that the subject itself is a constitutive element of objectivity (*ibid.*: 98).[30] Unfortunately, this interpretation is problematic because Adorno denies that the subject constitutes objects in his extensive critique of the fallacy of constitutive subjectivity. Against idealism, he maintains that the subject "is the agent, not the constituent, of object" (SO 254). More charitably, however, even as the object's agent, the subject's conceptual mediation of the object cannot be stripped away, eliminated or ignored, and this is what O'Connor intends. The subject's crucial mediating role with respect to objects also explains why Adorno refused to turn the preponderant object-ive world into a foundation or ground, warning in a passage to which I shall return that critical thought must not "place the object on the orphaned royal throne once occupied by the subject". Rather than turning the object into "an idol", critical thought aims "to abolish the hierarchy" between sub-ject and object (*ND* 181).

Nevertheless, these views about mediation do not fully explain why Adorno adopted a non-reductive and non-dualistic conception of the relationship between the knowing subject and its objects because Adorno ultimately grounds this epistemological relationship in his idea of natural history. When he takes up Marx's claims about the metabolism between our species and the natural world, Adorno acknowledges that human beings, like all other animals, have always been bound up with nature in their pursuit of material sustenance. At the same time, he insists that our affin-ity with nature as bodily, instinctual creatures does not mean that human beings can be reduced to nature because, in the course of their history, human beings also acquired consciousness. In fact, Adorno has a genetic explanation for the emergence of consciousness; he sees consciousness as a historical achievement.[31] In contrast to Searle's largely ahistorical account of consciousness, Adorno develops a rudimentary philosophical anthropol-ogy that reveals the extent to which consciousness is simultaneously bound up with nature and distinct from it.

Although this highly speculative account will be discussed later, I shall comment on it briefly here. A psychological force, reason and its agent, the ego, split off from nature for "purposes of self-preservation", and thereby became "nature's otherness" (*ND* 289). This point is illustrated in *Dialectic of Enlightenment*, where Horkheimer and Adorno describe Odysseus's cun-ning in his confrontation with the forces of nature. Since consciousness "branched off [*abgezweigt*] from the libidinous energy of the species" (*ND* 185), its affinity with the natural world does not entail a reductive view of consciousness. Still, consciousness never fully dissociated itself from instinct because its branching off was driven by instinct. We may have won our independence from nature by virtue of our capacity to abstract from it using reason but that independence will always be limited because nature itself – in the form of the instinct for self-preservation – calls "for some-thing more than conditioned reflexes" (*ND* 217).

Just as I accept O'Connor's account of our non-dualistic and non-reductive relation to nature, while questioning the grounds on which this account is based, I shall adopt O'Connor's description of Adorno's materialism as critical, although not for the reasons he gives. For O'Connor believes that Adorno's materialism is critical because it holds "*both* that the subject does not passively receive meanings from objects, and that the activity of the subject is circumscribed by the determinate independence of the object" (2004: 20). Moreover, O'Connor believes that Adorno's materialism is critical in a largely Kantian sense. Admitting that Adorno has an "unusual understanding of Kant's philosophy", O'Connor maintains that Adorno thinks Kant "provides the ingredients which are necessary for overcoming subjective idealism" (*ibid*.: 19). Here O'Connor observes that Adorno values Kant for his contribution to the critique of the fallacy of constitutive subjectivity.

At the beginning of this chapter, however, I argued that Adorno associates this critique with Marx when he equates it with the aim of historical materialism. Explicitly giving the word "critical" a Marxist gloss, Adorno asserts that what makes Marxism a "negative or critical system, a thoroughly critical theory" is Marx's claim that the "law of the [economic] system contains the downfall of that system, not its confirmation or self-preservation". Although Adorno denies that capitalism will necessarily be overcome as a result of its internal contradictions and persistent crises, he adopts Marx's idea that the world is "a system heteronomously imposed upon human beings as something foreign to them; it is the semblance of system and has nothing to do with their freedom" (*PT2* 262–3).

Adorno contends that Marx was notably ambivalent on the question of freedom. At times, he championed a constant "increase in productive forces and the ruthless domination of nature", including, by extension, the increasing domination of human beings. At other times, however, Marx opposed the work ethic in the name of the satisfaction of human needs, which he saw as the precondition for freedom (*PT2* 187). For Adorno, it is this latter concern for the realization of human freedom in a more rationally organized society that makes Marx a thoroughly critical theorist: Marx wanted to get beyond the so-called natural laws of society "into the kingdom of freedom"; he ultimately wanted to supersede "the notion of history as natural history" (*HF* 117). Adorno's materialism is critical because it shares Marx's aim to realize freedom, even as it stresses the incompatibility between freedom and our domination of nature. Freedom will be realized, if at all, only by overcoming our antagonistic and exploitative relation to nature.

Interestingly, Adorno has an equally ambivalent view of freedom: he rejects both free will and determinism on historical grounds. Determinism is wrong to deny free will outright because, in so doing, it implicitly endorses the commodification and reification of human beings. Determinism "acts as if dehumanization, the totally developed commodity character of labour power, were human nature pure and simple". But the champions of free will are wrong as well because they simply ignore the effects of commodification and reification on human behaviour. For Adorno, then, each extreme thesis is false because both proclaim identity. The doctrine of free will reduces human beings to pure spontaneity, and determinism is similarly reductive because it explains all human behaviour in terms of causes (*ND* 264). In fact, Adorno ends his lectures on moral philosophy with the desideratum that the highest point to which moral philosophy can rise today is "that of the antinomy of causality and freedom which figures in Kant's philosophy in an unresolved and for that reason exemplary fashion" (*PMP* 176).[32]

Rejecting the bald claim that human beings are free, Adorno nonetheless devised a philosophical framework that can accommodate human freedom when he denounced reductive and mechanistic materialism, while simultaneously endorsing a more dialectically inflected conception of matter and mind, nature and history. For once human beings acquired consciousness, we also acquired the capacity for self-reflection, a capacity that may eventually enable us more fully to distinguish ourselves from the natural world. Indeed, the following chapters will show that Adorno thinks that we shall be truly free only when we further develop this capacity, becoming more fully aware of our affinity with nature. Freedom depends on acquiring the critical, and self-critical, consciousness of our own natural history. We have not succeeded in emancipating ourselves from nature because we have not yet acknowledged the natural history that continues to shape us and our millenarian attempts to dominate nature.

As Adorno states frequently, human history displays an appalling continuity when seen in the light of our compulsion to dominate the natural world, other people and our own inner nature (*ND* 320). Unconsciously in thrall to instinct, we have become increasingly destructive and self-destructive. On the one hand, the nature on which we rely for our survival has been damaged, and continues to be damaged, by our very attempts to ensure our survival. Our untamed survival instincts now seriously jeopardize the future survival of all life on this planet. On the other hand, in our ceaseless struggles to preserve ourselves – whatever the cost – we continue to eviscerate the very selves for whose sake these struggles are waged when we renounce the satisfaction of our instincts and ignore our own natural history. These are just two of the paradoxes on which Adorno invites us to reflect with the aim of ascertaining how they might be overcome.

CHAPTER TWO

NATURE, RED IN TOOTH AND CLAW

Marx famously asserted that life is not determined by consciousness, but consciousness by life (Marx & Engels 1970: 47). On the orthodox interpretation of this assertion, Marx meant that socioeconomic conditions causally determine what Georg Lukács later called forms of objectivity or thought. Objecting to this interpretation, which implies that all consciousness is false – or ideologically distorted – consciousness, Adorno argues that "the definition of consciousness in terms of being has become a means of dispensing with all consciousness which does not conform to existence" (1967c: 29). When interpreted in a strictly deterministic fashion, Marx's distinction between base and superstructure was used repressively (in the former Soviet Union, for example) to undermine criticism by suggesting that it is impossible to think beyond the given. Against orthodox Marxism, Adorno wants to rescue the "baby" of criticism from the "bathwater" of false consciousness. To denounce all culture as false consciousness would wrongly extirpate "with the false, all that was true also, all that, however impotently, strives to escape the confines of universal practice, every chimerical anticipation of a nobler condition", thereby bringing about "directly the barbarism that culture is reproached with furthering indirectly" (*MM* 44).

In *Negative Dialectics*, however, Adorno gives Marx's claim about the priority of the material life process over consciousness a more positive reading. This claim should not be read as "metaphysics in reverse", that is, as though it authorized the reduction of consciousness to being, because Marx was primarily criticizing the "delusion that mind … lies beyond the total process in which it finds itself as a moment" (*ND* 200). Moreover, this interpretation of Marx is compatible with the first. For while Adorno believes that it is possible to think critically about socioeconomic conditions rather than merely reflecting them passively, he denies that we can completely transcend these conditions in thought. Even individuals who are critical of socioeconomic conditions are invariably shaped by them. In "On Subject and Object", Adorno again describes the individual's embeddedness in space, time and forms of thought as a type of imprisonment, arguing that our limited ability to see through our captivity is itself "determined by the forms" that captivity "has implanted in the individual" (SO 252).

Just as thought can never free itself from social and historical conditions, so it can never completely dissociate itself from the natural world because the "process" in which thought is situated is also a natural one. Human beings are part of nature: invariably oriented towards external nature, they are animated by their own internal nature in the form of instincts and needs. However, the nature of which we are inextricably part cannot be grasped in its immediacy. Adorno denounced what he called "peep-hole metaphysics" (*Guckkastenmetaphysik*) because it assumes that we can fully apprehend the world that lies beyond our concepts. After stating that this assumption has marred Western metaphysics from its inception (*ND* 139), Adorno insisted: "There is no peeping out". Whatever lies beyond thought "makes its appearance only in the materials and categories within [thought]" (*ND* 140). If nature is always mediated, it nonetheless remains distinct from its mediated forms.

Adorno borrowed some of his ideas about mediation from Hegel, while giving them a materialist twist. He not only rejected Hegel's attempt to reconcile mind and nature by progressively subsuming nature under mind, but adopted Kant's view that there is always a "block" or obstacle to our understanding of the natural world. This block points to "an irreducible residue": to something that is not identical with thought. Although he was as critical of Kant as he was of Hegel, Adorno maintained that the truth content in Kant's philosophy consists in "destroying the illusion of an immediate knowledge of the Absolute" (*ND* 140). Consequently, the barrier or block that denies reason unfettered access to the objective world also "prevents reason, spirit, the very thing that in the final analysis has separated itself off from manual labour, from being asserted in an absolute way" (*KCPR* 75).

Adorno's debt to Kant will be discussed in the next section of this chapter, when I examine some of the implications of the preponderance of the object for our conceptual mediation of nature. Since external nature is always mediated, I end this section by asking how nature might be understood as I review the attempts of Bernstein and Fredric Jameson to make sense of Adorno's conception of nature. The following section focuses on Adorno's ideas about internal nature. Insisting that human history "cannot be divorced from self-preservation, from the satisfaction of human needs" (*PMP* 94), Adorno contends that instincts continue to preponderate over thought, giving the lie to the supremacy of thought over being. Although I agree with Whitebook that Adorno has a Freudian conception of instinct, I criticize his contention that Adorno needs a concept of sublimation in order to reconcile mind and body, reason and instinct. I also provide an alternative reading of Whitebook's assertion that Adorno responds to the Freudian injunction to displace the ego with respect to the id with the aim of fostering greater autonomy. In the final section of this chapter, I summarize Adorno's ideas about external and internal nature and comment briefly on some of their more problematic aspects.

NATURE, THAT FEARSOME OBJECT

When Adorno asserts that Marx's well-known statement about the dependence of consciousness on being (or life) is not just metaphysics in reverse, he suggests that the existing priority of consciousness over life should not simply be reversed. Although the preponderance of the object can, at most, be attenuated, but never completely overcome, Adorno also rejects a reductive view of consciousness when he argues that it is wrong to speak about nature as "the absolute first, as the downright immediate compared with its mediations". Merely to invert Hegel's understanding of mind – by turning nature into the absolute *prius* – is mistaken because it ignores both nature's transience and its entanglement in our historically conditioned concepts and practices. Instead of seeing nature as static and inert, we should view "all nature, and whatever would install itself as such, as history" (*ND* 359).

Nature can be apprehended solely by means of concepts. Yet Adorno also insists that this mediated apprehension of nature "fails to absorb entity [*Seiendes*]" (*ND* 185). In fact, he seems to think that this point is relatively uncontroversial. He not only calls the failure of concepts to absorb objects a "purely privative and epistemological" fact, but believes that this failure amounts to "little more than the tautology that to think something is to think" (*ND* 171). Noting that Kant retains the idea of otherness in his concept of the noumenal *Ding-an-sich*, Adorno also speculates that Kant advanced the idea of things-in-themselves because he refused "to be talked out of the moment of the object's preponderance". Without otherness, Adorno warns, "what is known would be knowledge itself" (*ND* 184).

Although our conceptual mediation of things can make "no claim whatsoever to exhaust" them (*ND* 172), Adorno maintains that our indirect, or mediated, apprehension of the objective world "must always refer to some transmitted thing, without which there would be no indirectness" (*ND* 171). In other words, there is no mediation without immediacy. Moreover, experience itself discloses the existence of something that is not mediated.

On this point, O'Connor explains that there is "an irreducible, nonidentical moment" in experience. This moment, which evokes the particularity of the object, is both physical and non-conceptual. Experience reveals both the subject's own physicality and its "direct engagement with material reality". As a result, "the subject experiences something other than its own conceptuality" in its encounters with objects (2004: 71–2).[1]

Finke describes the epistemological significance of the object's preponderance in this way: the preponderance of the object "implies the acknowledgement of a surplus on behalf of the object allowing further conceptual disclosures and characterizations that can never be summed up in a final synthesis". On Finke's interpretation of this Kantian moment in Adorno's work, "[t]he object of experience" implies the "'thing itself' (*die Sache selbst*) as its condition, but where this thing remains non-identical to its expression within the conceptual space" (Finke 2004: 113–14). Although Adorno charges that Kant ultimately succumbed to a conception of knowledge as "a single tautology" – because the Kantian subject effectively knows only its own categories (*KCPR* 129) – Kant's idea of the *Ding-an-sich* rightly suggests that "the object of nature that we define with our categories is not actually nature itself" (*KCPR* 175–6).

Unlike Kant, however, Adorno does not think that the caesura or block that separates natural objects from our concepts of them is completely unbridgeable. For Adorno, the major problem with Kant's postulate of a noumenal realm is its radical separation of things-in-themselves from concepts. As a result, "it turns out that what remains of everything independent of the subject or that comes to the subject from outside is at bottom completely null and void". Borrowing a phrase from Bertolt Brecht, Adorno contends that things-in-themselves are nothing more than a "noble feature" in Kant's work; they "survive as a reminder that subjective knowledge is not the whole story, but they are without further consequence themselves" (*KCPR* 128). If Kant posits a noumenal realm on largely logical grounds, inferring its existence from inner perception, he no sooner posits it than he bars all knowledge of it. He confines the cognitive subject to examining its inner perceptions because these are allegedly all it can know.

According to Adorno, the greatness of Kant's *Critique of Pure Reason* lies in the clash of two conflicting motifs. On the one hand, Kant succumbed to identity thinking by submitting "synthetic *a priori* judgements and ultimately all organized experience, all objectively valid experience, to an analysis of the consciousness of the subject". If he recognized that our knowledge of objects is mediated, Kant wrongly concluded that we can apprehend only our own concepts and categories. On the other hand, Kant was a non-identity thinker *avant la lettre*. Rather than reducing everything that exists to our understanding of it, Kant "regards the idea that all knowledge is contained in humankind as a superstition". In Adorno's vivid gloss on the first *Critique*, Kant wanted to say that "to make an absolute of everything human is not significantly different from endorsing the customs of shamans who regard their own rites as objectively valid, even though in reality they are no more than subjective abracadabra". For Adorno, then, the *Critique of Pure Reason* contains both:

> an identity philosophy – that is, a philosophy that attempts to ground being in the subject – and also a non-identity philosophy – one that attempts to restrict that claim to identity by insisting on the obstacles, the *block*, encountered by the subject in its search for knowledge. (*KCPR* 66)[2]

The non-identity of concept and object, mind and nature, is the pivot around which Adorno's work turns. However, it should be stated once more that their non-identity does not imply that mind and nature, concept and object, are radically distinct. Irreducible to nature, the mind and its concepts are nonetheless immersed in, and part of, nature. Indeed, it is just Kant's failure to recognize the affinity between human beings and nature that mars his philosophy. Immediately after Adorno describes consciousness as "part impulse itself, and also part of that in which it intervenes", he remarks that, without this affinity between consciousness and its objects "which Kant so furiously denies", there could be no "idea of freedom, for whose sake he denies the affinity" (*ND* 265). Freedom presupposes the ability to act, but individuals can act only because they are also material, physical things, inhabiting specific social and historical contexts.

If something lies beyond our concepts, which concepts cannot fully grasp, Adorno stresses the object's preponderance in a decidedly unKantian fashion when he states that the qualities we experience in things (colours, tastes, smells, etc.) are not entirely subjective. So-called secondary qualities are also objective because they are "borrowed from the objectivity of the *intentio recta*", or from the subject's own corporeally mediated apprehension of objects. Since the subject has an affinity with objects by virtue of the fact that it is also something physical, the "subjective qualities in the object are all the more an objective moment" (SO 250). In an apparently paradoxical formulation, Adorno declares that it is just where "subjective reason senses subjective contingency" that "the primacy of the object shimmers through" (SO 254). Commenting on this idea, Bernstein aptly observes: "if subjects have an objective core, if the subject is … something other than a transcendental subject …, then this will be due to just those sensory/

perceptual qualities which it shares with objects that traditionally have been designated as merely subjective" (2001: 288).

Since subjective qualities are permeated with objectivity, Adorno believes that the very qualities that "the traditional critique of epistemology eradicated from the object and credited to the subject are due in subjective experience to the primacy of the object" (SO 250). Always also objective, the qualities we experience in objects must not – indeed, Adorno thinks they cannot – be stripped from objects in an attempt to grasp things-in-themselves. To try to strip objects of subjective qualities would not only ignore the preponderance of the object by abstracting from the subject's material encounter with objects as an embodied object itself, but would be self-defeating because objects can be apprehended only through these experienced qualities. In fact, if subjective mediations *were* eliminated, the object would effectively be conceived as a pure substratum, a *"subiectum"*, or in the same way that the transcendental subject has been conceived (ND 184).[3] Thus, when the subject posits a "pure" object, stripped of all the qualities and determinations that it experiences, it merely makes "the Other like itself through abstraction". Rejecting this abstract conception of objects, Adorno asserts that "the object of undiminished experience is more objective than that substratum" (SO 250).

Importantly, these ideas about the objectivity of subjective qualities also suggest that, while concepts can never exhaust objects, neither is conceptual mediation inherently defective. Since the cognitive subject and the concepts it wields are themselves "part of reality as a whole, a moment of reality", and "should not be hypostatized over against it" (MCP 68), they can, in principle at least, also disclose something veridical about things. In other words, Adorno never excludes the possibility that we can apprehend objects more adequately than we currently do. He implies as much when he states that "[i]f thought really yielded to the object, if its attention were on the object, not on its category, the very objects would start talking under the lingering eye" (ND 27–8). In Chapter 3, I shall show how it is possible to "listen" to objects when I explore Adorno's ideas about non-identity thinking. Briefly, non-identity thinking aims to rend the conceptual veil that masks objects; it does so, not by abandoning concepts, but by using concepts to forge a path towards the non-conceptual. Entrusting itself to experience, non-identity thinking tries to approximate conceptually the objects with which it is already "akin by virtue of its own objective being" (SO 254).

To resume: subjective experience could not occur in the absence of objects, but objects are always also mediated by concepts. Without concepts, "factual reality would be entirely vague and undefined: in Hegel's parlance, it would be a nothing" (KCPR 87). Since an object stripped of any "added thought or intuition" would be the "very reflection of abstract subjectivity" (SO 250), Adorno criticizes David Hume, whose epistemology "was subjectively oriented while still believing it could dispense with the subject". In response to Hume, Adorno insists once again that, if the object "lacked subject as a moment, then its objectivity would become nonsense". For the subject plays a more crucial role in shaping objects than even idealists believe (SO 257). As the object's agent (SO 254), the subject is an essential and ineradicable moment in objectivity. If one were to ignore the subject's contribution to the formation of an object, the object would "come apart diffusely like the fleeting stirrings and twinklings of subjective life" (SO 257).

Objects can be said to be "immediate" only if this word refers to something that is mediated by experience but is not exhausted by it, something without which, moreover, experience would not be possible. For his part, Hegel failed to recognize that mediation implies the existence of something immediate. Unlike Marx, Hegel "tends simply to accept that something that has evolved then disappears into the evolved reality". Once he has shown that a thing is mediated, immediacy becomes "no more than a piece of subjectivity, ... an instance of mind, ... something postulated by mind" (HF 136–7). By contrast, Adorno claims that mediation concerns our knowledge of objects or, more precisely, how we acquire knowledge of objects. But its counter-concept, immediacy, "is no modality, no mere definition of the 'how' for a consciousness". For immediacy is objective; it "points to that which cannot be removed by its own concept". Immediacy "stands for a moment that does not require cognition – or mediation – in the same sense in which cognition necessitates immediacy" (ND 172).

Rolf Tiedemann remarks in a footnote to Adorno's lectures on Kant's *Critique of Pure Reason* that Adorno was particularly interested in the section of Hegel's *Science of Logic* that describes the mediated relationship between form and matter. With respect to matter, Hegel wrote, form is "*posited* as relating itself to this its subsistence as to an other". For its part, matter "is posited as being related only to itself and as indifferent to other" (1969: 451). Yet matter "'is *implicitly* related to form' because it 'contains sublated negativity and is matter only through this determination'" (KCPR 279 n.16, quoting Hegel 1969: 451). Commenting on these ideas about the relationship between form and matter in the margins of his copy of *Science of Logic*, Adorno observed: "Very profound. In mediation the two elements are not 'equal'. Materialism" (KCPR 279 n.16).

This inequality also helps to explain why form and matter, concept and object, must be differently weighted. Stressing the preponderance of the object, Adorno states: "Mediation of the object means that it must not be statically, dogmatically hypostatized but can only be known as it entwines with subjectivity; mediation of the subject means that without the moment of objectivity it [the subject] would be literally nil" (*ND* 186). At the same time, Adorno insists that universal concepts and particular objects cannot exist without one another. Although they are not identical with universals, particulars are always "determined and thus universal". Conversely, the universal exists "only as the determination of the particular and [is] thus itself particular" (SO 257). When he examines Kant's claim that the only path available to us is a critical one, Adorno adds that his own arguments "terminate in the proposition that the *dialectical* path alone is open" (*KCPR* 159).

Adorno forges a dialectical path to acquire a better understanding of nature. In *Aesthetic Theory*, for example, he famously describes nature as the "mediated placeholder for immediacy [*vermittelte Statthalter von Unmittelbarkeit*]" (*AT* 62).[4] On this point, however, he has been misunderstood. When Steven Vogel (1996: 85) cites this description of nature in his provocatively titled *Against Nature*, he charges that Adorno contradicts himself: he posits nature as immediate while stating at the same time that nature is mediated.[5] But there are at least two problems with Vogel's objection. First, for Adorno, *all* objects – not just natural objects – are mediated placeholders for immediacy. Second, Vogel does not fully appreciate Adorno's view of natural things as existing both in themselves and for us (to use Hegelian terms). He counters this view with the claim that nature is nothing apart from its socially mediated forms. However, Adorno would respond to this claim by arguing that Vogel wrongly treats the "social" (which he nowhere defines) as "that on which everything is supported, on which everything depends and by which everything is oriented" (*MCP* 29).[6] Against this, Adorno contends that "society itself is determined by the things of which it is composed and … therefore necessarily contains a non-social dimension" (*HF* 122). To return to Jarvis's point: neither nature nor society is "an immediate given, a point at which theoretical inquiry" must stop (1998: 16).

Entangled in the material life process, our cognitive grasp of both society and nature is "intratemporal and historic, becoming as well as that which has become and in which becoming has accumulated" (*ND* 201). This also helps to explain why universal concepts can be described as particular. For concepts not only emerge in specific historical periods in response to particular problems and concerns, they may acquire different (sometimes radically different) meanings over time, or they may be superseded by other concepts. According to Adorno, who illustrates this point with reference to the concept of life, "even concepts abstract enough to seem to approach invariance prove to be historic" (*ND* 262). As abstract as the concept of life, nature too is a historical concept. Just as the natural world constantly changes, so too do the concepts we use to apprehend it. Neither nature nor our concept of it is static and immutable.

Using concepts to understand natural things, human subjects are themselves shaped by the historical and material life process they are trying to apprehend. Since our mediated relation to the natural world is always historically conditioned, concepts referring to nature have acquired what O'Connor calls a "historically sedimented character: an accumulation of uses and meanings". These uses and meanings are not only intersubjectively shared, but "sustained independently of any given subject – even the inventor of the meaning – in the social totality". In fact, what O'Connor says about the concept of freedom extends to the concept of nature as well. "Nature" is not just a human invention, it has "various connotations" which are generated by the "efforts of people – not least of philosophers – to articulate" ideas about nature. None of these connotations can be reduced to the intention of a single individual. A function of the activities of subjects, our ideas about nature are nonetheless "sustained in the social totality as experientially independent of subjects" (2004: 59–60).

Hence, nature acquires meanings within specific sociohistorical contexts. Owing to the changing conceptions of nature at different times and in different social contexts, "nature" has a sedimented history. And, of course, this raises the thorny question of how nature might be understood. Not surprisingly, this question has intrigued a number of commentators, including Jameson and Bernstein. As the latter observes in his discussion of the role of nature in Adorno's work: "Perhaps the dominant difficulty in thinking through Adorno's deployment of nature is that, as he is intensely aware, there is very little, if any, 'nature' in evidence at all; all the nature we come across has already been, inevitably, socially mediated" (2001: 189). But Bernstein is not long deterred by the difficulties that accompany any attempt to understand Adorno's conception of nature. For Bernstein, a "substantive answer to what Adorno means by 'nature' could not be simpler except for the fact that its cognitive and rational status is both difficult and obscure: nature refers to what is living as opposed to what lacks life" (*ibid.*: 191).

On Bernstein's view, then, "nature" refers to living or animate beings. He bases his interpretation on a passage in *Dialectic of Enlightenment* that criticizes enlightenment's extirpation of animism, its disenchantment of the world (*DE* C:5, J:2–3). However, Bernstein's identification of nature with the animate – or the living – is problematic for more than one reason. First, although Horkheimer and Adorno did denounce enlightenment's conflation of "the animate [*Lebendige*] with the inanimate" (*DE* C:28, J:21), its crude objectification of the "spirits of human beings" (*DE*, C:28, J:21), it is something of a leap to infer from this denunciation that they identified

42

nature exclusively with the animate because they criticized myth as well, rejecting its attribution of life to inorganic things, its spiritualization of inanimate objects. Their critique of both enlightenment and myth (along with Adorno's later criticisms of the fallacy of constitutive subjectivity) renders suspect Bernstein's claim that Adorno tries "to resurrect a legitimate anthropomorphism, an anthropomorphic nature that is somewhere between the mythic extremes of myth, 'which compounds the inanimate with the animate', and enlightenment, 'which compounds the animate with the inanimate'" (2001: 196–7).[7] In fact, the critical thesis that myth turns into enlightenment and enlightenment reverts to myth suggests that both conceptions of nature must be overcome. Fear of nature characterizes both: enlightenment is just the mythic fear of nature that has turned radical (*DE* C:16, J:11). As I shall argue later in this chapter, Adorno champions, not a compromise between myth and enlightenment, but an entirely new form of enlightenment that would help to reconcile mind and body, concept and object, thereby making freedom possible.

Yet Bernstein also qualifies the idea that Adorno identifies nature with the animate when he associates the animate with an object's "individuated intricacy and power in excess of its phenomenal appearing", or with its "nonidentical excess". On Bernstein's view, "animism is the ascription to individuals of an excess in virtue of which they become nonsubstitutable for one another" (2001: 193). Here Bernstein appears to agree with Jameson, who also equates nature with the non-identical (1990: 9–10).[8] Moreover, this interpretation seems to be based on a passage in *Aesthetic Theory* where Adorno describes natural beauty as "the trace of the nonidentical in things under the spell of universal identity" (*AT* 73). But this reading of Adorno is equally problematic, not just because Adorno is referring to natural beauty – not to nature *tout court* – but also because (as stated in my brief rejoinder to Vogel) *all* objects are non-identical with respect to our concepts of them. In other words, to equate nature with the non-identical does not adequately differentiate natural objects from other objects. Adorno explicitly rejects this conception of nature when he criticizes Marx for calling the non-identical by the "crude, too narrow name of 'nature'" (*ND* 178). In her remarks on this passage, Stone observes that "the non-identical extends more widely than nature, so that cultural items *and* natural beings are irreducibly particular" (2006: 242).[9]

Bernstein mistakenly uses the word "non-identical" in a substantive, rather than relational, sense to refer exclusively to (organic) things.[10] More problematically still, he describes the non-identical as the "deity 'in' the object" (2001: 193). If Adorno thinks we have demonized nature throughout our history, Bernstein seems to believe that Adorno wants to deify it. As tempting as this reading of Adorno may be, I have already shown that Adorno refuses to place the object – natural or otherwise – "on the orphaned royal throne once occupied by the subject". He refuses to turn the object into "an idol [*Götze*]" when he argues that critical thought should attempt to abolish the hierarchy between subject and object, not to reverse Kant's Copernican turn towards the subject, or to bless what has heretofore been worst cursed (*ND* 181). If Adorno tries to give the Copernican turn an axial twist (*ND* xx), the twist is a heuristic device only; it is similar in some respects to the deconstructive manoeuvre of reversing hierarchical relations with the ultimate aim of abolishing them altogether. To be sure, the relationship between subject and object will always be asymmetrical – as Anke Thyen puts it – because the preponderance of the object is also "grounded genetically: spirit and consciousness originally derive from nature itself" (Thyen 2007: 207). However, Adorno wants to attenuate this preponderance by reconciling subject and object, mind and matter, human beings and nature.

In one account of how we might more adequately apprehend objects, Adorno revises Edmund Husserl's phenomenological procedure:

> The "to the things themselves" that philosophical phenomenology had dreamed like a dreamer who dreams he's waking up can only come true for a philosophy that stops hoping to acquire knowledge with the magical stroke of eidetic intuition, and instead thinks through the subjective and objective mediations. (1998o: 13)

Objects can be apprehended only by "reflecting, at every historical and cognitive stage, both upon what at that time is presented as subject and object as well as upon their mediations" (SO 253). For Adorno, then, the task of acquiring a more complete understanding of natural things requires that we reflect thoroughly on our conceptual and practical engagement with nature. Only by scrutinizing the ways in which we have historically attempted to apprehend nature can we improve that apprehension. A similar idea is conveyed in Adorno's lectures on metaphysics: "There is no knowledge that can repudiate its mediations; it can only reflect them" (*MCP* 129). Again, this indirect – mediated – approach to things will not necessarily distort them because, in principle, the cognitive subject's own objectivity makes possible a more adequate apprehension of objects.

What is strikingly consistent in Adorno's reflections on our mediated relation to nature is his contention that we have almost invariably adopted an antagonistic stance towards it, thereby revealing our fear of nature.

44

Among other places, Adorno made this point in his 1962 essay "Progress": "reason, which wants to escape nature, first of all shapes nature into what it must fear" (P 152).[11] Throughout human history, nature has been seen as overwhelmingly powerful, even life-threatening. Since nature is regarded as a fearsome Other, human beings have tried to tame it, to bring it under their control, by force, if necessary. Arguing that this conception of nature is now anachronistic because "technology has virtually made self-preservation easy" (*ND* 349), Adorno also contends that our persistent attempts to subsume nature under concepts for the purpose of controlling, manipulating and exploiting it, reveal that nature continues to inspire fear, dread, even terror. *Pace* Marx, who asserted in *The German Ideology* that human beings have overcome their primitive, "animal consciousness" of nature, Adorno complains that we persist in regarding nature as "a completely alien, all-powerful and unassailable force" (Marx & Engels 1970: 51).[12]

However, it is important to add here that Adorno never denied that nature has also been conceived as pure, innocent, noble, wholesome, sublime – or in Soper's words, "as both the best of friends and the worst of foes". But Soper cogently argues that, even when viewed positively, nature is often seen as antithetical to human traits (1995: 71).[13] Furthermore, many positive conceptions of nature are associated with domination and control. For example, the ideas of Kant and Edmund Burke about the sublimity of nature, along with their Romantic counterparts, "must be viewed as complex reactions to the Promethean achievements of the day in knowing and subduing a 'chaotic' nature". Thus, even the idea of the sublime:

> is the expression of anxiety, but also the aesthetic 'luxury', of a culture that has begun to experience its power over nature as a form of severance from it, while Romanticism only finds expression against the background of a certain mastery of its forces and a consequent concern for the alienation it entails. (*Ibid.*: 227)

In the latter case, "the romanticization of nature in its sublimer reaches is … a manifestation of those same human powers whose destructive effects it laments" (*ibid.*). To cite Adorno's own gloss on Kant's idea of the sublime, Kant thought of nature's sublimity in terms of submission and domination: the feeling of the sublime is "a peculiar vibration between the powerlessness felt by the empirical person in face of the infinitude of natural forces, and on the other hand, the joy of mind, as the essence of freedom, in being superior to and stronger than this natural power" (*MCP* 125).[14] Even when experienced as sublime, then, nature remains an alien power to be brought under human control.

Given this recurring conception of nature as Other and alien, Adorno feels justified in making the ostensibly hyperbolic statement that nature does not yet exist (*AT* 74). Although this statement could be interpreted in a variety of ways, it can also be construed in Hegelian terms: for us, nature does not yet exist in itself. Summarily reduced to "the stuff of labor and the reproduction of life" and, equally problematically, to the "substratum of science" (*ibid.*: 65), nature has not yet developed in accordance with its own inner dynamic. Since nature has a purposiveness "other than that posited by humanity" (*ibid.*: 288), we not only fail to respect nature's alterity and aseity when we treat the natural world instrumentally, as though it were a mere means to the end of our own survival, but we have also damaged nature. Nature does not yet exist because it "has been repressed and drawn into the dynamic of history" (*ibid.*: 131).

As a force that appears to jeopardize our survival, nature conjures up something alien. In contrast to the objects we have created for our own use and enjoyment, nature often plays the role of our absolute and antithetical Other. Owing to this conception of nature as that which we are not (or which is not what we are), our apprehension of natural things is more problematic than our apprehension of other kinds of objects. Consequently, when Adorno states that there are times in which we may come close to the objects we are trying to think,[15] it is unlikely that he considers nature to be among these objects. To cite Bernstein: "all the nature we know is of the wrongly mediated kind" (2001: 190). But our dualistic conceptions of subject and object, mind and body, nature and history effectively mask nature in the self as well; they belie the fact that human beings are also natural beings. Although non-human nature will remain other than what we are to the extent that we are not entirely reducible to it, it has usually been seen as completely Other: whatever nature is said to be, we have stubbornly defined ourselves as both superior to nature and its opposite.

THE UNDERGROUND HISTORY OF HUMANITY

If we have demonized the natural world by turning it into an alien Other, something similar can be said about our relation to our own internal nature. Throughout our history, we have opposed ourselves to nature both without and within. Where external nature has been instrumentalized with the aim of taming and controlling it, we have often renounced or repressed internal nature. As Horkheimer and Adorno argued in *Dialectic of Enlightenment*, the progressive mastery of external nature also required mastery of nature in ourselves (*DE* C:54, J:42). On this point, Whitebook observes that the domination of both inner nature and outer nature are inherently violent. Even as they forcibly impose unity on the diversity of external nature, human beings try "to impose the same violent synthesis ... on the polymorphous diffuseness of the id; the *principiuum individuationis* is violent per se" (2004b: 93).

Of course, Adorno borrows extensively from psychoanalysis in his discussion of internal nature; he relies on Freudian terminology and a Freudian conception of the dynamics of psychical life. Indeed, one reason why his materialist theory is distinctive is because it encompasses human psychology. According to Buck-Morss, Adorno found Freud's work compatible with materialism because he recognized that a materialist moment had been "'present in Freud from the very beginning'" – a moment that appears (among other places) in Freud's "'fundamental concept of genital desire [*Organlust*]'" (1977: 205 n.163).[16] Sara Beardsworth expands on this idea when she remarks that psychoanalysis arose and developed in response to the suffering experienced by individuals who fail to recognize and accommodate the material dimension of their lives, and who are therefore fundamentally deceived about their own constitution (2007: 380).

But it was not just Freud's materialism that Adorno prized. For, as Martin Jay notes in his excellent introduction to Adorno's work, Adorno (along with other critical theorists) never wavered in his belief that psychology had "a legitimate place in making sense of the totality of human relations". If Adorno and his coworkers were prepared to acknowledge the "irreducible tensions" between Marx and Freud, what led them to draw on psychoanalysis was "the unexpected rise of an irrationalist mass politics in fascism, which was unforeseen by orthodox Marxists". And, even after the defeat of National Socialism, "psychological impediments to emancipation" remained visible in "the manipulated society of mass consumption that seemed to follow in its wake" (1984: 85). But Chapter 1 showed that Freud was indispensable for yet another reason: what particularly recommended Freud to Adorno was his recognition that human history is also a natural history.

To be sure, Adorno was not an orthodox Freudian, and he often complained that Freud was a conservative thinker. In *Minima Moralia*, for example, he criticized Freud not only for treating reason as a mere superstructure, but for consigning pleasure to the "repertoire of tricks for preserving the species". Viewing pleasure as "a cunning form of reason", Freud failed to consider "that moment in pleasure which transcends subservience to nature" (*MM* 61). Yet even as he advanced these criticisms, Adorno was discussing the psychology of anti-Semitism with Freudian social psychologists (Müller-Doohm 2005: 292), while writing essays that relied extensively on psychoanalysis and offering a staunch vindication of it. If, in one of his more famous aphorisms, Adorno stated that "nothing in psychoanalysis is true but the exaggerations" (*MM* 49), he also insisted that critical thought requires an element of exaggeration (*MM* 126). Admitting that he himself was exaggerating the sombre side of the human predicament, Adorno declared that, in so doing, he was following the maxim that "only exaggeration per se today can be the medium of truth" (1998f: 99).[17]

In his defence of Freud, Whitebook states that Freud hoped the ego would eventually learn to accommodate itself to its instinctual life. Yet Freud's idea of displacing the id with respect to the ego – formulated in the phrase "where id was, there ego shall be" – appears to contradict his equally well-known assertion that the ego is not master in its own house. If the first injunction seems to promote ego autonomy, the second suggests that such autonomy cannot be achieved. Despite the apparent contradiction, however, Whitebook convincingly shows that these assertions are not as incompatible as they may first appear. For Freud thinks that the ego can displace the id only on the condition that it is decentred with respect to it (Whitebook 1995: 92). Rather than achieving mastery over the id by completely "dissociating itself from and suppressing the id's instinctual material", the ego achieves "this end and enriches itself at the same time and to the same extent by establishing 'free intercourse'" with the id (*ibid.*: 117).[18]

On Whitebook's view, Freud regards the decentration of the ego "as a major advance in the 'project of enlightenment'". Understood "in the Piagetian sense of a *reorientation*", decentration dislodges narcissistic egocentrism, thereby improving our perspective on ourselves and the world (*ibid.*: 93). It contributes to the project of enlightenment by ridding us of the narcissistic illusion of our omnipotence, thereby obliging us to recognize, *inter alia*, that we are finite, corporeal beings who cannot claim special entitlement for ourselves either as individuals, or as members of racial or ethnic groups (*ibid.*: 94–7 *passim*). Recognizing that it is not master in its own house fortifies the ego because the ego "requires austere strength of a certain order to tolerate the narcissistic injuries demanded by psychoanalytic knowledge and to come to terms with [its] grandiosity" to the extent that this is possible (*ibid.*: 99).

Whitebook also claims that Adorno endorses the Freudian project of decentring the ego. Before I examine this claim, however, it is important to note that Adorno frequently objects to the Freudian injunction "where id was, there ego shall be". In *Minima Moralia*, for example, he charges that, with this injunction, Freud vacillated "between negating the renunciation of instinct as repression contrary to reality, and applauding it as sublimation beneficial to culture" (*MM* 60). Later, Adorno complains that Freud made the "doctrine of the renunciation of instincts his own with his principle of the domination of the id by the ego" (*PMP* 138). Here, too, Adorno seems to believe that Freud wanted to displace the id with the ego.[19]

Nevertheless, these criticisms of Freud do not detract from Whitebook's insight that Adorno tries to advance the Freudian project of decentring the ego. Like Freud, Adorno wants to foster greater ego autonomy even as he recognizes that we are, and will remain, natural creatures driven by need and instinct. Autonomy – which would manifest itself, *inter alia*, in thinking and speaking for oneself, in questioning established opinions and institutions, in criticism and self-criticism – is impeded by narcissistic pathologies in the West, pathologies that only encourage adaption and conformity to existing states of affairs. Although Whitebook mistakenly claims in one essay that Adorno adopts Freud's "official" position – namely that the repressive, defensive ego is strong and rational (Whitebook 2004a: 81)[20] – he actually describes Adorno's view as well when he argues that Freud wanted to dislodge the weak, narcissistic ego, which easily falls under the sway of instincts and is highly susceptible to manipulation and control by external agencies and forces.

Thus, decentration would not dislodge or displace an already strong ego in order to give the id freer reign. Rather, by enabling the ego to come to terms with its narcissistic grandiosity, decentration would strengthen the weak ego, allowing it to deal more adequately with the demands of both the external world and its own instincts. Indeed, ego weakness is only exacerbated by current conditions. Although ego formation was always a precarious achievement, the ego today largely fails to develop "its intrinsic potential for self-differentiation" and regresses "towards what Freud called ego libido". In this regressive state, "[w]hat actually wanted to get beyond the unconscious ... reenters the service of the unconscious and may thus even strengthen its force". According to Adorno, then, the already overburdened ego "cannot perform at all adequately the function allotted to it" in our irrational society. It is "constantly taxed beyond its powers" in its attempts to respond to the demands of "both the libido and ... self-preservation" (1968: 86–7, trans. mod.).[21]

In a further divergence from Freud, Adorno denies that a reconciliation of the ego with its drives is possible under existing conditions. Autonomy will be achieved only when society has been transformed in such a way that we are liberated from the lifelong struggle to satisfy our needs. As long as we must devote our entire lives to acquiring the means necessary to survive, we will remain the pawns of society because society depends on the principle of individual self-preservation; this principle enables society to function (*ND* 312). Taking up Marx's criticisms of Adam Smith's claim that the pursuit of private interest promotes the general interest, Adorno agrees that private interest is "'already a socially determined interest, one that can be pursued only on the terms laid down by society and by the means provided by society'" (*ND* 335). Tethering individuals to self-preservation, to the pursuit of their material sustenance under anarchic and volatile economic conditions, late capitalism ensures that individuals focus exclusively on their egocentric interests all the better to advance its own (*ND* 343).

When he emphasized the historical character of instinct, Adorno remarked that our instincts and needs are now harnessed to, and shaped by, powerful social, psychological and economic forces. In fact, he claimed that our narcissistic understanding of ourselves as free and autonomous would suffer a severe blow if we were candidly to admit to ourselves that we are dominated by exchange relations to such a degree that we have become their pawns (*ND* 312). Manipulated and exploited by advertising and marketing agencies with their sophisticated psychotechnologies, our instincts express themselves in needs "which have today become wholly a function of profit interests" (1967e: 77). Since instinctual gratification has been diverted almost entirely into commodified channels, the dictum that the ego is not master in its own house also refers to the preponderance over individuals of instincts that are now entangled in exchange relations.

Adorno acknowledges that Freud was disinclined to view instincts as historical, teaching instead that "the unconscious, from which even consciousness and the objective forms of spirit are fed, ... is ahistorical" (P 156). Yet Adorno also argues that psychoanalysis does not preclude the historicality of instinct. In "Freudian Theory and the Pattern of Fascist Propaganda", for example, he states that Freud "pointed to historical trends" throughout his work in "the choice of his subject matters, and the evolution of [his] guiding concepts". If he failed to explore the social forces that contribute to the development of pathologies such as narcissism, Freud did develop "within the monadological confines of the individual the traces of its profound crisis and [its] willingness to yield unquestioningly to powerful outside collective agencies" (1978: 120). A similar defence of Freud appears in "Education after Auschwitz", where Adorno contends that the discontent to which the renunciation of instinct gives rise "also has its social dimension, which Freud did not overlook though he did not explore it concretely" (1998c: 193).[22]

Interpreting renunciation as a socially conditioned phenomenon, Adorno argues that Freud's idea of renunciation "goes hand in hand ... with the direction of civilization, ... with the basic tendency of an urban civilization that is bourgeois in the broadest sense, that is to say, orientated towards work" (*PMP* 136). Although Freud could not have foreseen that renunciation would increase to the point where it would become intolerable, intensifying the rage against civilization and making resistance to it all the more "violent and irrational" (ibid.), one of his more profound insights is that civilization produces and reinforces its opposite: aggression (ibid.: 191). And, as Freud had shown in "Group Psychology and the Analysis of the Ego" (1985b), this aggression may be discharged blindly, or more actively channelled by religious organizations, the military, and the state to target out-groups.[23]

Of course, Adorno defended Freud's instinct theory in his early essay "Die Revidierte Psychoanalyse" where he criticized the ego psychology of revisionists. In response to their objection that Freudian psychoanalysis perfunctorily divides the psyche into ahistorical instincts, Adorno stressed the dynamic aspects of Freudian theory, and countered that it is the revisionists who have an ahistorical conception of the psyche. The revisionists do with character traits what they allege Freud did with instincts; they dehistoricize them. Furthermore, when they separate the ego from its genetic connection to the id, they mistakenly ascribe "a being-in-itself" to the properties of the psyche, failing to understand that the ego itself has evolved (1972c: 22). When they reject Freud's instinct psychology, revisionists also deny the role that civilization plays in repression and overlook the discontent and unhappiness to which repression gives rise.

On Adorno's view, Freud's insights into the cultural conflicts that are caused by repression reveal far more about the nature of history than the revisionists' "zealous appeal to environmental factors" (ibid.: 23). Revisionists also posit these factors as influences that act externally on individuals, forgetting that the individual is itself a product of society. It is in this context that Adorno points again to the implicitly historical character of instincts:

> [Since] external influences reinforce and bring to light only those tendencies which are already preformed in the individual, … psychology can become more adequately aware of the social mechanisms which have produced the individual, the more deeply it sounds out the critical zones inside the individual.
>
> (Ibid.: 27)

Psychoanalysis can locate "the point where the social principle of domination coincides with the psychological one of the repression of instincts both ontogenetically and phylogenetically" by focusing on the libido as something presocial (ibid.).

A similar idea is expressed in "Sociology and Psychology:" since inner and outer life are now torn apart, Freudian theory, which "turns its back on society and idiosyncratically concentrates on the individual and his archaic heritage, says more about the hapless state of society than one which seeks by its 'holistic approach' or an inclusion of 'social factors' to join the ranks of a no longer existent *universitas literarum*" (1967e: 70). Individuals cannot be reconciled with society by theoretical fiat because there is now a very real, socially conditioned, antagonism between their needs and social demands. Consequently, the resolution of the antinomy between the individual and society will remain "mere ideology as long as the instinctual renunciation society expects of the individual can neither be objectively justified as true and necessary nor later provides him with the delayed gratification". Citing Benjamin, Adorno adds that, in our antagonistic society, "each individual is nonidentical with himself, both social and psychological character at once, and, because of the split, maimed from the outset" (1968: 96).[24]

More generally, when he comments on the predominance of our archaic heritage, or the weightiness of our own internal nature, Adorno again rejects the claim that the conscious ego and its rational faculties constitute "an autonomous second source of psychic life in addition to the id". Although the ego "separated itself off [*sich verselbständigt*]" from the instincts as "the result of a genetic process", this only means that the ego is "both so much instinct and something else" (*ibid.*). The conscious ego "arose out of existence, as an organ for staying alive", and reason developed as the privileged instrument for self-preservation. To repeat an earlier point, the human mind became something other than instinct, only by reflecting existence in order to satisfy survival imperatives (*MM* 243).

This account of the emergence of consciousness helps to explain why Adorno describes the separation of the human mind from non-human nature as both mere semblance and something real (SO 246). If the dualism of mind and body, ego and id, fosters a distorted understanding of ourselves, Adorno also casts the mind's "rejection of what it denies for its own identity's sake" in a more positive light when he asserts that dualism reflects "the mind's historically gained 'self-consciousness'" (*ND* 202). Always also instinctual, the ego nonetheless dissociated itself from instinct as it developed its capacity for reflection and self-reflection. Once it had acquired this capacity, the mind could "no more be leveled down to existence than existence could be leveled down to the mind" (*ND* 201). Thus the separation of ego and instinct is not just real because it reflects our (flawed) self-understanding; it is also real because the ego is not fully reducible to instinct. At the same time, however, the dualism of ego and instinct, mind and body, remains mere semblance because all "mental things are modified physical impulses". On this point, Adorno agrees with Friedrich Schelling: "urge [*Drang*] … is the mind's preliminary form" (*ND* 201–2 *passim*). An outgrowth of its drives, the mind is "not what it enthrones itself as, the Other, the transcendent in its purity, but rather is also a piece of natural history" (P 156).

In "Weighty Objects", Whitebook provides a psychoanalytic interpretation of this semblance of dualism between mind and body, ego and instinct. Here he remarks that the ego was originally formed "in opposition to the immediate spontaneity of the impulse;" it was "established and maintained by expelling the impulse 'to the zone of unfree bondage to nature'" (2004c: 66, quoting *ND* 22), thereby creating "a boundary between itself and internal nature as 'its inner foreign territory'" (*ibid.*, quoting Freud 1975c: 57). However, once it renounced the immediate gratification of its impulses in the interest of survival, the ego also began to deny that it was a creature of instinct and need. From the ego's perspective, instinct "now assumes the meaning of an unconscious, involuntary, and reflexive phenomenon, that is, of nature and unfreedom" (*ibid.*: 66). And, as Whitebook also argues, this renunciation and "extrojection" of instincts and needs, which was:

> only supposed to be a mediate means to the mastery of external
> nature and the creation of the material conditions for human
> happiness, in fact deprives the whole process of any intrinsic end,
> except self-preservation, and, in the long run, not only makes
> that happiness inaccessible but jeopardizes survival as well.
> (1995: 148)[25]

Whitebook also cites the passage in *Dialectic of Enlightenment* where Horkheimer and Adorno famously stated that Europe has two histories: a "well-known, written history and an underground history" (*DE* C:231, J:192). Human history can be told, not as the Hegelian story of reason progressively transcending nature, but as the story of reason submitting to nature in its very attempts to transcend it. In fear of the forces of nature both within and without, we have tried to subdue and control them in order to preserve ourselves. This behaviour gives the lie to our sense of ourselves as superior to nature, as stronger and more powerful than nature by virtue of our rational faculties. In her own psychoanalytic reading of this situation, Beardsworth speaks of the emergence of "an obsessional ego or 'rational' subject in opposition to nature". Stringently opposing itself to nature, the ostensibly sovereign rational subject "unwittingly reenacts the numb human reactions of archaic patterns of self-preservation". Indeed, it is our "fearful aversion to nature" that "forms the perpetually disavowed ground of enlightened modernity and its rational subject" (2007: 380).[26]

Adorno has a distinctive account of instinct. Rejecting Kant's conception of the will, he coins the term "addendum" (*das Hinzutretende*) to refer to instinct (*Trieb*) or impulse (*Impuls*). Where Kant would have considered the addendum to be opposed to the will as pure practical reason, Adorno wants to reinstate what Kant tried to banish or excommunicate from the will on the grounds that there would be no will at all without the addendum, the will's ostensible Other (*ND* 229). Here again, Adorno argues that our impulses are not completely alien to the ego because "the ego itself consists in libidinous energy that has split off and turned to the testing of reality". Moreover, our impulses make freedom possible by releasing us from the "spiritual prison of mere consciousness" and enabling us to "take a leap … into the realm of objects" (*HF* 237).[27]

The addendum is the "rudiment of a phase in which the dualism of extramental and intramental was not thoroughly consolidated yet, neither volitively bridgeable nor an ontological ultimate". Since it undercuts the Cartesian dualism of *res extensa* and *res cogitans*, the addendum is both "intramental and somatic in one" (*ND* 228–9). In fact, when Adorno insists that these two aspects cannot be separated out entirely (*HF* 235), he implies that instincts should not be conceived in purely biological terms. Although Whitebook alleges that Adorno sometimes employed an exclusively biological conception of instinct in order to emphasize "the moment of non-identity between individual and society" (1995: 194), Chapter 1 showed that Whitebook compares Adorno's conception favourably to Freud's when he asserts that both Adorno and Freud view instinct as "a frontier entity on the border between the mental and the physical" (*ibid.*: 260).

The addendum not only points back to an earlier stage of history in which human behaviour was largely reactive and reflexive, but also points forwards to a stage where nature and mind may finally be reconciled. In a passage that has interested many commentators, including Whitebook (*ibid.*: 260–61) and Bernstein (2001: 254–7), the addendum is described as "a flash of light between the poles of something long past, something grown all but unrecognizable, and that which some day might come to be" (*ND* 229). If, in the distant past, our behaviour was purely reflexive, impulse later found itself in the service of the ego principle (*HF* 237), albeit as an element that appeared alien to the ego. In the future, however, Adorno would like to see neither the primitive state of undifferentiatedness from nature – the "terror of the blind nexus of nature" – nor the delusional separation of subject and object in which the subject summarily reduces the object to itself, thereby "forgetting how much it is object itself" (SO 246). Instead, he endorses communication between what has historically been differentiated (SO 247).

Both Adorno and Freud claim that freer intercourse between ego and id would contribute to the process of enlightenment by promoting greater autonomy. Clarifying this idea, Whitebook remarks that Freud's idea of autonomy prescribes "an 'active situation'" where the ego is no longer "heteronomously, that is to say, passively, determined by the id" (1995: 118). Rather than reacting defensively to its impulses, the ego would accommodate itself to its instinctual life by incorporating instinctual forces into its structure (2004c: 71). Moreover, Whitebook asserts that sublimation is the key to this accommodation. Borrowing from the work of Hans Loewald, he maintains that sublimation may make possible a "fully embodied integration of the ego and the drives" (1995: 258).

This integration of the ego and its drives depends, in part, on recognizing the preponderance of the object, a preponderance that Freud also stressed when he insisted on the centrality of the body, while denying that one could have immediate access to "the soma itself" (Whitebook 2004c: 63). Nevertheless, since Adorno was so leery about the concept of sublimation, he was unable to provide better conceptual illumination about how to reconcile psyche and soma (*ibid.*: 70); he lacked "the theoretical resources to alternatives of psychic synthesis that would constitute new forms of postconventional selfhood" (*ibid.*: 59). In fact, Whitebook also alleges that, despite his explicit rejection of sublimation, Adorno implicitly relied on it when he speculated about the future reconciliation of ego and instinct (*ibid.*: 60).[28]

Yet Whitebook unwittingly captures Adorno's own views about decentring the ego when he notes, all too briefly, that *Dialectic of Enlightenment* suggests that mindfulness of nature in the self is "an antidote to the domination of internal nature and the reification of the self" (2004b: 95; see also *DE* C:40, J:32). For Adorno strongly commends mindfulness of nature in later work as well, although it is important to note that he no longer refers to remembrance – *Eingedenken* – of nature, but to "the self-reflection [*Selbstbesinnung*] of the subject's natural side" (*ND* 397). Equally important, this critical self-awareness is the antidote to domination that Whitebook thinks sublimation alone can provide. (Indeed, Whitebook never explains how mindfulness of nature can be interpreted as a form of sublimation.) Reconciliation with nature requires that individuals reflect on themselves as part of nature – in particular, on their compulsive attempts to dominate nature – both to acquire a better understanding of their dependence on nature, and to achieve a greater degree of autonomy with respect to it. The ego will become more autonomous only when it recognizes that it is not omnipotent, not completely master in its own house, but driven by impulses that it can neither dispense with nor eradicate.

In an argument that may initially appear contradictory, Adorno asserts that "we are no longer simply a piece of nature" only "from the moment that we recognize that we are a piece of nature". To acknowledge our affinity with nature is already to transcend nature because the "little piece of our nature that is not nature, is in actuality identical with consciousness of self". Consciousness of self, which takes the form of critical reflection on the self as part of nature, simultaneously enables us to distinguish ourselves from other animals because it marks our specific difference from them. Refusing to reduce history to nature, Adorno observes that human beings are the only animals capable of self-reflection: "any being that stands outside of nature and might be described as a human subject can be said to possess consciousness of self, the capacity for self-reflection in which the self observes: I myself am part of nature" (*PMP* 103–4 *passim*). In fact, Chapter 4 will show that Adorno regards the development of our capacity for self-reflection as one of the more positive features of modernity.

Accordingly, Adorno bypasses Freud's notion of sublimation and champions a more conscious and rational form of reconciliation. If sublimation can be described as active, it is neither undertaken consciously by the ego for the most part, nor is it, on one Freudian account at least, accessible to most individuals.[29] In fact, Beardsworth further objects that Whitebook views sublimation as a form of identification – or, more broadly, internalization – in which libido is withdrawn from an object when the ego internalizes features of it, narcissistically absorbing them into itself (2007: 370). Understood in this way, sublimation does not reconcile "the rational and moral subject with excised nature" (*ibid.*: 373).[30] Instead, it involves a mimetic identification with objects, and leads to the "marked emergence of the death drive" (ibid.: 372). In sublimation, "the moral subject and extrojected nature ... *collapse into one another*"; this allows the superego to act "with the impulsive and unconscious tyranny that hitherto characterized the id" (*ibid.*: 373).

In light of these problems, Beardsworth proposes that transference love – in Julia Kristeva's sense of that term – can help to establish freer intercourse between the ego and its drives (*ibid.*: 386). Like Whitebook, however, Beardsworth also fails to appreciate the pivotal role that Adorno gives to reason: freer intercourse between ego and id will be established only after self-preserving reason begins to reflect critically on its instinctive domination of nature. Reason is the "organon" of progress because reason alone can overcome its limitations by recognizing them as such. Praising Kant for preserving the unity of reason, Adorno argues that "a nature-dominating and a reconciling level do not exist separate and disjunct within reason, rather both share all its determinations". For nature-dominating reason can invert into its other by reflecting on itself, by applying reason to itself in such a way that, "in its self-restriction", it "emancipates itself from the demon of identity" (P 152).[31]

Like Hegel, who argued that "very fact that we know a limitation is evidence that we are beyond it, evidence of our freedom from limitation" (1971: 23–4), Adorno believes that reflection on our instinctual life is a necessary condition for emancipating ourselves from the increasingly self-destructive pursuit of our own individual survival. In *Negative Dialectics*, he declares that rational insight into our affinity with nature is the crux of a dialectics of enlightenment (*ND* 270). Here he revives the central thesis of *Dialectic of Enlightenment*, namely that a thorough critique of enlightenment's instinctually driven subjugation of nature may "prepare the way for a positive notion of enlightenment which will release it from entanglement in blind domination" (*DE* C:xvi, J:xviii). Genuine enlightenment would involve recognizing that our perennial attempts to dominate nature, which account for the rise and fall of entire civilizations, have been impelled by nature. Enlightenment also requires that we begin to communicate with this excluded Other.

At the same time, our affinity with nature should not be regarded as a "positive, ontological determination" because this would allow the dialectic of enlightenment to "grind it to bits as a relic, a warmed-up myth that agrees with domination" (*ND* 270). To foster reconciliation, what communicates through affinity must also be distinguished from what it resembles. Consequently, reflection on nature in ourselves involves both acknowledging our resemblance to nature as instinctual, embodied creatures, and respecting nature's heterogeneity. The mark of a truly enlightened mind, mindfulness of nature in ourselves may also make it possible for us more fully to differentiate ourselves from non-human nature by freeing us "from the blind pursuit of natural ends", and freeing us for "alternative actions". This is why Adorno views mindfulness of nature as the harbinger of freedom: freedom depends on nature becoming conscious of itself (*PMP* 104).

BOUNDARIES OF THE SAYABLE

In his criticisms of Adorno at the end of the first volume of *The Theory of Communicative Action*, Habermas charges that Adorno expands "instrumental reason into a category of the world-historical process of civilization as a whole". Obscuring "the contours of the concept of reason", Adorno's conception of history was "fixated on the relation of subjectivity and self-preservation" (1984: 366). Where Habermas views history from the perspective of progressively evolving communicative interaction, Adorno focuses on the human animal's instrumental engagement with the natural world in its struggle for survival. In this allegedly monolithic account, Adorno "shifts the primordial history of subjectivity and the self-formative process of ego identity into an encompassing historico-philosophical perspective". As a result, he regards the whole of human history as the history of "a reason that is instrumentalized for the purpose of self-preservation, which is posed as an absolute end" (*ibid.*: 380). Reiterating these criticisms in *The Philosophical Discourse of Modernity*, Habermas maintains that, for Adorno, the "compulsion toward rational domination of externally impinging natural forces" obliges human beings to follow "the course of a formative process that heightens productive forces without limit for the sake of sheer self-preservation" (1987: 110).

These criticisms have some truth to them. Although self-preservation has taken different forms throughout our history, Adorno views human history generally as characterized by the struggle for survival. In his 1955 essay "Sociology and Psychology", he contends that "the word 'existence' in usage uncontaminated by philosophy means equally the fact of being alive and the possibility of self-preservation in the economic process" (1967e: 71). Although I cannot respond to Habermas's counter-claim here, namely that human beings primarily preserve themselves by means of communicative action,[32] Adorno contends that labour is the principal means by which human beings preserve themselves. In other words, he adopts a largely Marxist perspective, which he enriches with Freudian psychoanalysis. Where Marx targeted Hegel and others for failing to recognize that the first premise of human existence is that human beings must work to produce the means to satisfy their basic human needs (Marx & Engels 1970: 48), Freud observed that human life has as one of its two foundations "the compulsion to work, which was created by external necessity" (1975a: 38). To date, our history has largely consisted in the activities that have enabled us to provide ourselves with the necessities of life.

Reason has been an indispensable tool in the procurement of these necessities. In fact, Adorno maintains that, despite his prevarication on this issue, even Kant recognized that "reason cannot be divorced from self-preservation, from the satisfaction of human needs" (*PMP* 94). Consequently, Habermas's charge that Adorno sees human history as the history of the species's attempts to preserve itself by deploying reason also rings true. This conception of history is accentuated in a passage of *Dialectic of Enlightenment* that was cited in the Introduction: world history can by no means be understood in terms of the development of abstract categories such as freedom and justice. Rather, a serious history (*ernsthafte*

Geschichte) of the human race would deem "ideas, prohibitions, religions, and political creeds" to be of interest "only insofar as, arising from diverse conditions, they increase or decrease the natural survival prospects of the human species on the earth or within the universe" (*DE* C:222–3, J:184–5).

Although Adorno advocates mindfulness of nature in the self, Jan Rosiek remarks that it is often difficult to determine whether the nature of which he enjoins us to be mindful is our own nature or external nature. Rosiek goes on to argue that this "undecidability" actually reinforces the point that Adorno wants to make, "namely that we ourselves are made of the stuff of nature" (2000: 384). Given Adorno's ideas about internal nature, it should be somewhat clearer of what "stuff" he thinks we are made. Internal nature comprises drives that Adorno conceives in a largely Freudian fashion as both psychic and somatic in one, even as he emphasizes their socially mediated and historical character. Just as external nature is always mediated by our historically conditioned concepts and practices, so our internal nature is shaped and conditioned by social and historical factors. Mindfulness of nature in the self entails mindfulness of the diverse ways in which our behaviour is impelled by historically conditioned drives, especially the instinct for self-preservation, which lie on the boundary between psyche and soma.

Since Adorno adopts Freud's instinct theory, his ideas about internal nature stand or fall with Freud's. However, Freud's ideas are problematic for a variety of reasons. Even Whitebook, who thinks that Freudian theory can provide "a point of departure for reincorporating the body into Critical Theory" (1995: 84), concedes more than once that, with his conception of instinct as lying "on the border between body and psyche, image and word, sayable and unsayable", Freud pressed up "against the boundaries of the sayable" (*ibid.*: 164). Freud's dual conception of instinct, which tries to preserve the distinction "between the object of biological and the object of psychoanalytic investigation", tends to make his theory more, rather than less, obscure (*ibid.*: 187).[33] To take the full measure of Adorno's ideas about internal nature, one would therefore need to unravel the complexities in Freud's with the aim of offering a better defence of both.

Adorno adds a further degree of complexity to Freudian theory when he conceives of instinct both as a hybrid of mental and physical components, and as fundamentally shaped by social and historical factors. Yet, even as he criticizes Freud's ahistorical conception of instinct, Adorno finds something positive in it. It is not just that Freud unwittingly reveals the real antagonisms that undermine the relationship between the individual and society. For the truth content "in Freud's notion of the archaic and indeed possibly 'timeless' nature of the unconscious" consists in the idea that "concrete social circumstances and motivations cannot enter it without being altered and 'reduced'". In other words, by insisting on the unchanging nature of our instinctual life, Freud is attempting to support the claim that reality is always "'translated' into the language of the id", or that it invariably undergoes "modification upon entering the unconscious" (Adorno 1968: 80).

Reality is translated into the language of the id, but the reverse is also the case: the id is invariably modified in its contact with reality. In fact, Adorno thinks that Freud's faulty conception of instinct as timeless and ahistorical had a social origin; instincts appear to be ahistorical only because their development has been arrested by social forces (*ibid.*). Adorno made a similar point earlier. The needs in which instincts are expressed are not static; they seem static today only because society itself has acquired a "stationary character". If we succeed in making society more rational, needs themselves will be transformed. Indeed, Adorno thinks that needs will change decisively once the production process is devoted unconditionally and unrestrictedly to their satisfaction (1972d: 394). Describing neuroses as the pillars of society in *Negative Dialectics*, Adorno also claims that there are "instincts spurring human beings beyond the false condition; but the neuroses tend to dam up those instincts, to push them back toward narcissistic self-gratification in the false condition" (*ND* 298).

If it is difficult adequately to characterize the instincts that make up our underground natural history because instincts are always socially mediated, it is just as difficult to say much about external nature for many of the same reasons. Moreover, our apprehension of both internal and external nature has long been distorted by our antagonistic relation to nature, by our view of nature as a hostile Other, as alien. Only an entirely new mode of cognition would make it possible to gain greater insight into the natural world by taking into account our own affinity with nature while refusing to reduce nature to our concepts of it. As the following chapter will show, Adorno calls this mode of cognition non-identity thinking; he adopts a dialectical conception of objects – including natural objects – as non-identity through identity (*ND* 189).

To conclude this chapter, however, I shall review briefly some of the points I have made here. Since the "suppression of nature for human ends is a mere natural relationship …, the supremacy of nature-controlling reason and its principle is a delusion". Proclaiming itself "Baconian master of all things, and finally their idealistic creator", the subject "takes epistemological and metaphysical part in this delusion". Indeed, the deluded subject may be compared to the master in Hegel's master–slave dialectic. For in its thought and activity, the master merely reveals "the extent to which, in consuming the object, it is beholden to the object" because its preten-sion to sovereignty is made under the "spell" of what it believes is under its own spell (*ND* 179–80). To desist from merely identifying nature with ourselves, we must first come to terms with our own affinity to nature (*ND* 269). Again, to rise above nature in any meaningful sense, we must finally come to terms with the extent to which we are, and will remain, instinc-tual, embodied creatures, and hence part of the natural world that we have historically attempted to dominate. And, as Rosiek points out, this is what Adorno calls the experience of the sublime. Reconciling human beings with their natural history, "the experience of the sublime reveals itself as the self-consciousness of human beings' naturalness" (*AT* 198, cited in Rosiek 2000: 384).

CHAPTER THREE

THOUGHT THINKING ITSELF

Adorno ventured the claim that the entire programme of Western philosophy consists in self-reflection: "philosophy in general has been the implementation of just this νόησις νοήσεως that he [Aristotle] ascribes to the divine principle as the primal image of all philosophy" (*MCP* 94–5).[1] He repeats this claim in his lectures on Kant's *Critique of Pure Reason*: "philosophy is really a matter of 'thinking on thinking', as Aristotle defined it" (*KCPR* 82). But if self-reflection has been the lifeblood of philosophy, Adorno insists that it is not an end in itself. Denouncing Western reason because it effectively condemns thought to thinking itself, he argued that, to escape the sphere of immanence, of narcissistic navel-gazing, thought must become self-critical. He stressed the need for critical self-reflection throughout his work, and dignified it with the name "metaphysics". Metaphysics should not limit itself to the "self-reflection of thought and of the pure forms of thought". As self-critical, metaphysics must question the tacit, unexamined "thesis of the whole metaphysical tradition", namely "whether thought and its constitutive forms are *in fact* the absolute" (*MCP* 99).

Metaphysics must question whether, and to what extent, thought can transcend the sphere of concepts to grasp objects. Although philosophy's confidence in its ability to transcend concepts is as "doubtful as ever", it is both one of philosophy's "inalienable features and part of the naïveté that ails it". Without this naive confidence, however, philosophy must "capitulate, and the human mind with it" because, if thought were condemned to thinking only itself, "there would be no truth; emphatically, everything would be just nothing" (*ND* 9). Reinterpreting Kant's famous dictum that concepts without percepts are empty, Adorno wanted to abolish concept fetishism, or the "autarky of the concept", by showing how concepts are "entwined [*verflochten*] with a nonconceptual whole". If they were not

62

entwined in the non-conceptual, concepts would not be concepts of any-thing at all and would therefore be empty (*ND* 12).

Criticizing Hegel, Adorno insists that concepts are defined by that which is outside themselves, because on their own they do not exhaust themselves. Consciousness itself is "a piece of the spatio-temporal world, a piece without any prerogatives over that world and not conceivable by human faculties as detached from the corporeal world" (*ND* 401). Yet Adorno also admits that his negative dialectics resembles Hegel's dialec-tics in one respect: it too is circular, but only to the extent that unfold-ing a concept (*die Entfaltung des Begriffs*) involves reaching back to the non-conceptual objects that spawned it, and to which it continues to refer, in such a way that the differences between concept and object are not submerged, or do not "perish", in the concept. In the thinking Adorno champions, a concept should "lead to its otherness without absorbing that otherness" (*ND* 157). To paraphrase Robert Hullot-Kentor, Adorno wants to plumb the capacity of thought to allow nature to break in on the mind that masters it.[2]

Adorno makes this point in a different way in his interpretation of Karl Kraus's ostensibly conservative epigram: the origin is the goal. Rather than proposing a return to a prelapsarian state, Kraus can be interpreted as say-ing that "nothing is original except the goal", or that "it is only from the goal that the origin will constitute itself". The goal is to disclose the "life of the ephemeral [*das Leben des Ephemeren*]", or the life of particular, transi-tory, non-conceptual things (*ND* 155–6).[3] For its part, of course, the life of ephemeral natural things has not yet been disclosed because the material particulars to which "nature" refers have been suppressed by being sub-sumed under this, and other, concepts and subsequently manipulated and controlled as mere instances of more general kinds.

Again, Adorno wants to undo this suppression of nature, not by hyposta-tizing non-conceptual particulars, but by cancelling the subject's claim to be first (*ND* 139), and respecting "that which is to be thought – the object – even where the object does not heed the rules of thinking" (*ND* 141). Neither mere thought objects, nor immediately given as they are in them-selves, natural things will be disclosed only when the compulsion to achieve identity has been overcome. As with other concepts, unfolding the concept of nature involves using this concept to reach back to the natural things from which it is derived while sustaining the difference between them, a difference that has now all but vanished in the concept.

Adorno's ideas about non-identity thinking suggest nothing less than a radically different way of thinking about nature that would revolutionize the current, identitarian, mode of thought, which subsumes natural objects under concepts without remainder. Yet O'Connor reveals that non-identity thinking is not a completely novel cognitive paradigm; it is derived from the structure of existing experience because that structure already contains a critical logic that implicitly challenges our destructive and self-destructive interaction with the environing natural world (2004: 76). (For his part, Bernstein claims that identity thinking is parasitic on non-identity thinking [2001: 279].) Equally important, Adorno believes that non-identity thinking may help to redeem damaged life. In this respect, non-identity thinking is a form of metaphysics because metaphysics "is always also an attempt to *rescue* something", or to save by means of concepts what appears to be threatened by concepts (*MCP* 19). With non-identity thinking, Adorno wants to use concepts to forge a path towards the fragments and ruins of wounded nature with the aim of rescuing nature from its misappropriation in identity thinking.

This path will be explored here. To begin, I shall examine Adorno's account of the historical development of Western reason, placing special emphasis on the history of its subsumptive, identitarian employment of concepts. This account is not fully developed, but it does help to contextualize Adorno's critique of the prevailing identitarian mode of cognition, a mode of cognition that also afflicts science. After reviewing Adorno's critique of identity thinking, I shall outline his alternative to it. Since Bernstein has the most fully developed gloss on non-identity thinking, his interpretation will be examined closely. I shall argue that Bernstein has grasped important aspects of non-identity thinking but that he neglects one of its central dimensions, namely its prospective, speculative and emphatic orientation towards things. To anticipate my argument, Bernstein does not adequately address Adorno's claim that non-identity thinking apprehends objects by means of possibility, "the possibility of which their reality has cheated the objects and which is nonetheless visible in each one" (*ND* 52). Following this assessment of Bernstein, I discuss other aspects of non-identity thinking, including its determinate negation of existing states of affairs and its employment of constellations of concepts. The chapter ends by showing how non-identity thinking may help to redeem damaged nature.

A BRIEF HISTORY OF REASON

In a section of *Dialectic of Enlightenment* entitled "On the Critique of the Philosophy of History", Horkheimer and Adorno implicitly endorse Darwinian theory. In so doing, they reject the view that *Homo sapiens* suddenly erupted in nature, or that the emergence of our species was the result of a leap – a view they call "*die Theorie des Seitensprungs*", or the theory of spontaneous generation (Horkheimer & Adorno 1969: 234–5).[4] Agreeing with Darwin that nature makes no leaps – at least with respect to the natural history of *Homo sapiens* – Horkheimer and Adorno contend that human beings evolved slowly over millennia. Moreover, reason played a crucial role in the evolution of our species as "an instrument of adaptation" to the environing world. Reason can be compared to the teeth on a bear since both serve the same purpose; reason just serves the purpose of adaptation more effectively, turning human beings into "animals with more far-reaching powers" (*DE* C:222–3, J: 184–5).

These ideas also appear in the Odyssey section of *Dialectic of Enlightenment*, where reason manifests itself in the cunning of Odysseus in the face of the powers of nature. Odysseus developed his cunning as a means to the end of self-preservation. To survive, he needed to placate natural forces that were far more powerful than himself. Only his "consciously contrived adaptation to nature", that is, his shrewd decision to conform to nature's laws sufficiently to enable him to escape their full force, could bring nature "under the control of the physically weaker" (*DE* C:57, J:44). But if reason originated as an organ of adaptation to the natural world, it remains an adaptive response to a world that continues to be perceived as hostile. Human beings are still imprisoned in the natural context, even and especially as organisms that assert themselves against the organic (*DE* C:54, J:42).

Adorno refers infrequently to Charles Darwin in later writing, but he returns to these ideas about the evolution of reason throughout his work. In "Marginalia to Theory and Praxis", for example, he states once again that the ego's rational faculties "came into being in the first place as an instrument of self-preservation, that of reality-testing" (MTP 272). Viewing self-preservation in Freudian terms as a life instinct, Adorno remarks in *Negative Dialectics* that this instinct contributed to the development of at least one species that did not simply respond passively and reflexively to its environment. If the human animal exhibited the compulsive, reactive behaviours common to all other animals, these behaviours turned into something qualitatively different as we evolved. In human beings, the compulsive mechanism that underlies all animal behaviour was transformed into "the repressing agent", or the ego (*ND* 223).[5]

In his psychoanalytic account of the emergence of reason, Whitebook explains that the unity of the self is compulsive because it is "achieved by dragooning all the diffuse and conflicting forces of inner nature into its service and regimenting them according to the external demands of 'the ego principle'" (2004c: 68). Driven by survival instincts, *Homo sapiens* began to develop an ego when other instincts were banished to "the zone of unfree bondage to nature" (*ND* 222). In other words, the compulsive extrojection of instinct eventually turned into "the self of self-preservation" (*ND* 217). This idea was first advanced in *Dialectic of Enlightenment*, where human history is described as the history of the introversion of sacrifice, or the history of renunciation (*DE* C:55, J:43). To survive, we repressed or renounced many of our instincts; this sacrifice of instinctual gratification was subsequently transformed into subjectivity (*DE* C:56, J:43). Although it remains bound to nature, the "identical, enduring self … is the product of a hard, petrified sacrificial ritual in which the human being, by opposing its consciousness to the natural context, celebrates itself" (*DE* C:54, J:42).

Over time, human beings acquired the capacity for speech, the ability to form and manipulate concepts. Seeing something positive in this, Horkheimer and Adorno point out that concepts enabled the human animal to "seize the identical in the flux of phenomena". With concepts, the same species can be isolated "in the alternation of specimens, or the same thing in altered situations". If the lives of other animals are "unrelieved by the liberating influence of thought", speech allows human beings to escape from the "dismal emptiness of existence", making resistance to it possible (*DE* C:246–7, J:205). These ideas reappear in *Negative Dialectics*. Owing to the universal and abstract character of concepts, there is a breach between concepts and objects. This breach has had many negative effects, but it also allowed human beings to "recoil into what not merely 'is'" (*ND* 202). Indeed, Adorno describes all thought as "an act of negation, of resistance to that which is imposed upon it"; thought is "a revolt against being importuned to bow to every immediate thing" (*ND* 19).

Thought can transcend existing conditions owing to the abstract universality of its concepts. But thought also initiates what Adorno describes as a practical impulse that may aid in transforming existing conditions. Thinking that is "more than the organization of facts and a bit of technique" always has "a practical telos" (MTP 265). In thought that is worthy of the name, human beings distance themselves from the environing world, if only unwittingly, thereby refusing passively to accept the already given. Examples of resistive thought range:

> from the primitive who contemplates how he can protect his small fire from the rain or where he can find shelter from the storm to the Enlightenment philosopher who construes how humanity can move beyond its self-incurred tutelage by means of its interest in self-preservation. (MTP 264–5)

As I shall show later in this chapter, non-identity thinking deploys concepts in just this critical and potentially emancipatory way.

In *Dialectic of Enlightenment*, the human species's relative autonomy with respect to nature is attributed to its capacity to recognize "the logic of either-or, of consequence and antinomy". Here, however, Horkheimer and Adorno focus on the negative aspects of thought, while insisting once more that we enjoy only a limited degree of autonomy with respect to nature owing to our own natural history. The repression of internal nature, which led to the formation of the self or ego, is rooted in the compulsion to tame external nature. This compulsion also incites thought to subsume natural objects under universal concepts without remainder, banishing or excommunicating non-human nature (*DE* C:39, J:31). In other words, identity thinking (a term that is not used in *Dialectic of Enlightenment*) is yet another instance of our irresistible urge to subjugate nature. Explicitly describing identity thinking as compulsive in *Negative Dialectics*, Adorno declares that his version of dialectics is devoted to breaking the compulsion to achieve identity (*ND* 157) because that compulsion distorts our apprehension of the natural world even as it binds us to nature in ways that are increasingly self-vitiating.

In keeping with their conception of reason as an organ of adaptation to the environing natural world whose primary aim is self-preservation, Horkheimer and Adorno claim that ideation, or representation (*Vorstellung*), is only an instrument that allows human beings to distance themselves from nature "in order thus imaginatively to present it to themselves – but only … to determine how it is to be dominated". Resembling a material tool, something that is "held on to in different situations as the same thing, and hence divides the world, as the chaotic, manysided and disparate, from the known, the one and identical", the concept is just an "ideal tool, fit to do service for everything, wherever it can be applied". An instrument that facilitates domination, "thought becomes illusory whenever it seeks to deny its function of separating, distancing, and objectifying" (*DE* C:39, J:31).

Horkheimer and Adorno foreground thought's "divisive" function with respect to objects in their account of the development of language. In the mythical worldview, words and things were not fully distinguished from one another; this helps to explain why human beings believed that words could exert power over things. Over the course of our history, however, words and things were increasingly distinguished, and myths began to lose their explanatory force. The transitional period is illustrated in the *Odyssey*, when Odysseus saved his life in his encounter with Polyphemus by playing on the double meaning of the word "*Oudeis*", which signifies both "nobody" and Odysseus himself. To avoid being eaten by the Cyclops,

Odysseus divorced expression from intention, words from what he wanted to achieve by using them. He learned that words "distance themselves from every fulfilling content and at a distance refer to every possible content – both to Nobody and to Odysseus himself" (*DE* C:60, J:47).

This discovery of the abstract generality of words in relation to objects heralds the emerging rift between subject and object. By outwitting the Cyclops, Odysseus also acquired a sense of himself as distinct from nature. Yet, his was also a pyrrhic victory because it was bought at the cost of self-denial, the denial of nature in himself. Odysseus effaced himself when he called himself "Nobody": he acknowledged himself to himself by denying himself; he saved his life by losing himself (*DE* C:60, J:47–8). Distancing himself from nature by means of language with the aim of ensuring his survival, Odysseus ultimately carved out an ego that was devoid of content. Self-identity was achieved but it was purely abstract and formal because the ego was eviscerated; self-identity amounts to little more than the Fichtean abstraction I = I. Ironically, the self sacrifices itself in the very name of survival by opposing itself to nature both within and without.

Historically, enlightenment has merely perpetuated these problems. Driven by instinct to distinguish itself from nature by objectifying it, enlightenment thought is just "nature made audible in its estrangement". In enlightenment's compulsive attempts to master nature as something alien and other, its enslavement to nature persists, and "the mythical forces of nature reproduce themselves in expanded form" (*ND* 348). Adorno comments many times, and in different ways, on the irony of this situation, which other philosophers have concealed ideologically, or simply ignored. So, for example, even the Kantian subject, whose freedom supposedly marks its superiority to nature, is an indissoluble part of nature; its self-aggrandisement is simply a reaction to the experience of its own impotence with respect to nature. Instinctive and unconscious, this reaction impedes self-reflection (*ND* 180).

The claim that human beings are superior to nature is, at bottom, just "a spiritualized continuation of Darwin's struggle for existence". According to Adorno, "the supremacy of nature-controlling reason and its principle" is a delusion because our ceaseless attempts to dominate nature reveal that we are as imprisoned in survival instincts as other animals. In other words, the "suppression of nature for human ends is a mere natural relationship" (*ND* 179). If imprisonment in instinct helps to "explain the special ferocity of rhinoceroses", it also explains "the unacknowledged and therefore more dreadful ferocity of *homo sapiens*" (*ND* 180). Tolerating nothing outside ourselves, imprisoned within our concepts and conceptual schema, we now summarily identify nature with our concepts in order to predict its behaviour and control it for our own ends. "In fear", Adorno writes, "bondage to nature is perpetuated by a thinking that identifies, that equalizes everything unequal" (*ND* 172).

IDENTITY THINKING AND ADORNO'S CRITIQUE OF SCIENCE

In the late 1950s and throughout the 1960s, Adorno continued to develop his critique of the prevailing mode of cognition in the West. Indeed, Bernstein observes that identity thinking was criticized as early as *Dialectic of Enlightenment*, even though it was not given that name. What was called "the principle of immanence" in *Dialectic of Enlightenment* was later called identity thinking. This principle entails that an object is known "only when it is classified in some way", or "when it is shown, via subsumption, to share characteristics or features" with other objects. Similarly, "an event is explained if it can be shown to fall within the ambit of a known pattern of occurrence, if it falls within the ambit of a known rule or is deducible from (subsumable by) a known law". For their part, concepts, rules and laws have a cognitive value only when they are "subsumed under or shown to be deducible from higher-level concepts, rules, or laws" (Bernstein 2001: 87). Summarizing these points, Bernstein writes:

> Cognition is subsumption, subsumption is necessarily reiterable, and reiteration occurs through cognitive ascent from concrete to abstract, from particular to universal, from what is relatively universal, and thereby still in some respect particular, contingent, and conditioned, to what is more universal. (*Ibid.*: 88)

Subsuming objects under concepts, identity thinking orders, organizes and arranges these concepts in systems that describe objects in terms of those features that make them controllable and amenable to manipulation. Yvonne Sherratt remarks that Adorno criticizes such systems because they ignore the non-conceptual content that informs them; because they become worlds in themselves governed by their own laws; and, finally, because they suggest that the "internal world of detached signs actually 'is' the Object" (2002: 121). Sherratt also comments on the resemblance between this hypostasis of the conceptual system and the Freudian mechanism of projection. As in fantasy, the subject does not actually engage with anything beyond the system. Since "the system *is* the object", the subject fails to go beyond the system to the object. It remains enclosed within its conceptual constructs precisely because "the system comes to replace the Object as the 'Object' for the Subject's mind" (*ibid.*: 123).

The impulses that led human beings to create these self-enclosed systems originated in "the premental, the animal life of the species". The objects of scientific and philosophical systems find their counterpart in the human animal's prey; the manipulator of concepts was originally a fearful, hungry predator whose rage against its prey served to frighten and paralyse it. This primitive "anthropological schema" subtends even the most abstract epistemological systems (Fichte's idealism is mentioned). In such systems, everything that reminds philosophers of nature is deemed inferior, evil; this allows thought "to devour it without misgivings". The philosophical system is just "the belly turned mind, and rage is the mark of each and every idealism". Yet, the more our ideational schemes and practical actions "follow the law of self-preservation", the less we admit the primacy of that law. If we were to acknowledge the role that self-preservation has played, and continues to play, in our lives, our "laboriously attained status as a *zoon politikon* would lose all credibility" (*ND* 22–3 *passim*).

Driven to subordinate particulars under universals, we continue to substitute unity for diversity, simplicity for complexity, permanence for change and identity for difference. Thought is satisfied merely to bring objects under its conceptual yoke. Once we have identified particular objects with our concepts of them, and arranged these concepts within explanatory frameworks, there is supposedly nothing more of importance to be said. Consisting in the claim that diverse objects fall under concept "X", identity thinking effectively obliterates the particularity of objects, their differences from one other, along with their individual histories and development. Classifying, ordering and explaining the external world by ranging it under concepts that are organized systematically, the goal of identity thinking is – to quote Nietzsche, who interpreted this behaviour as a manifestation of the physiological will to power – to *make* all being thinkable, to force it to yield and bend to us (1982a: 225).

Despite the element of coercion or force in cognition, no object is ever a pure instance of a concept; objects are always more, and other, than the concepts under which they are subsumed. To give an admittedly trivial example: to say of "Y" that it is a cat abstracts from the animal's sex, weight, age, colouring, gait, physical condition, whether it is short- or long-haired, its habits, food preferences, personality, intelligence, modes of expression, relationships with humans and other animals and so on – in short, it abstracts from everything that makes that cat a singular creature. Such thinking also has an ideological dimension: the ideological aspect of identity thinking is revealed "in its permanent failure to make good on the claim that the non-I is finally the I". This helps to explain why Adorno thinks that ideology critique is central to philosophy: it involves "a critique of constitutive consciousness itself" (*ND* 148).

The natural and social sciences can be criticized as ideological to the extent that they too perpetuate the fallacy of constitutive subjectivity. Adorno's criticisms of Karl Popper in *The Positivist Dispute in German Sociology* reveal some of his concerns. In science, as Popper conceives it, the scope of concepts is reduced to an abbreviation of particular existent facts, failing to lead beyond their compass (Adorno *et al.* 1976: 58). On this point, Adorno echoes Husserl in *The Crisis of European Sciences*: with its almost exclusive reliance on facts, the prevailing notion of objectivity fosters the "widespread acceptance of a philosophical and ideological positivism" (Husserl 1970: 6). Furthermore, the facts that science tries to register with its supposedly neutral, descriptive-explanatory concepts are themselves constructed with these concepts. Blind to the inadequacies of its conceptual mediation of objects, science has become idealistic. It is often satisfied with the "pure identity of thought with itself", failing to register the heterogeneity of objects with respect to its abstract schema. The truths that science offers are illusory because "the pure non-contradiction, to which [science] contracts, is simply a tautology–the empty compulsion to repeat, which has developed into a concept" (Adorno *et al.* 1976: 58).

Like Husserl, Adorno also rejects the equation of reason with the activities of quantification and calculation. Even Plato, who first introduced mathematics as the "model of method", stressed the qualitative moment of reason. Plato preserved the qualitative moment "as the substrate of that which is to be quantified", while warning that if this moment were ignored, reason would "recoil into unreason". Since Descartes, however, science has tended to ignore quality in favour of measurable quantities. In time, quantitative measurement became the primary model for rational activity. Criticizing this model, Adorno argues that to equate reason with quantification misses the essential moment in reason. Reason does not simply consist in the subsumption of discrete particulars under universal concepts or mathematical formulae. Underlying this subsumptive operation is the capacity to distinguish between particulars: "to aggregate what is alike means necessarily to segregate it from what is different". And, to perceive difference, dissimilarity or unlikeness is to perceive quality. When it ignores qualititative distinctions, thought becomes "emasculated and at odds with itself" (*ND* 43–4 *passim*).

These criticisms resurface in Adorno's critique of the concept of causality. Pointing to the equivocation in the word "*ratio*", which means both reason and cause, Adorno observes that causality "presupposes the formally logical principle – or better, perhaps, it presupposes noncontradictoriness, the principle of naked identity – as a rule for the material cognition of objects, even though evolution might historically have taken the opposite course"

(*ND* 233). This concept, which in Kant is a function of subjective reason, acts as a principle of unity, a single law for all nature. Alleged to be the law of nature, causality "is transferred [*übertragt*] from reason to objects", and "palmed off as cognition of them". As a result, judgements about "causal connections turn into tautologies". Reason employs these judgements "to determine what it effects anyway, as the faculty of laws" (*ND* 247 *passim*).

With causality, we learn what identity has done to non-identity. The concept of causality not only has "its *fundamentum in re* in identity" but, as a "mental principle", it "mirrors the real control of nature". Reason finds causality in nature whenever it attempts to control nature. This compulsion to control is reason's own "spellbinding principle" (*ND* 269). Adorno even goes so far as to speculate that, if it were free from the compulsion of identity, thought might "dispense with causality, which is made in the image of that compulsion" (*ND* 234). As contentious as this claim is, Italo Testa observes that John McDowell also speculates about the "possibility of not identifying nature with the realm of law", while questioning the identification of the realm of law with causality (2007: 480).[6] Yet, there are major differences between Adorno and McDowell. Among other things, McDowell believes that we differ from other animals because our lives are not "enslaved" to immediate biological imperatives (see McDowell 1994: 115–17).[7] In fact, for McDowell, "first" nature ultimately drops out of the picture.[8]

Owing to its subsumptive, identitarian deployment of concepts and mathematical formulae, Adorno questions the degree to which science understands nature. He does not deny that science "works", or that it often succeeds in predicting events and in manipulating and controlling objects. Instead, he complains that scientific knowledge has as its sole criterion "the fact that it works". Since science currently renounces "any attempt to make any statement about the nature of things, and about what things really are" (*KCPR* 134), it might begin to work better if it prevented its abstractions from liquidating the particular, by identification (*ND* 265). Scientists should acknowledge the preponderance of the object, the asymmetrical relationship between concept and object. For knowledge always involves a relation to things that are not conceptual and cannot be captured fully by concepts.

Kant's idea that our knowledge of things-in-themselves is blocked or obstructed represents a "historical watershed" in philosophy because Kant had "a kind of premonition" that "science does not necessarily represent the last word about nature". According to Adorno, "it is a metaphysical experience implicit in the doctrine of the block in the *Critique of Pure Reason* that the object of nature that we define with our concepts is not actually nature itself". Yet, our knowledge of nature is now "so preformed by the demand that we *dominate* nature (something exemplified by the chief method of finding out about nature, namely the scientific experiment) that we end up understanding only those aspects of nature that we can control". As we trawl nature with our conceptual nets, and catch "more and more things in them", there is nonetheless "a sense in which nature … seems to keep receding from us". In fact, "the more we take possession of nature, the more its real essence becomes alien to us" (*KCPR* 175–6).

Adorno also objects that the emphatic or normative element of thought is completely absent from science. Science explicitly abjures all value-judgements in the name of its allegedly neutral and dispassionate pursuit of truth. Against this, Adorno argues that science's claim to value-neutrality is ideologically suspect because science implicitly legitimates existing states of affairs when it confines itself to examining them uncritically. On Adorno's view, the scientific pursuit of truth should be guided by the more emphatic idea "of a true society" (Adorno *et al.* 1976: 27). Science should embrace the normative goal of enhancing human and non-human nature, rather than trying to increase the profit margins of the owners of the means of production by manufacturing ever more effective, but destructive, means to exploit nature.

Despite these criticisms, however, Adorno does have a more positive view of science. If he criticizes science for committing the fallacy of constitutive subjectivity, he also wants to overcome the "fateful" or "disastrous" (*verhängnisvoll*) division of labour between philosophy and the natural sciences. Since subjective concepts are not cognitive ultimates, it may yet be the case that cognition can break through them. And the natural sciences may provide a model for this breakthrough (*ND* 187–8). Adorno even suggests that philosophy might defer to physics to understand how cognition can break through concepts. With Albert Einstein, physics "burst the visual prison as well as that of the subjective apriority of space, time and causality". Physics is now more faithful to our experience of the world because experience itself teaches the possibility of such a prison break by arguing "for the primacy of the object and against its own omnipotence" (*ND* 188). Science implicitly respects the preponderance of the object. In the modern sciences, "*ratio* peers over the wall it itself erects", catching "a snippet of what does not agree with its own ingrained categories" (SO 251). O'Connor explains that Adorno is referring here to the "ability of the object to surprise our expectations and to be unpredictable". The element of unpredictability leads to theories being "overthrown by evidence that could not be reduced to the theory" (2004: 53).

It may one day be possible to "transcend the official separation of pure philosophy and the substantive or formally scientific realm". However, this will happen only by using "the strength of the subject to break through the fallacy of constitutive subjectivity" (*ND* xx). Just as science implicitly respects the preponderance of the object when it revises its hypotheses in light of new evidence, undermining the autarchy of its own concepts, so philosophy displays a similar regard for the object's preponderance by incessantly renewing itself in the experience of its subject matter in order to do justice to things (1998g: 131). In one formulation of this task, Adorno declares that concepts should be used to transcend concepts (*ND* 15). The next section of this chapter is devoted to examining how concepts may transcend themselves in non-identity thinking.

NON-IDENTITY THINKING

As opposed to identifying a thing with a concept, non-identity thinking "seeks to say what something is". Remarking on the apparent contradiction, Adorno concedes that, in saying "it is", non-identity thinking does identify; it even identifies to a greater extent than identity thinking. But non-identity thinking identifies in other ways because it does not merely classify objects by subsuming them under universal concepts (*ND* 149). To cite Husserl's well-known dictum, non-identity thinking aims at the things themselves; it immerses itself in "things that are heterogeneous to it, without placing those things in prefabricated categories" (*ND* 13). Rather than philosophizing about concrete things, Adorno asserts, "we are to philosophize … out of these things" (*ND* 33). When it philosophizes out of things, non-identity thinking transcends concepts by disclosing elements of affinity between its concepts and non-conceptual objects – an affinity that makes concept formation possible in the first place. In non-identity thinking, these "elements of affinity – of the object itself to the thought of it – come to live in identity" (*ND* 149).

Non-identity thinking attempts to show that non-conceptuality is inalienable from the concept (*ND* 137). As Bernstein remarks, non-identity thinking is more fully self-aware precisely because it acknowledges that concepts are immersed in, and part of, the natural world (2001: 291). In fact, Bernstein believes that non-identity thinking marks an "axial turn" towards objects (*ibid*.: 233). The direction of conceptuality should be turned towards non-conceptuality because concepts are not just generated in our embodied contact with material things, but continue to evoke these things owing to their meaning in which their mediation by the non-conceptual survives (*ND* 12). In what follows, however, I shall argue that it is not sufficient to focus on this axial turn; non-identity thinking involves more than a turn towards the non-conceptual.

Bernstein's account of non-identity thinking is insightful and sugges-
tive; it amply rewards repeated readings. Yet his account is incomplete. To
be sure, Adorno stressed the ethical import of a non-instrumental cognitive orientation towards nature and the objective world generally, but
he did not restrict non-identity thinking to revealing the non-conceptual
dimension of concepts, or to disclosing their "intuitive moment suitably
enlarged" (Bernstein 2001: 280). Nor does non-identity thinking consist solely in finding an analogue in the conceptual realm for constraints
imposed on perception by non-conceptual objects (*ibid.*: 300). In fact, by
interpreting non-identity thinking as an attempt to highlight the material
basis of thought, Bernstein deifies the object, violating Adorno's injunction
to abolish the hierarchy between concept and object, mind and nature (*ND*
181). Ironically, he also overlooks the properly ethical – and redemptive –
dimension of Adorno's thought.

Bernstein's reconstruction of Adorno's ethics ignores the thoroughly dialectical cast of Adorno's work. Since an Adornian ethics would no more
be grounded in nature than it would in culture,[9] it must embrace both the
dependence of culture on nature and the mediation of nature by culture
(including concepts). Concepts have a twofold relation to objects. On the
one hand, they depend on non-conceptual material particulars that give
them their content and are the source of their power to name objects. On
the other hand, concepts transcend non-conceptual particulars by virtue
of their abstract universality. They may simply substitute themselves for
particulars, as in identity thinking, but they may also transcend particulars
in a different, and more constructive, way.[10] Adorno alludes to this positive
sense of transcendence when he writes in the passage cited at the beginning of this chapter that negative dialectics grasps its objects by means of
possibility (*ND* 52).

Bernstein's interpretation of this passage is revealing. On his view, the
possibility that negative dialectics wields is the possibility for meaning
that late capitalist society has betrayed (Bernstein 2001: 345). Moreover,
Bernstein seems to believe that this betrayed possibility can simply be read
off objects by redirecting concepts towards their material axis: the damage
inflicted on objects is cognizable owing to "structures of meaningfulness"
in objects themselves (*ibid.*: 306).[11] To return to objects their possibility for
meaning, it is sufficient to return to concepts their power to name these
structures (*ibid.*: 345). For his part, however, Adorno argues that naming
is not sufficient. In fact, he complains that naming can come too close to
objects by succumbing to "the fetish of the irrevocability of things in being".
Bernstein is certainly aware of this problem. He realizes that objects "are
not simply so and not otherwise", or that objects "have come to be under

certain conditions" (*ND* 52). But to return to objects their "possibility for meaning" involves more than understanding how they came to be what they are – in ethical terms, injured or damaged. Non-identity thinking also has proleptic orientation, which anticipates improved state of affairs. In this case, concepts indicate how things might develop under better conditions.

Negative dialectics is resolutely critical; it indicts damaged life by means of the orientation that some concepts afford towards the unrealized possibilities that inhere in it. Its ability to indict damaged life is a function of thought itself in so far as thought inherently resists mere things in being (*ND* 19). Although Bernstein rightly wants to restore the material axis of concepts, he neglects their critical, resistive and speculative force. For concepts also have the power to reveal that "nothing particular is true", that "no particularity is itself, as its particularity requires" (*ND* 152). Concepts wield this power only when their immersion in things includes "the freedom to step out of the object, a freedom which the identity claim cuts short" (*ND* 28).

Adorno had already explained in *Minima Moralia* that it is just this critical and speculative approach to objects that distinguishes his work from positivism. When it fails to detach itself from objects, "thought loses not only its autonomy in the face of reality but, with it, the power to penetrate reality". The cognizing subject not only exists "at a remove from life", as Adorno states frequently. For the subject can engage with things only if it remains at a remove from them. To express what exists, thought requires "an element of exaggeration, of over-shooting the object, of self-detachment from the weight of the factual, so that instead of merely reproducing being, it can, at once rigorous and free, determine it" (*MM* 126–7).

In *Negative Dialectics* Adorno speaks about the "longing" (*Sehnsucht*) of the universal concept to become identical with the particular thing. This longing reflects the inadequacy of objects with respect to our concepts of them. Non-identity thinking thematizes this inadequacy while simultaneously attempting to redress it. Adorno illustrates this point in his discussion of the emphatic concept of freedom. Individuals are both more and less than free. They are always more than free because freedom is, at best, only one of their attributes. At the same time, individuals are less than free because the concept of freedom "feeds on the idea of a condition in which individuals would have qualities not to be ascribed to anyone here and now" (*ND* 150). Thus, non-identity can be said to contain identity in two respects. The first involves what might be called an identification with things through immersion in their particular features. In the second, however, non-identity can be said to contain identity in the prospective longing of the concept to be identical with the thing (*ND* 149).[12] Here, concepts have a speculative orientation; they aim at what would be different (*ND*

153). In both cases, however, "it is the task of philosophy to appropriate on behalf of the concept that element of identification *with* the thing itself–as opposed to the identification *of* the thing" (Adorno 2008: 92).[13]

Negative dialectics involves the "[r]eciprocal criticism of the universal and of the particular". It judges *both* "whether the concept does justice to what it covers" *and* "whether the particular fulfills its concept". Although the particular must be given its due, Adorno also insists that it should satisfy at least some of our concepts of it. These two critical operations jointly "constitute the medium of thinking about the nonidentity of particular and concept" (*ND* 146). To remain content with the judgement that the concept does (or does not do) justice to what it "covers" would amount to abandoning "the medium of virtuality, of anticipation that cannot be wholly fulfilled by any piece of actuality". When it abandons interpretation, thought becomes "untrue" (*MM* 127). But Adorno also argues that, to trivialize the universal concept by treating it like a "soap bubble" would make it impossible for theory to grasp "the idea of conditions which, in giving individuals their due, would rid the universal of its wretched particularity" (*ND* 199). The particular will satisfy its concept only by making good on the potential immanent in it – a potential that some emphatic concepts may invoke or intimate.

Thus, non-identity thinking "contains" identity in a peculiar fashion. Attempting to make good on "the pledge that there should be no contradiction, no antagonism" between the object and our concepts of it (*ND* 149), non-identity thinking prospectively identifies an object with emphatic concepts. These concepts point forwards to changed conditions, such as the condition of a free society in which individuals would develop their potentials unfettered. By alluding to conditions that do not exist here and now, some concepts detach themselves from damaged life, "overshooting" what exists to grasp it critically in light of its better potential. To cite Herbert Marcuse, emphatic concepts designate potentialities in a concrete historical sense because they synthesize "experiential contents into ideas which transcend their particular realizations as something that is to be surpassed, overcome" (1964: 214). They "conceptualize the stuff of which the experienced world consists, and they conceptualize it with a view of its possibilities, in light of their actual limitation, suppression and denial" (*ibid.*: 215).

Like Marcuse, Adorno was also critical of operational definitions of objects because these definitions strip concepts "of what philosophical terminology used to call" their idea (*ND* 151). The idea underlying concepts is a "negative sign" that lives in the "cavities between what things claim to be and what they are" (*ND* 150). The "truth moment" in identity thinking consists in highlighting this disparity between what ought to be and what is, while pledging to abolish it by working towards conditions in which concept and thing may finally be identified (*ND* 149). And, as Gillian Rose observed, Adorno called this prospective apprehension of damaged life "rational identity thinking" (1978: 44).[14]

Even affirmative identity thinking, with its pragmatic "nature-controlling element ... joins with a utopian element" to the extent that it too suggests that an object "is to be what it is not yet" (*ND* 150). In all judgements what the speaker means "is always the entity due to be judged *beyond* the particular included in the judgment – otherwise, according to its own intention, the judgment would be superfluous" – but "this intention is precisely what it [the particular] does not satisfy". It is in this context that Adorno declares that no particular is as its particularity requires (*ND* 152). Dialectical cognition must also experience the inadequacy of thought and thing in the thing itself (*ND* 153) because the "substance of the contradiction between universal and particular" is that the non-conceptual particular "is not yet – and that, therefore, it is bad wherever established". Holding fast to what concepts usually ignore in particulars, negative dialectics also retains the "'more' of the concept" *vis à vis* particulars (*ND* 151). Indeed, Adorno declares that "[w]hat is, is more than it is". This "more" is "not imposed upon the object but remains immanent to it, as that which has been pushed out of it". He continues: "In that sense, the nonidentical would be the thing's own identity against its identifications" (*ND* 161).

Determinate negation, which Adorno called "right thinking" in his lectures on *Negative Dialectics* (2008: 28), allows concepts to evoke something other than what exists. Although Bernstein seems to recognize this at times,[15] he does not give determinate negation the central role it deserves in his construction of an Adornian ethics. If thought inherently resists mere things in being, its resistance is all the more powerful when its ideas are forged in the crucible of our painful experiences of damaged life. For by negating these negative experiences, we may succeed in envisaging conditions under which suffering might end. Pain and negativity are "the moving forces of dialectical thinking" (*ND* 202) because, through them, we may glean reality's better potential.

With respect to the idea of freedom, Adorno states that it is just "nature-controlling sovereignty and its social form, domination over people, that suggest the opposite to our consciousness: the idea of freedom" (*ND* 220). The shape of freedom "can only be grasped in determinate negation [*bestimmte Negation*] in accordance with the concrete form of a specific unfreedom" (*ND* 231). Our ideas of freedom emerge in the negation of what is negative, of the unfree conditions in which we live. Hence, freedom is impeded by the very conditions that our idea of freedom presupposes. Conceived in relation to extramental reality, our idea of freedom offers "a polemical counter-image to the suffering brought on by social coercion; unfreedom is that coercion's image" (*ND* 223). Negating those aspects of historical reality that cause suffering by perpetuating unfreedom, this idea can also be used critically to indict an unfree reality.

In *Eclipse of Reason*, Horkheimer made a similar remark about the historical derivation of emphatic concepts: "At all times", he wrote, "the good has shown the traces of the oppression in which it originated". The idea of human dignity is a case in point: this idea was "born from the experience of barbarian forms of domination" (1974: 177). Although neither Horkheimer nor Adorno explicitly mentions them, they invite us to think of movements such as abolitionism and universal suffrage, where the unfree conditions that caused suffering also spawned ideas about conditions under which oppression might end. Again, emphatic ideas of freedom arise within oppressive situations as resistance to repression (*ND* 265). There are fragments of good in the world, but these only appear through a glass darkly; they are glimpsed by those who resist (in thought, action, or both) injustice, unfreedom, intolerance and oppression. Modernity's rational potential manifests itself wherever individuals confront and contest the limits to their freedom, in conditions that reduce them to mere cogs in the wheels of the economic machinery, and in their struggles against the multifarious forms of oppressive state power.[16]

Emphatic concepts intimate what might yet be: the better potential that lies within damaged life. In so doing, they cast a negative light on existing conditions, revealing that these conditions do not make good on the potential they contain. Making this point in "Individuum und Organisation", Adorno admits that we "may not know what people are and what the correct arrangement of human affairs should be". Yet "we do know what [people] should not be and what arrangement of human affairs is false". It is only in this critical understanding of the negative aspects of the human predicament that "the other, positive, one is open to us" (1972b: 456). This idea reappears in a 1969 radio lecture, "Critique", where Adorno offers his own variation on Baruch Spinoza's famous proposition: all determination is negation. In response to Spinoza's claim that truth is an *index sui et falsi*, Adorno counters that "the false, once determinately known and precisely expressed, is already an index of what is right and better" (1998b: 288).[17]

However, Hammer is mistaken when he states that the determinate negation of false conditions gives rise to incontestable or incontrovertible ideas about what is right and better: an *a priori* that can be wielded critically (2006: 85). Rather, by negating specific circumstances at particular points in time, determinate negation evokes historically conditioned and limited ideas about improved states of affairs. In *Minima Moralia*, for example, Adorno observed that we derive our ideas about what is possible from our historically situated critique of damaged life. In criticism, we fashion, entirely from contact with objects, perspectives on the world that displace and estrange it. On the one hand, estrangement through the lens of possibility is easy to achieve to the extent that "consummate negativity, once squarely faced, delineates the mirror-image of its opposite". On the other hand, estrangement is also very difficult because our ideas about the "opposite" of negativity are educed from the same "distortion and indigence" that we are trying to escape (*MM* 247). To put this idea in another way, our critical perspectives are not just shaped, but tainted, by the historical conditions we criticize.

This is one reason why Adorno rejects Hegel's claim that the negation of the negation yields something positive. Even if it were possible to imagine all things radically altered, our images of these things would be chained to ourselves and "to our present time as static points of reference, and everything would be askew" (*ND* 352). But Adorno also charges that to "equate the negation of negation with positivity is the quintessence of identification" (*ND* 158). A critique of damaged life may indicate what is right and better, but it does so only obliquely. The negation of the negative remains negative because, at best, positivity is only indirectly outlined by critique. A critical negation of existing states of affairs, determinate negation discloses something equally negative: that what exists is not yet what it ought to be, and that what ought to be does not yet exist. In other words, the negation of the negation only yields more negativity.

Fotini Vaki takes issue with Adorno on this point. According to Vaki, the labour of the negative in Adorno's work consists in setting "the object against its own internal tensions, contradictions and inconsistencies, manifesting thereby the object's failure to fulfill its own concept". Arguing that Adorno embraces the first dimension of Hegel's determinate negation, Vaki thinks that he dismissed the second – the view that the negation of the negation will lead to "more coherent and complete forms of life and consciousness" (Vaki 2005: 111) – because he wrongly believed that Hegel thought history was destined to come to a standstill (*ibid.*: 112–13). Nevertheless, Adorno did not reject the second dimension of determinate negation because he took issue with Hegel's obscure thesis of the end of history. Instead, what Adorno contests in Hegel's account of determinate negation is the claim that the negation of the negation always yields something positive, that the real will become rational of necessity.

Vaki also questions how far critical theory can go "by relying only on the recognition of contradictions" (*ibid.*: 114). She objects that the standpoint from which Adorno criticizes social reality "is only glimpsed indirectly in a completely unspecified way", and that he never clarifies the concrete conditions under which his emphatic ideas would be realized (*ibid.*: 116).

However, Adorno would readily concede these points: he explicitly states that materialism gives the *Bilderverbot*, or ban on images, a secular form because it does not permit utopia to be pictured in an entirely positive way. But a further problem arises: for even as Adorno admits that it is not possible at present fully to conceptualize or imagine substantively improved conditions, he appears to ignore the ban on images when he states, *inter alia*, that the perspective vanishing point of his materialism is "the spirit's liberation from the primacy of material needs in their state of fulfillment" (*ND* 207).

Elizabeth Pritchard explains that determinate negation enabled Adorno to arrive at ideas about improved conditions, but only in the form of an inverted image of damaged life (2004: 187).[18] At one and the same time, the determinate negation of damaged life allowed him to dismiss an "outright description of the absolute (positive theology)", and to flout "the prohibition upon such description based on the purportedly 'wholly other' character of the absolute (negative theology)". With determinate negation, Adorno wanted both to "reveal the features of damaged life that preempt redemption" and to "indicate something determinate about that redemption, without thereby presuming its immanent arrival" (*ibid.*: 193). Moreover, Pritchard cogently argues that Adorno refused to accept a complete ban on images because such a ban would risk leaving the status quo unchallenged: it would bar any and all attempts to conceive of alternatives (*ibid.*).[19]

To the charge that determinate negation affords only a limited glimpse of conditions that transcend existing ones, Adorno would counter that nothing more can be achieved because there is no more secure standpoint for critique. Since the good life can be glimpsed only "in resistance to the forms of the bad life that have been seen through and critically dissected", it is not possible to envisage anything beyond this negative stance (*PMP* 167–8).[20] In another vivid metaphor Adorno states that critical thinkers must do "what the miner's adage forbids: work their way through the darkness without a lamp, without possessing the positive through the higher concept of the negation of the negation, and immerse themselves in the darkness as deeply as they possibly can" (*MCP* 144). By problematizing critique in this way, Adorno also exacts humility from those who might otherwise claim to occupy a superior standpoint. Critics must scrutinize their concepts carefully. Even those who "will not be stopped from differing and criticizing" are not authorized to put themselves in the right because their criticism is sullied by the reality they want to change (*ND* 352). Still, determinate negation offers the only viable critical leverage on damaged conditions by making it possible to think beyond them to a limited extent, indicating directions for change.

Since the transcendence of existing conditions feeds on nothing but the experiences we have in immanence (*ND* 398), Adorno describes transcendence in a characteristically aporetic fashion. On the one hand, those who attempt to "nail down transcendence can rightly be charged ... with ... a betrayal of transcendence" because any attempt to "nail down" what surpasses existing conditions will fail. On the other hand, "if the possibility, however feeble and distant, of redemption in existence were cut off altogether, the human spirit would become an illusion, and the finite, conditioned, merely existing subject would eventually be deified as carrier of the spirit" (*ND* 400). As noted earlier, there is an implicitly emancipatory moment in all thought. Thought that refuses to "have its law prescribed for it by given facts transcends them even in the closest contact with objects" (*ND* 17). But if all thought is implicitly critical, it becomes explicitly so by negating the negative: damaged life.

Adorno admits that determinate negation is an entirely subjective process. Yet he also claims that the moment of determinate negation "is the strongest argument for the adequacy [*Zulänglichkeit*] of emphatic knowledge" (*ND* 159 n.). Jarvis indirectly makes sense of this claim when he remarks that we have no access to "some kind of immediate objectivity wholly free of subjective mediation". In other words, it is not "possible to guarantee objective knowledge simply by stripping away those elements of cognition considered to be subjective, as if they were an accidental extra" (Jarvis 1998: 183). This idea that knowledge contains an ineradicable subjective dimension that does not necessarily compromise it applies to knowledge acquired with emphatic concepts as well. If subjective concepts generally may have a purchase on objectivity, so too an emphatic apprehension of objects, of the suppressed potential immanent in them, is not irredeemably defective. In fact, Adorno contends that "the resistance of thought to mere things in being, the commanding freedom of the subject, intends in the object even that of which the object was deprived by objectification" (*ND* 19).

Although emphatic ideas are often used ideologically to legitimate existing conditions, they may also reveal the disparity between what society claims to be and what it currently is. *Contra* Bernstein, who states that, for Adorno, actual possibility is unattainable (2001: 434–5), Adorno believes that resistive thought can disclose real possibilities that social conditions belie to the extent that it negates what, specifically, is damaging in these conditions. Again, like Marcuse, Adorno adopts (with the caveats noted above) Hegel's idea that the possible "can be derived from the very content of the real" (Marcuse 1999: 150). To give but one example (which will be discussed briefly in Chapter 4), the state of technology is now such that it points to the real possibility of liberating ourselves from the compulsive pursuit of self-preservation. For Adorno: "The more enhanced the forces of production, the less will the perpetuation of life as an end in itself remain a matter of course. The end, as a prey to nature, becomes questionable in itself while the potential of something other is maturing inside it" (*ND* 349).

Immediately after describing determinate negation as subjective, Adorno adds that the moment of determinate negation actually "supports the possibility of a metaphysics beyond the Hegelian one" (*ND* 159). In his lectures on metaphysics, he makes a similar remark: determinate negation is "the only form in which metaphysical experience survives today" (*MCP* 144). Throughout its history, metaphysics has involved "an attempt to save – and to save by means of concepts – what appeared at the time to be threatened precisely by concepts, and was in the process of being disintegrated, or corroded" (*MCP* 19). As mentioned earlier, metaphysics rescues objects when it discloses the damage done to them, using concepts that evoke their better potential. On a more literal interpretation, determinate negation supports the possibility of metaphysics by enabling thought to go beyond what physically exists, to transcend the given.

To resume, Adorno's negative dialectics is a dialectics of both immanence – the always only partial immersion in things – and the partial transcendence of things through emphatic concepts derived by means of determinate negation. Although philosophy should immerse itself in "things that are heterogeneous to it without placing those things in prefabricated categories" (*ND* 13), philosophers who merely attempt to mirror the objects they are trying to think will fail to grasp them because an object "only opens itself up to the subjective surplus in thought" (*ND* 205). Philosophers can reveal the uniqueness and singularity of particular things only by reflecting critically on their conceptual mediation of them in an attempt to rend the conceptual veil that distorts them. But they also determine things more actively, using concepts to disclose unrealized possibilities in things, possibilities gleaned through immersion in them.[21] In this respect, Hullot-Kentor likens Adorno to Hegel: for both, thinking "is how the mind is bound up in what it is at the same time separate from, and the being bound up is itself a determination of the separation as determinate negation" (Hullot-Kentor 2006: 164).

When he rejects dualistic conceptions of the cognizing subject and the object it seeks to know – which express the antagonism between human beings and nature in epistemological form – Adorno remarks that epistemological dualism may itself be overcome by means of the "determinate negation of the individual moments whereby subject and object are turned into absolute opposites". "In truth", he observes, "the subject is never quite the subject, and the object never quite the object; and yet the two are not pieced together out of any third that transcends them". Although the "division, which makes the object the alien thing to be mastered and appropriates it, is indeed subjective", it is also the case that "no critique of its subjective origin will reunify the parts, once they have split in reality". At one and the same time, then, we must critically maintain the "duality of subject and object ... against thought's inherent claim to be total", while recognizing that a radically dualistic conception of reason and nature is equally false (*ND* 175 *passim*). This idea reappears in "Reason and Revelation:" reason "must attempt to define rationality itself, not as an absolute ... but rather as a moment within the totality, though admittedly even this moment has become independent in relation to the totality" (1998k: 138).

In the course of this discussion of the role of determinate negation in non-identity thinking, I may have given the impression that non-identity thinking consists in wielding emphatic concepts in an isolated and piece-meal fashion. This impression can be corrected by examining a dense and elliptical section of *Negative Dialectics* where Adorno proposes that constellations of concepts be deployed to apprehend objects (*ND* 162–3).[22] David Kaufmann interprets this section in the following way: since each concept is particular, it necessarily "misses its mark in the object", and "other concepts need to be mobilized to correct its insufficiencies". Although these concepts will, in turn, suffer from the same problem, they will do so in a "slightly different way". By arranging concepts in a constellation, however, we may be able to "form an asymptotic approximation of the truth of the object" (2004: 170). In Adorno's own words, when concepts are clustered around an object, they "potentially determine the object's interior". Constellations of diverse concepts may illuminate "the specific side of the object, the side which to a classifying procedure is either a matter of indifference or a burden" (*ND* 162). Again, given Adorno's ideas about mediation, he can consistently deny that the determination of a natural object by a constellation of concepts will invariably obscure what that object is "internally".

Stone offers a more historically sensitive gloss on the rationale behind the deployment of constellations when she focuses on the following assertion: "Becoming aware of the constellation in which a thing stands is tantamount to deciphering the constellation which, having come to be, the thing bears within itself" (*ND* 163). For Adorno, "the specificity of any thing consists in the sedimentation of history in it". In the course of history, "any thing enters into multiple relations with other things; each such relation shapes and marks this thing; each thing, therefore, exists as a precipitate of its complex history". Optimally, concepts will provide "a chart or map" of these "sedimented past relations". Although Stone mis-takenly thinks that relations between concepts in a constellation should simply "mirror the relations between the many aspects of the thing" (2006: 241), she tries to do justice here to Adorno's claim that concepts should transcend concepts.

Interestingly, Adorno thinks that we can learn from science how objects may be unlocked by their constellation. In *Negative Dialectics*, he praises Max Weber's employment of ideal types; these are sociological concepts that are "gradually composed' from 'individual parts ... taken from historic reality'" (*ND* 164). Remarking on Adorno's debt to Weber, Axel Honneth states that, in:

> Weber's essay "Objectivity", we read, in almost word-for-word agreement with Adorno, that the ideal type should be under-stood as "the synthesis of a great many diffuse, discrete, more or less present and occasionally absent *concrete individual* phenom-ena into a unified *thought* construct. (2005: 53)[23]

In *The Protestant Ethic and the Spirit of Capitalism*, Weber illustrates his constellative approach to objects by gathering diverse concepts around capitalism – acquisitiveness, the profit motive, calculation, organization, bookkeeping – to express what the concept of capitalism "aims at, not to circumscribe it to operational ends" (*ND* 166).[24]

If constellations like these form a subjectively created context, Adorno again refused to view the subject as an invariable source of distortion when he stated that this subjective context can be read "as a sign of objectiv-ity", or as a sign of the "spiritual substance [*geistigen Gehalts*]" of things (*ND* 165).[25] For truth emerges in "a constellation of subject and object in which both penetrate each other". Criticizing Martin Heidegger, Adorno declares that truth "can no more be reduced to subjectivity than to that Being whose dialectical relation to subjectivity Heidegger tends to blur" (*ND* 127). Furthermore, truth is not something static; it is not given once and for all. To apprehend the truth of natural things, philosophy must con-stantly renew itself "in the experience of the subject matter". Thus, truth is "a constantly evolving constellation" (Adorno 1998g: 131), and objects are "infinitely given as a task" (SO 253).

Bernstein too emphasizes the moral dimension of this task, arguing that "[n]egative dialectics as a whole is a response to damaged sensuous par-ticularity" (2001: 361). Indeed, Adorno describes truth in a more emphatic way when he asserts that the condition of all truth lies in "the need to lend a voice to suffering" (*ND* 17). Philosophy can do "justice to the experience of nature only when … it incorporates nature's wounds" (*AT* 68). To return to a remark made by Stone, constellations lend a voice to suffering by showing that natural things "have been damaged, prevented from existing in their spontaneous forms" (Stone 2006: 243). To this, I would add that a constellation can reveal the damage done to natural things only on the condition that at least some of its concepts are emphatic in character, that is, when at least some of its concepts point to possibilities in nature that existing conditions have betrayed (*ND* 52). Among the concepts that form a constellation, then, are ideas that gesture towards the possibilities in non-human nature in order to ascertain what things might become if the conditions that now damage them were ameliorated in such a way as to enable them to flourish. And, as Adorno states repeatedly, these emphatic ideas of undistorted nature arise "only in distortion, as its opposite" (*MM* 95).

In its determinate negation of wounded nature, philosophy resembles artworks because both attempt to rescue nature by negating its repression through reflection (*AT* 288).[26] But, since art determines its object as "indeterminable", it "requires philosophy, which interprets [art] in order to say what it is unable to say" (*AT* 72). This point is made frequently: "Every artwork, if it is to be fully experienced, requires thought and therefore stands in need of philosophy" (*AT* 262). But philosophy and art must be distinguished for another reason. For if philosophy refuses to abandon "the longing that animates the nonconceptual side of art", it is also the case that a "philosophy that tried to imitate art, that would turn itself into a work of art, would be expunging itself" (*ND* 15). In contrast to art, "philosophy cannot survive without the linguistic effort" because the "organon of thought" is language (*ND* 56). Consequently, Bernstein is right to argue that the claim, advanced by some, that Adorno wanted "to displace reason with aesthetic praxis and judgement" represents "a massive misunderstanding and distortion of his thought" (2001: 4).[27]

More generally, philosophy must reflect critically upon its concepts, including concepts that refer to nature, with the ultimate aim of enabling "a mutual approximation of thing and expression", to the point where the difference between them fades. In this attempt to approximate material particular and abstract universal, philosophy reveals its utopian bent because to want "substance in cognition is to want a utopia" (*ND* 56). In another formulation of the goal of negative dialectics, Adorno states that his "cognitive utopia would be to use concepts to unseal the nonconceptual with concepts, without making it their equal" (*ND* 10). Expressing this idea in a starkly aporetic way, he writes that the goal of a "changed philosophy would be to become aware of likeness by defining it as that which is unlike itself" (*ND* 150).

THINKING NATURE

Michael Theunissen (1983: 51) believes that Adorno follows Marx when he postulates "the necessity of universal compulsion for the realization of freedom".[28] However, in *Negative Dialectics*, Adorno cites, not Marx but Hegel, insisting that he differs from Hegel only in intent. Unlike Hegel, who saw identity (the identity of identity and difference) "as the ultimate, the absolute", Adorno contends that prospects for transforming late capitalist society into a realm of freedom presuppose the experience of identity as "a universally coercive mechanism which we … ultimately need in order to free ourselves from universal coercion, just as freedom can come to be real only through coercive civilization, not by way of any 'Back to nature'" (*ND* 147).

It would nonetheless be wrong to conclude that Adorno wanted to justify or legitimate universal coercion when he described it as necessary. In fact, he challenged what he called the theodicy of conflict (*HF* 52), or the theodicy of suffering, when he denied that our antagonism to nature was historically necessary and denounced the view that "failure, death and oppression are the inevitable essence of things". Against this fatalistic view, Adorno countered that suffering is both avoidable and criticisable (2008: 104), that history need not have followed a coercive course (*ND* 321), and that this course can be changed at any time (*HF* 68). But since Western history has largely been coercive, exploitative and oppressive, it has "necessarily" given rise to concepts such as freedom, justice and democracy, which are derived from the very conditions they oppose and would not have arisen in their absence. The conditions that now prevent the realization of modernity's rational potential point dialectically to their own reversal because that potential resides within these negative conditions and can be disclosed by reflecting critically on our suppression of nature both within and without.

Adorno traces some of these ideas back to Kant. In "Idea for a Universal History with a Cosmopolitan Purpose", Kant taught that "the entanglement of progress … in nature's hold upon the domination of nature, in short, in the realm of unfreedom, tends by means of its own law toward the realm of freedom". Stating that Hegel derived his own idea of the cunning of reason from this, Adorno also observes that Kant regarded the reconciliation of reason and nature as "immanent in the antagonistic 'development' because he derived it from a design that nature harbors for human beings" (P 149).[29] Although Kant dogmatically ascribed this design to nature, and wrongly regarded nature as static and inert (*HF* 151), Adorno notes with approval that "Kant comes closest to the concept of reconciliation in the thought that the antagonism terminates in its abolition" (P 150).

Adorno called this salutary reversal of fortune the dialectic of progress, and went on to describe it this way: "While the perpetual oppression that unleashed progress always arrested it at the same time", it is nonetheless the case that "this oppression – as the emancipation of consciousness – first made the antagonism and the full extent of the deception recognizable". Since experiences of oppression encourage those who suffer from oppression to envisage conditions in which oppression might be abolished, oppression is actually "the prerequisite for settling the antagonism" (P 150). Indeed, Bernstein remarks that injustice "is the medium of real justice". Justice in its emphatic sense is derived from "the always practical, always eventful, always political struggle for the elimination of injustice" (2005: 303).

Non-identity thinking involves the determinate negation of existing states of affairs; it relies for its critical force on ideas that have been forged in resistance to damaged life. These ideas may include the resistive concepts that emerged in the struggles waged by women to emancipate themselves from patriarchy. As Horkheimer and Adorno had already observed in *Dialectic of Enlightenment*, women have historically been regarded as purely natural, biological beings who are not subjects in their own right. Since women have been perceived as the image of nature in a world that is geared to mastering nature, mastery over nature has included mastery over women, often through force or violence (*DE* C:248, J:206). But the myriad forms of physical and psychological violence inflicted on women *qua* nature for centuries have also elicited ideas and concepts that may be used critically to counter both the reduction of women to the status of natural things and the denigration of physical and biological differences. Deployed in a constellation, these ideas may foster new ways of thinking about what it is to be human with a view to freeing us from the oppressive social practices that summarily reduce women to natural objects while completely dissociating men from the natural world.

More generally, all forms of oppression involve casting groups and individuals as Other than what the oppressor is. And, in human history, nature has played the role of Other *par excellence*. It is therefore not surprising that, when individuals and groups are marginalized within, or excluded from, society, they are often portrayed as bestial or animal-like, inhuman or not fully human, instinctive and irrational. In virtually all cases, the oppressor targets an individual or group as *merely* natural.[30] For example, in totalitarian movements such as Nazism, members monopolize "all the so-called sublime and lofty concepts, while the terms they use for what they persecute and destroy–base, insect-like, filthy, subhuman and all the rest– they treat as anathema" (*MCP* 123). In this case, identity thinking takes the form of applying concepts to human beings that refer to other natural things in order to justify dominating, manipulating and controlling them. Once an individual or group is identified with nature, there is no indignity that may not be visited upon it in order to subjugate it. Rape, torture, segregation, confinement and enslavement are just some of the ways in which "nature" has been brought to heel.

Nevertheless, all those who have been coercively identified with nature, and are seen as lesser, or other, than human, may, by virtue of their painful experiences of that coercion, forge concepts and ideas that help to vindicate both nature and themselves. Here too, Adorno agrees with Horkheimer in *Eclipse of Reason*: "language reflects the longings of the oppressed and the plight of nature" (1974: 179). Our ideas of justice, equality and freedom are just "nature's protestations against her plight" (*ibid*.: 182). Nature may eventually overcome its plight in a more positive way than the one Horkheimer described – where oppressed nature lashes out irrationally against its oppression, only to reinforce it – when the idea of humanity is reconfigured to supersede the antagonism between the animal and the human, instinct and reason, body and mind that has served to justify oppression for thousands of years.

In *Negative Dialectics*, Adorno explicitly compared the subject of identity thinking to Hegel's master in the master–slave dialectic (see *ND* 179–80).[31] However, Bernstein reveals that the master–slave dialectic is an underlying theme in *Dialectic of Enlightenment* as well. For both Adorno and Hegel, "[r]eason (the master concept)" must recognize its dependence "on object (the slave intuition)" because reason is "systematic misrecognition" when it attempts "to detach itself from reliance on nature by mastering it". As it has played itself out in history, the dialectic of enlightenment can be seen as a "fundamental expression of the dialectic of desired independence from nature and disavowed dependence" (2004: 25–6). On Hegel's account, however, the master must overcome his dependence on the slave, who represents "mere" nature and mediates his relation to nature, and the slave must overcome her dependence on nature by transforming nature through her labour. In each case, then, dependence on nature is entirely negative (*ibid*.: 25).

For Adorno, by contrast, our dependence on nature is negative only when we disavow it. By continuing to disavow nature in ourselves, our compulsive attempts to control nature now threaten to destroy what they are meant to preserve. In Adorno's version of the master–slave dialectic, the slave will win her freedom, not by viewing herself as completely distinct from nature (as her male masters have done), but by gaining a fuller appreciation of the extent to which she depends on nature as an embodied being. At the same time, since the slave already enjoys a relative degree of autonomy with respect to nature (an autonomy gained both by manipulating nature to fulfil her master's desires, and by delaying the gratification of her own needs in the service of her master), her emancipation requires that she acquires a better understanding of the degree to which she is independent of nature, while finding less repressive and exploitative ways to express that independence.

Once we realize that "[a]bsolute domination of nature is absolute submission to nature", we may be able to "arch beyond" our largely sado-masochistic relation to nature by means of self-reflection (P 152). Becoming more fully cognizant of our own creatureliness – evident, *inter alia*, in the evolution of our species – we may finally bring to a halt our domination of nature "through which domination by nature continues" (P 150). By extension, thought should also begin to think critically about itself by asking whether "thought and its constitutive forms are *in fact* the absolute" (*MCP* 99). Adorno made this point again in *Negative Dialectics*: "If negative dialectics calls for the self-reflection of thinking, the tangible implication is that if thinking is to be true – if it is to be true today, in any case – it must also be a thinking against itself" (*ND* 365). Only critical self-reflection can prevent the subject "from building walls between itself and the object, from the supposition that its being-for-itself is an in-and-for-itself" (*ND* 31).

Thinking about thought therefore entails thinking about nature as that from which reason emerged but to which it cannot be reduced, that from which concepts are formed but with which they are not identical and, finally, as that with which thought may eventually be reconciled. For reconciliation to occur, human beings and non-human things should be regarded neither as an undifferentiated unity, nor in their current hostile antithesis. Again, reconciliation would involve the communication of what is differentiated (SO 247). Borrowing a phrase from Baron von Eichendorff, Adorno expressed this idea poetically: in a reconciled condition, human beings would grant proximity to the "beautiful alien" (*das schöne Fremde*),[32] while simultaneously allowing the alien Other to remain "distant and different, beyond the heterogeneous and beyond that which is one's own" (*ND* 191). However, reconciliation cannot be achieved by means of thought alone. Non-identity thinking is not sufficient for reconciliation because reconciliation ultimately depends on altering the relationship between an equally problematic iteration of universal and particular, namely the relationship between society and the individuals it comprises. As Chapter 4 will show, to think differently, individuals must first be able to live differently.

CHAPTER FOUR

ADORNO'S ENDGAME

Indissolubly entwined, nature and history preponderate over individuals and their cognitive activity. Nature preponderates over cognition because our cognitive faculties serve primarily as instruments of adaptation to the natural world. Our concepts themselves are tied to non-conceptual reality; they emerge and develop in our embodied encounters with material objects (*ND* 11). By extension, nature preponderates over individuals as corporeal beings, driven by instinct and need. Now as in the past, self-preservation runs wild, and reason ends by regressing to nature (*ND* 289). For its part, history preponderates over cognition, not just because our concepts are intersubjectively sustained constructs with socially conditioned and sedimented histories, but because – as Adorno often put it – individuals are imprisoned in prevailing modes of thought. Finally, this chapter will show that late capitalist society preponderates because it shapes the process of individuation, ensures the material survival of individuals and defines their relation to nature as members of the labour force.

Under the monopoly conditions that characterize late capitalism, individuals stand in much the same relation to society as particulars stand to universal concepts. Adorno suggests this throughout his work when he refers to society as the "universal". Where identity thinking summarily subsumes objects under concepts, society reifies individuals, expunging their idiosyncrasies by subsuming them under abstract exchange relations.[1] Adorno emphasizes the isomorphism between identity thinking and exchange relations when he observes that exchange is "fundamentally akin to the principle of identification" because it serves as the "social model" for this principle. Like identity thinking, which ignores the particularity of natural things by treating them as mere instances of more general kinds, exchange "imposes on the whole world an obligation to become identical, to become total" (*ND* 146).

Thought has always been shaped by both survival imperatives and economic conditions. If identity thinking can be traced all the way back to the emergence of language as an instrument for bringing nature to bay, it also changed as it modelled itself on the historically specific modes of abstraction that Marx outlined in the first chapter of *Capital* when he charted the development of exchange relations in the West. Commenting on the preponderance of exchange relations in human life, Jameson notes that Adorno takes up Marx's claim that the mode of abstraction that defines a historically specific form of value – from barter to monopoly capitalism's exchange relations – also affects civilization "across the whole range of distinct human activities (from production to the law, from culture to political forms, and not excluding the psyche and the more obscure 'equivalents' of unconscious desire)" (1990: 149).

With the development and spread of increasingly abstract exchange relations, cognition succumbed completely to identity thinking. Although Habermas mistakenly charges that Horkheimer and Adorno detach reifying exchange relations from "the special historical context of the rise of the capitalist economic system" (1984: 379), he is right to make the contrary claim that identity thinking acquires world-historical influence, or universal significance, only under capitalism "through the differentiation of the medium of exchange value" (*ibid.*: 378). To be sure, Adorno recognizes that "society's law of motion has been abstracting from its individual subjects for thousands of years, degrading them to mere executors, mere partners in social wealth and social struggle" (*ND* 304), but he also complains that identification reaches extreme proportions with the advent of monopoly capitalism, which now extends its influence across the globe. Like Marx, Adorno distinguishes between societies in which exchange is episodic and fragmentary, and those where virtually all nature and most aspects of human life have become commodified.

When it reduces human beings to agents and bearers of exchange value, late capitalist society adversely affects the process of individuation. Viewing individuation as a largely positive achievement, Adorno contends that the individual's subordination to exchange relations compromises its potentially emancipatory capacity for self-reflection and seriously undermines its prospects for changing its destructive and self-destructive relation to nature. In fact, this relationship has become so destructive that Adorno predicted the catastrophic annihilation of nature as a whole. In the next section of this chapter, I shall examine Adorno's account of the process of individuation in order to make sense of his ostensibly exaggerated claim that the individual "owes society its existence in the most literal sense" (*MM* 154). The following section explains why late capitalism now thwarts, with potentially disastrous consequences, more mutually beneficial relations between individuals and the natural world. Finally, this chapter will outline Adorno's response to the question "What is to be done?" For Adorno not only believed that self-preservation could be made more rational, but he explored the prospects for transforming socioeconomic conditions with a view to repairing the damage these conditions have inflicted on human and non-human nature. Critical of both impediments to individuation and forms of collective action today, Adorno nonetheless thought that some individuals could play an important role in initiating the social transformations that are needed to avoid catastrophe.

THE RISE AND FALL OF THE INDIVIDUAL

Adorno devoted much of his work to examining the tremulous process of individuation, and the waning prospects for self-determination and self-actualization in the West. Championing the individual as a potentially resistive and critical force, he complained in *Dialectic of Enlightenment* that individuation has never been fully achieved because the "class-determined form of self-preservation" continues to maintain us "at the level of mere species being" (*DE* C:155, J:125). Odysseus is the prototype for the modern individual (*DE* C:43, J:35) because he represents one of the first attempts to shake off the primal mud of species being. Nevertheless, we have already seen that this attempt backfired because Odysseus eviscerated the self he was trying to preserve by suppressing his instincts and opposing himself to nature as its Other in order to dominate it.

If Odysseus is the prototype for the modern individual, Shakespeare's Hamlet is its more fully developed counterpart. Commenting on Hamlet's difficulties in reconciling reflection and action, Adorno asserts that "the category of the bourgeois individual, the autonomous, independent individual, can be said to have appeared for the first time" in *Hamlet* (*PMP* 112). According to Adorno, "*Hamlet* is as much the proto-history of the individual in its self-reflection as it is the drama of the individual paralyzed into inaction by that reflection" (MTP 260). With his ruminations on his own impermanence, his mortality, Hamlet represents "the first wholly self-aware and despondently self-reflecting individual" (*MCP* 136). He marks a watershed in Western history because he heralds the "beginning of the self-emancipating modern subject's self-reflection" (*ND* 228). Nevertheless, Shakespeare's Hamlet was eventually eclipsed by Beckett's Hamm.[2] As monopoly conditions developed under capitalism, the individual rapidly declined.

Adorno did not comment extensively on the material conditions that gave rise to individuation and self-reflection. However, he remarked, very generally, that the principle underlying our exchange-based society "was realized only through the individuation of the several contracting parties". The *principium individuationis* is not just rooted in capitalist society, it is literally "the principle of that society, its universal" (*ND* 343). From this, one may surmise that the individual emerged as capitalism was supplanting the feudal economy. In fact, Adorno also observed in "Individuum und Organisation" that, once "the free market economy displaced the feudal system", capitalism required "entrepreneurs and free wage labourers". These developed, "not only as professional, but also as anthropological types". At the same time, "concepts arose – like those of personal responsibility, foresight, the self-sufficient individual, the fulfilment of duty, but also rigid moral constraint, an internalized bond with authority". It is in this 1953 essay that Adorno first endorsed the generally accepted view that "the individual itself – as the word is currently used – scarcely goes back much further than Montaigne or Hamlet, at best to the early Italian Renaissance" (1972b: 450).

The capacity for sustained self-reflection, which Hamlet exemplifies in his soliloquies, accompanied the birth of the modern individual: the individual was "constituted as a unit by its own self-reflection, the Hegelian 'self-consciousness'" (*ND* 218). Individuation and heightened self-reflection are coeval and coequal under capitalism because individuation involves the "individual's monotonous confinement to her particular interest" (*ND* 348). To survive under the fiercely competitive conditions that characterized the first liberal stage of capitalism, human beings were obliged to become self-regarding and self-reliant to an unparalleled degree. To cite Raymond Geuss: "the modern individual is a product of the market: each individual is essentially defined and constituted by his or her own 'self-interest', which is the form the impulse toward self-preservation takes in a market society" (2005: 12). Confined to the sphere of self-interest under capitalism, individuals must fend for themselves: to survive, they must identify, promote and defend their interests against competing ones.

In other words, individuals were free under liberal capitalism only as "economically active subjects"; they were free only to the extent that the economic system fostered their autonomy to promote competition. This is why Adorno believes that their autonomy was "potentially negated at the source" (*ND* 262). At the same time, he concedes that capitalism did allow the individuals it shaped to acquire a limited degree of autonomy and freedom. In a psychological gloss on these ideas, Adorno notes that the family – the "most effective agency of the bourgeoisie" – spawned resistive behaviours as children measured their strength against their fathers by rebelling against the reality principle they represented. This resistance to parental authority probably strengthened children as individuals, and possibly even produced them as individuals (*MM* 23). Examining this situation under a wider social lens, Adorno maintains that, in our antagonistic society, "the relationship between generations" is "one of competition, behind which stands naked power" (*MM* 22).

However, these claims about the role of the male parent in promoting the development of strong egos do not (as some commentators believe) imply that we should return to the earlier stage of capitalism, nor are they simply nostalgic. To counter these interpretations, it should be stressed that Adorno realized that a return to the earlier stage of liberalism was impossible in any case, while insisting that the only autonomy individuals have ever enjoyed had largely been a function of economic conditions. But he also argued that a more substantive form of autonomy will emerge only when the psychic agency in which parental commands are internalized – the superego – is sublated "as something truly heteronomous and alien to the ego". As Freud also recognized at times, the superego represents "blindly, unconsciously internalized social coercion" (*ND* 272). Since the superego allows society to extend repressively into the psychology of individuals (Adorno 1968: 79), Adorno controversially declared that, in a "state of universally rational actuality [*ein Zustand allseitiger rationaler Aktualität*] ..., no superego would come into being" (*ND* 273).

The conditions that once promoted a limited degree of individual autonomy have changed dramatically. As a result of these changes, the little autonomy that individuals formerly enjoyed has almost completely evaporated. If our autonomy was always "a function of a society based on exchange", late capitalist society now undermines the individual by means of integration (*ND* 262). Of course, even during capitalism's liberal heyday, individuals were "mere executive organs of the universal". Under recent conditions, however, they have become "irrelevant to a degree which no one could anticipate". The principle of individuation still prevails, "and thus all the evil instincts of a person imprisoned in her ego", but the function of the individual is now equated with her functionlessness, or with her powerlessness in relation to late capitalist society (*ND* 343).

Adorno travestied this situation in *Minima Moralia*. Although individuals persist and are "even protected and gaining in monopoly value", they have been reduced to exhibition pieces, "like the foetuses that once drew the wonderment and laughter of children", because they no longer have any semblance of autonomy with respect to economic conditions. Condemned by history to be mere tools of capitalism, individuals are now "dragged along, dead, neutralized, and impotent as ignominious ballast" (*MM* 135). Here Adorno underscored the lifelessness of the lives that individuals lead today: the optimal organization of relations of production requires the coordination of people from whom all vestiges of life have been drained. Ironically, we are prepared to subordinate ourselves to exchange relations, which drain us of life by reducing us to so many commensurable units of value, in order to stay alive. Consequently, "[t]he will to live finds itself dependent on the denial of the will to live: self-preservation annuls all life in subjectivity" (*MM* 229). In his commentary on this passage, Jarvis remarks that, the more "thoroughly developed the means of production and its associated division of labour, the less living labour can set its own goals: the less, indeed, living labour is living" (1998: 71).

Some of the economic factors that led to the decline of the individual are described in Adorno's early essay "Reflections on Class Theory". When competition among the bourgeoisie resulted in monopoly conditions, many entrepreneurs were forced to sell their business concerns to competitors. Obliged to exchange their labour for wages or a salary to survive, the economically disenfranchised bourgeoisie formed a new mass class with the proletariat; the interests of this entire class now conflict, at least in principle, with those of the owners of the means of production and their political allies. In a Hegelian claim about the *Aufhebung* – or sublation – of classes under monopoly capital, Adorno maintains that Marx's concept of class must be preserved because "the division of society into exploiters and exploited, not only continues to exist but gains in force and strength". But the concept must also be called into question "because the oppressed who today, as predicted by [Marxist] theory, constitute the overwhelming majority of humankind, are unable to experience themselves as a class" (RCT 97). So, while class stratification persists, the composition of classes has changed, and the subjective awareness of belonging to a class has all but vanished.

In his 1965 essay "Society", Adorno continued to insist that "society remains class society" (1969–70: 149, trans. mod.), because "the difference between the classes grows objectively with the increasing concentration of capital" (*ibid.*: 150). Three years later, in "Late Capitalism or Industrial Society?", he rejected the industrial society thesis because it implies that the world is:

> so completely determined by the unprecedented growth in technology that the social relations that once characterized capitalism – namely the transformation of living labour into a commodity, with the consequent conflict between classes – have now lost

their relevance or can even be consigned to the realm of super-
stition.   (2003a: 111)

Although this thesis characterizes forces of production today, relations of
production remain capitalist because people are:

> still what they were in Marx's analysis ...: appendages of the
> machine, not just workers who literally have to adapt themselves
> to the nature of the machines they use, but far beyond that, figu-
> ratively, workers who are compelled right down to their most
> intimate impulses to subordinate themselves to the mechanisms
> of society and to adopt specific social roles without reservation.
>   (*Ibid.*: 117, trans. mod.)

Moreover, Adorno accepted Marx's appraisal of class membership in terms
of the ownership of, and control over, the means of production (*ibid.*: 112).
He also thought that class stratification was more pronounced in North
America (*ibid.*: 115).

In contrast to Marx, however, Adorno observes that workers now have far
more to lose than their chains because their standard of living has improved.
The establishment of the welfare state, which Marx did not foresee, is partially responsible for this improvement. Along with shorter work days and
improved working conditions, workers enjoy "better food, housing and
clothing; protection for family members and for workers in their old age;
and an increase in average life expectancy". Here Adorno agrees with other
members of the Institute for Social Research: the welfare state has given
workers a more financially stable and materially comfortable existence. Like
other critical theorists, however, he argues that the welfare state contributes
to the invisibility of classes by masking class relations. The higher standard
of living also mollifies workers, precluding the possibility that hunger will
compel them to join forces and engage in revolutionary activity (RCT 103).
Borrowing a phrase from "The Communist Manifesto", Adorno maintains
that, with the welfare state, the ruling class effectively secures "for 'slaves
their existence within slavery' in order to ensure its own" (RCT 105).

With the transformation of class society into mass society, reification
has increased. On the cognitive level, once again, reification consists in the
attempt to "relate all phenomena, everything we encounter, to a unified
reference point and to subsume them under a self-identical, rigid unity,
thus removing them from their dynamic context" (*KCPR* 114, trans. mod.).
On the societal level, reification has a similar character because it transforms human beings and their life activity into "formally commensurable

variations of the exchange relationship" (*MM* 229). Reduced to so many instances of exchange value, individuals now find themselves under what Adorno calls a "spell". "In human experience", he writes, "the spell is the equivalent of the fetish character of the commodity. The self-made thing becomes a thing-in-itself, from which the self cannot escape any more" (*ND* 346). Spellbound, individuals tend to think of themselves and others as "the same", while becoming increasingly less tolerant of differences. This levelling tendency (which writers as diverse as Friedrich Nietzsche, Søren Kierkegaard, Alexis de Tocqueville, and Martin Heidegger also described) is just one of the effects of reification.

To survive, individuals must constantly adapt to an inherently unpredictable, unstable and often volatile economy. Spending their lives in pursuit of the means necessary to ensure their survival, individuals self-destructively promote and strengthen the very economic forces that make a mockery of their individuality. Jarvis makes this point succinctly: "The more obvious it becomes that the economic basis of any individual's life is liable to annihilation, and the more real economic initiative is concentrated with the concentration of capital, the more the individual seeks to identify with and adapt to capital" (1998: 83). Adaptation to the conditions that make individuals as expendable as many of the commodities they produce or consume is reinforced by sophisticated psychotechnologies in advertising and the culture industry, and by the prevailing positivist ideology, which legitimates existing conditions with its constant refrain: that is just the way things are.[3] By these means, the needs of individuals in the newly emergent mass class are harmonized with commodified offers of satisfaction in the capitalist marketplace. In fact, Adorno complains that "making-oneself-the-same, becoming civilized, fitting in, uses up all the energy that might be used to do things differently" (RCT 109).[4]

Since, under monopoly conditions, "the distinction between exploiters and exploited is not so visible as to make it obvious to the exploited that solidarity should be their ultima ratio", conformity to approved models of behaviour and existing offers of need satisfaction now appears more rational than collective action against exploitation (RCT 97). Failure to conform is not just regarded with suspicion; it has the more serious consequence of exposing "offenders to the vengeance of society even though they may not yet be reduced to going hungry and sleeping under bridges" (1967e: 71). A similar observation was made in *Dialectic of Enlightenment*: "Anyone who does not conform is condemned to an economic impotence which is prolonged in the intellectual powerlessness of the eccentric loner" (*DE* C:133, J:106). Reinforced by the mass media and other institutions and agencies (such as the educational system), conformity and adaptation are

98

motivated by fear: "the fear of being cast out, the social sanctions behind economic behaviour" (1967e: 71).

When he contrasts the earlier stage of liberal capital with monopoly conditions, Adorno observes that individuals now have little choice but to surrender the task of self-preservation to the capitalist economy and the welfare state. This surrender is necessary because, without it, "the individual would be unable to preserve himself in more highly developed social conditions". However, it also pits "the general rationality" of capitalism against "the particular human beings" whom this rationality "must negate to become general" (*ND* 318). Offering a psychological reading of this problem, Adorno remarks that, since the task of self-preservation has been taken in charge by economic and political institutions, late capitalist societies can dispense with "the mediating agencies of ego and individuality" that were fostered in the more competitive liberal phase of capitalism. They now encourage the formation of weak and submissive egos, arresting differentiation by exploiting "the primitive core of the unconscious" (1968: 95).

Today, the ego "is necessarily burdened with tasks that are irreconcilable with the psychoanalytic conception of the ego". On the one hand, the ego must "understand reality and operate consciously". On the other hand, it "must set up unconscious prohibitions and … remain largely confined to the unconscious" in order to comply with the "often senseless renunciations" that society imposes upon it. Here Adorno stresses the aporetic character of the ego: its "cognitive activity, performed in the interest of self-preservation, has to be constantly reversed, and self-awareness foregone, in the interest of self-preservation". Although ego formation was always a precarious achievement, the ego now fails to "develop its intrinsic potential for self-differentiation", regressing "towards what Freud called ego libido". In this condition, "[w]hat actually wanted to get beyond the unconscious … reenters the service of the unconscious and may even strengthen its force" (*ibid.*: 87). This regression accounts for the development of narcissistic pathologies in which the ego's "self-preserving function" is, "on the surface at least, retained but, at the same time, split off from that of consciousness and thus lost to rationality" (*ibid.*: 88, trans. mod.). Given narcissistic ego weakness, effective resistance to the destructive exploitation of both inner and outer nature has disappeared almost entirely.

Resistance is further compromised because narcissism and reification have damaged the interpersonal relationships that might, under improved conditions, allow individuals to form healthy social bonds, thereby making collective action more effective.[5] The reifying effects of the exchange principle on human sociality manifest themselves in many ways, including the tendency to derive a sense of social identity from the display of symbols that signal the socioeconomic status of their bearers. In this case, class struggle is displaced by the struggle for social prestige. For its part, narcissism is equally debilitating. With their weak egos, narcissists band together in groups, identifying with leaders on whom they project traits of their aggressive and unbridled superego introjects. (Indeed, Adorno often stressed the aggressive character of the narcissistic superego.) On Freud's account in "Group Psychology and the Analysis of the Ego" (1985b), which Adorno took up in "Freudian Theory and the Pattern of Fascist Propaganda", love of self is transferred to leaders who reanimate these introjects. Like Freud, Adorno also emphasized the fragile nature of this social bond, which disintegrates when the leader abandons the group.

Accordingly, Adorno offers two related accounts of the damage inflicted on interpersonal relations under capitalism. Whereas narcissism helps to explain why individuals would form groups in which they subordinate themselves to their equally narcissistic leaders, reification means that interpersonal relations develop on the flimsy basis of social markers and status symbols, or that social relations degenerate into relations between things. Compensating for the legitimate feelings of helplessness and powerlessness that individuals experience today, the display of these markers and symbols also serves a narcissistic function by turning individuals, "either in fact or imagination, into members of something higher and more encompassing to which they attribute qualities which they themselves lack and from which they profit by vicarious participation" (1993b: 32–3). Like the followers of demagogic leaders, who "seek a compensatory identification with the power of the collective" (1998h: 111), those who use social markers to distinguish themselves from others derive a narcissistic sense of satisfaction from belonging to an exclusive group that they regard as superior to other groups.

Paradoxically perhaps, reification and narcissism have the additional effect of alienating individuals from one other. Forming pseudo-collectivities in which they are all "the same" – as mere instantiations of both exchange value and their manipulated drives – individuals are simultaneously atomized and dissociated from one another by an "unbridgeable chasm" (1972c: 35). Social alienation arises precisely because interpersonal relations are secured by nothing more solid than abstract exchange relations and frail narcissistic affiliations. Since they find it difficult to form and sustain strong social bonds, individuals have become disconnected monads without windows who self-destructively but stubbornly "balk at their real dependence on the species as well as at the collective aspect of all forms and contents of their consciousness" (ND 312). This widespread sense of social isolation, fostered at the very heart of pseudo-collectivities, is yet another reason why resistance occurs only infrequently and is often ineffective.

Summarizing these points, Adorno states: "Collectivism and individual-ism complement each other in the wrong direction" (*ND* 284). Encouraged to identify themselves with their functions as workers and consumers in the capitalist marketplace, and driven by instincts whose satisfaction is diverted almost entirely into commodified channels, individuals develop pathological social bonds that simply reinforce their sense of isolation. And fear of financial insecurity plays a large part in thwarting their resistance to conditions that are as irrational as they are unnecessary. Even in the rare cases where they have not completely internalized prevailing social norms, individuals submit to society's demands because they fear losing their live-lihoods and social status. As a counterpart to this, with its cradle to grave provisions, the welfare state compensates for social and economic power-lessness, keeping individuals relatively content with their lot. This helps to explain why Adorno grants an element of truth to Hegel's notion of world spirit: it offers a "distorted sense of the real predominance of the whole" over individuals (*ND* 304). Adorno therefore seems to offer little hope that resistance to domination will succeed.

THERE'S NO MORE NATURE

Society's increasing disregard for the lives of individuals marks the direction of history. Mere pawns in a world "whose law is universal individual profit", we submit to forms of integration that are so complete and far-reaching that Adorno compared them to genocide, "the absolute integration". "Even in his formal freedom", Adorno remarked, "the individual is as fungible and replaceable as he will be under the liquidators' boots" (*ND* 362). Bourgeois individualism, which celebrates the individual as the substance of society, now masks an entirely different reality: the predominance of the universal exchange principle and its homogenizing and levelling effects on needs, behaviour, thought and interpersonal relations. Individuals today act as a collective, albeit a damaged, and therefore ineffective one (*ND* 344). Their virtually complete integration helps to explain the emergence of totalitarian movements. So, in *Minima Moralia*, Adorno spoke about the "straight line" that leads from thraldom to reifying exchange relations to "Gestapo tortur-ers and the bureaucrats of the gas-chambers" (*MM* 183).

Now the largely helpless pawns of economic and political forces that ruthlessly advance their particular interests in profit and power across the globe, individuals remain "too much in thrall to the biological life of which consciousness is itself a kind of derivative, a diverted energy" (*MCP* 132). Struggling all their lives to procure the necessities of life, individuals have little choice but to sell their labour power to those who are in a position to buy it; they must constantly learn new skills or upgrade old ones to keep pace with new technologies; they must search for employment with every change in the labour market, and in many cases move or emigrate to find work. And, to satisfy their needs, they must use their wages or salaries to purchase whatever commodified offers of satisfaction are affordable and available on the market. To stay alive, then, individuals are obliged to perpetuate the very conditions that make their existence precarious. Indeed, under monopoly conditions, self-preservation demands that individuals adapt to an economic system that has little interest in keeping them alive *qua* individual. "For capital", as Jarvis remarks, "the individual's self-preservation is not itself a matter of any importance" (1998: 83).

When he condemns capitalism's damaging effects on the lives of individuals, Adorno also objects that late capitalist society is self-defeating. By compressing "the particular until it splinters, like a torture instrument", society is working against itself because "its substance is the life of the particular" (*ND* 346). In fact, Adorno goes much further than simply underlining the indifference of capital to the preservation of the individuals whose activities of production and consumption sustain it. Ostensibly geared towards the preservation of its subjects, late capitalism destroys individuals in the more literal sense when it disregards the needs of its living human substratum in its relentless pursuit of profit. Stressing the gravity of our situation, Adorno warns that the primacy of volatile economic forces, which the owners of the means of production defend on the largely specious grounds that they serve the interests of society as a whole, now "has its vanishing point in the death of all" (*ND* 320).

But the death of all will have a related cause. For our material survival is not only tied to the performances of an inherently unstable economy and the often fickle largesse of the welfare state; it depends equally on the continued viability of the natural world. Like the individual, however, nature too is moribund. As Beckett foresaw in *Endgame*, we face a catastrophic situation in which "there's no more nature" (1958: 10). In his commentary on this play, Adorno states that reification and the annihilation of nature are of a piece: "the complete reification of the world ... is indistinguishable from an additional catastrophic event caused by human beings, in which nature has been wiped out and after which nothing grows any more" (1991: 245). Since our survival instincts are now running amok, it is by no means beyond the realm of possibility that we will destroy the natural world along with ourselves. Whether the death of all results from a nuclear war waged in self-defence, or from plundering the earth in pursuit of profit, is irrelevant. Both are equally possible; indeed, the latter prospect is becoming increasingly likely. The relative indifference of the owners of the means of production to these eventualities, along with our voluntary servitude to capital, make the end of life on this planet an all too plausible scenario.

If Hamlet's self-reflection deepened the rift between the thinking subject and the natural world that Odysseus's cunning first opened, Beckett's Hamm is left with the dregs. In contrast to Hamlet, who pondered whether it was better to live or to die, Hamm welcomes death because his life has become absurd, a grotesque caricature of itself. Indeed, Adorno remarks that all that remains of the human subject today "is its most abstract characteristic: merely existing, and thereby already committing an outrage" (*ibid.*: 251). Reduced to the pursuit of its mere survival, the moribund individual now perpetuates itself by destroying the natural world on which its life depends. Today, "[l]ife's sole remaining content is that there shall be nothing living. Everything that exists is to be made identical to a life that is itself death, abstract domination" (*ibid.*: 245).

Adorno insists that we be presented with the bill for our destructive and self-destructive domination of nature. To counter our conceit that we are utterly distinct from, and superior to, nature, the mind's own natural growth should be acknowledged by tracing it back to material scarcity (*PT2* 173). But it is not just a matter of acknowledging that reason grew out of instinct. For it should also be clear that the labour we perform to ensure our survival is itself "necessarily dependent on something other than itself, on nature". Human history and nature are intertwined because "[l]abor – and in the last analysis its reflective form, spirit, as well – cannot be conceived without the concept of nature, any more than can nature without labor: the two are distinct from and mediated by one another at the same time" (1993a: 23).

Adorno adopts Marx's view here. As Marx stated in the *Economic and Philosophic Manuscripts of 1844*, we "can create nothing without *nature*, without the *sensuous external world*" (1964: 109). Chapter 1 showed that Marx took up the idea, prevalent in nineteenth-century science, of the metabolism between human beings and nature. Although he did not develop this idea, Marx recognized that human beings must remain in continuous interchange with nature if they want to survive (*ibid.*: 112). This point is made again in *Capital*:

> Labour, then, as the creator of use-values, as useful labour, is a condition of human existence which is independent of all forms of a society; it is an eternal natural necessity which mediates the

metabolism between human beings and nature, and therefore
human life itself.   (1976a: 133)

In his commentary on Marx's ideas about this metabolic interchange,
John Foster observes that human beings "produce their own historical
relation to nature in large part by producing their means of subsistence"
through socially conditioned labour (2000: 72–3 *passim*). Marx regarded
self-preserving labour as "a process between man and nature, a process by
which man, through his own actions, mediates, regulates and controls the
metabolism between himself and nature". In *Capital*, Marx contends that, in
labour, we "confront the materials of nature as a force of nature" by setting
in motion the natural forces which belong to our bodies (1976a: 283, cited
in Foster 2000: 141). And, as Marx had already stated in the *Manuscripts*,
the fact that our "physical and spiritual life is linked to nature ultimately
means that nature is linked to itself" because we are inextricably part of
nature (1964: 112).

With the development of capitalism, however, our metabolism with
nature was seriously compromised (see Marx 1976a: 637, cited in Foster
2000: 156). Indeed, Foster argues that Marx was deeply concerned about
environmental issues such as soil degradation, air and water pollution, "the
depletion of coal reserves", and "the destruction of forests" (Foster 2000:
165). A similar point is made by Moishe Postone. One of the consequences
of the constant expansion of our productive capacities "is the accelerating
destruction of the natural environment" which Marx criticized in *Capital*
and elsewhere. Since production uses up increasing amounts of raw materials, our relation to nature has become a "one-way process of consumption,
rather than a cyclical interaction". Production now consists in "an accelerating transformation of qualitatively particular raw materials into 'matter',
into qualitatively homogeneous bearers of objectified time" (Postone 1993:
311–12 *passim*).

Marx also recognized that, to survive under capitalism, workers must
collaborate in a process that may well lead to the destruction, not just of
themselves, but of all living things. For their part, Horkheimer and Adorno
complain that "the whole machinery of modern industrial society is just
nature bent on dismembering itself" (*DE* C:253, J:210). Denouncing late
capitalist society as a "wholesale racket in nature" (*DE* C:254, J:211), they
sound the alarm when they speculate that humanity's "destructive capacity
risks becoming so great that a clean sweep will be made if the race is ever
exhausted". We shall either "tear each other to pieces", or take "all the flora and
the fauna of the earth" with us and, "if the earth is then still young, the whole
thing will have to be started again at a much lower stage" (*DE* C:224, J:186).

Conceived and manipulated as something that exists exclusively for us, nature has been drawn into human history and, in many cases, irreparably damaged by its entwinement with it. Our cavalier attitude towards nature – the wholesale racket in nature – has damaged nature, damage we can gauge by the suffering it causes to both human and non-human nature: by the extinction of entire species of plant and animal life, by the destruction of natural habitats, and the death of more than one hundred areas in the oceans, to give only three examples. What Adorno says about identity thinking is equally true of our practical relation to nature: the closer we come to an object, the more we have tended to shape it in our own image and drive it away, "much as civilization has driven the wildest and most exotic animals into the most inaccessible jungles" (*KCPR* 176).

In fact, identity thinking is only indirectly responsible for damaging the natural world because such thinking is itself fundamentally conditioned by our practical engagement with nature in labour.[6] If, to cite Alfred Schmidt, Marx thought that human beings "construe the world, in the various spheres of their culture, on the model of their contemporary struggle with nature" (1971: 30), Adorno arrives at a similar view when he examines the claim that "knowledge really just repeats what has always existed in the actual process of human labour". Although he denies that cognition is causally determined by this process, he does argue – albeit without developing this point – that cognition is "a kind of reflex" of this process. In fact, Adorno contends that, "when consciousness reflects upon itself, it necessarily arrives at a concept of rationality that corresponds to the rationality of the labour process" (*KCPR* 172).[7] To borrow a phrase from Nietzsche, when it "conceptually mummifies" living things (1982b: 479), identity thinking mirrors the labour process that subsumes nature wholesale under abstract exchange relations.

I criticized Bernstein in the preceding chapter for fetishizing damaged life by equating non-identity thinking almost exclusively with an immersion in things, while ignoring its speculative dimension, its proleptic orientation towards objects. Bernstein effectively views non-identity thinking as the mimesis of moribund life when he asserts that the "transcending impulse of consciousness" is exhausted in "the orientation of the material axis of the concept" (2001: 426), or in "an encounter with a sensuous particular where that particular is experienced in its own right and not as an example or token of anything else" (*ibid.*: 428). Against views like these, Samir Gandesha argues that mimesis has become "a morbid imitation of, and consequent adaptation to, a nature that, by virtue of the process of rationalization and disenchantment, has become lifeless" (2004: 465).[8] In labour as well, individuals who have been drained of life turn nature into something as lifeless as they themselves have become. Confronting them on the practical level as resistant, unwieldy and fearsome, nature is treated in the labour process as entirely unreverberant. To borrow a phrase from *Endgame*, all is now "corpsed" (Beckett 1958: 20).

SELF-PRESERVATION MADE RATIONAL

In the *Manuscripts*, Marx complained that, as long as survival remains paramount for workers under capitalism, the purely natural functions of eating, drinking, excreting and reproducing will remain their "sole and ultimate ends". Workers feel themselves to be freely active only in these animal functions, while in their human functions they no longer feel themselves to be "anything but an animal" (1964: 111). Adorno agrees: workers are confined to the biological pursuit of preserving their lives under capitalism. Rather than being a means to a further end, the preservation of the individual has become an end in itself. As a result, the "present condition is destructive: a loss of identity for the sake of abstract identity, of naked self-preservation" (*ND* 279). This situation has become so perilous that, to preserve ourselves, we not only participate in the destruction of the natural world on which our survival depends, but accept our own abasement into something "absolutely fungible and replaceable". Insignificant and superfluous, we have nothing "but this atomized self which lives our life" (*MCP* 109–10).

Yet Adorno also denied that the parlous situation in which we now find ourselves was inevitable or necessary. If the continuity of human history lies in the growth of our destructive powers, Adorno questioned whether our antagonistic relation to the natural world was "a piece of prolonged natural history", or whether, "even if it evolved, it followed from the necessities of the survival of the species and not contingently, as it were, from archaic arbitrary acts of seizing power". Criticizing both Hegel and Marx for dismissing "all doubts about the inevitability of totality", Adorno insisted that such doubts cannot but arise for those who want to change the world (*ND* 321). He was also largely persuaded by the view that history is contingent, if only on heuristic grounds:

> Only if things might have gone differently; if the totality is recognized as socially necessary semblance, as the hypostasis of the universal pressed out of individual human beings; if its claim to be absolute is broken – only then will a critical social consciousness retain its freedom to think that things might be different some day. (*ND* 323)

106

In fact, it is more in keeping with what Adorno described as the impending catastrophe to suppose that it originated in an equally "irrational catastrophe" (*ibid.*).

Similar ideas are expressed in "Progress", where Adorno states more forthrightly that the economic conditions that threaten our survival are "man-made, and therefore revocable" (P 156). He also considers how catastrophe might be avoided in his lectures on metaphysics. If "everything we call culture consists in the suppression of nature and any uncontrolled traces of nature" (*MCP* 118), Adorno shows (in a proto-deconstructive manoeuvre described in Chapter 2) that this hierarchical relationship between the dominator and the dominated can be reversed: the dominators of nature are themselves dominated by nature because domination is impelled by nature itself in the form of the instinct for self-preservation. To advance beyond our current predicament, where those who exploit nature in the name of progress are also its victims, we must first acknowledge that what now counts as progress has become self-vitiating.

Genuine progress will not occur through the "abstract negation" of domination. Instead, we can begin to change our destructive and self-destructive relation to nature by means of determinate negation. Here, too, Adorno follows Marx who (to cite Postone 1993: 372) thought that radical social change was "rooted in the possibility of a determinate historical negation" of existing conditions.[9] The possibility of wresting free of both exchange relations and the equally subsumptive abstractions of identity thinking is "effectuated by the pressure of negativity", or by the damage these abstractions have inflicted on both human and non-human nature. In the first instance, however, the negation of the pressure of negativity takes the form of critique. By reflecting critically on its compulsive attempts to dominate nature, reason negates domination. Through such critical self-reflection, reason may arch beyond its own submission to nature and become reconciled with nature. Again, reason alone – the principle of "societal domination" that has been inverted into the subject – can abolish domination (P 152).

If critical self-reflection enables us to arch beyond domination, it may also transform self-preservation by directing this instinct towards more fully rational ends. Indeed, Adorno insists that reason can never sever its links with self-preservation. Human behaviour can be deemed rational only "in so far as it serves the principle that has been regarded … as the true fundamental principle of every existent being: [*suum*] *esse conservare*, self-preservation" (*PMP* 137). In other words, reason should retain, even strengthen, its links with self-preservation. As Kaufmann remarks, it is not self-preservation *per se*, but the "limited rationality of self-preservation …

107

that leads to the irrationality of a reason devoted entirely to means, to *how* things should be done rather than to *what* should be done" (2004: 175). Rather than vainly attempting to overcome survival instincts, reflection on the self as a part of nature may enable us to reconcile ourselves with, and accommodate ourselves to, our underground instinctual life.

Adorno applies determinate negation to the current, irrational, form of self-preservation. Since it is "only as reflection upon ... self-preservation that reason would be above nature" (*ND* 289), he hopes that we will acquire "the potential for that self-reflection that could finally transcend the self-preservation to which it was reduced by being restricted simply to a means" (MTP 273). However, self-reflection will transcend self-preservation – which is now restricted to preserving the lives of individuals – only when we consciously direct our survival instincts towards the goal they implicitly contain: the preservation of the species as a whole. Citing Weber, Adorno remarks that, once it has emancipated itself from "the contingency of indi-vidually posed ends", the "subject of *ratio*, pursuing its self-preservation, is itself an actual universal, society – in its full logic, humanity". What is "inexorably inscribed within the meaning of rationality" is the preservation of humanity (MTP 272). Emphatically conceived, reason "should not be anything less than self-preservation, namely that of the species, upon which the survival of each individual literally depends" (MTP 273).

Nevertheless, if self-preservation should be extended to encompass the preservation of the species, Adorno also warns against hypostatizing the species for reasons that echo his concerns about the plight of indi-viduals under late capitalism. Although it is "part of the logic of the self-preservation of the individual that it should ... embrace ... the preservation of the species", it is also the case that embracing the preservation of the species is problematic because "there is an intrinsic temptation for this universality to emancipate itself from the individuals it comprises". Even on the condition that species reason is liberated "from the particularity of obdurate particular interest", the species may subsequently "fail to free itself from the no less obdurate particular interest of the totality". Since this conundrum concerning the relationship between the individual and the species has not yet been resolved, Adorno considers it to be "a problem of the greatest possible gravity" (*HF* 44–5).

In the final analysis, the preservation of humanity requires the transfor-mation of society: self-preservation has its end "in a reasonable organiza-tion of society" (MTP 272). Today society is irrational because it continues to increase "all apparatuses and means of quantifiable domination at the cost of the goal, the rational organization of humankind" (1998k: 138, trans. mod.). But the pressure of negativity makes itself felt here as well because the prospect of establishing humanity as the subject of its own history has really only opened up in the face of its extinction (P 145). Since existing conditions now threaten to destroy all life on earth, we are compelled to think about how society might be rationally organized to ensure the preservation of all nature, including our own species. Progress is dialectical because "historical setbacks, which themselves are instigated by the principle of progress ... also provide the condition needed for humanity to find the means to avert them in the future" (P 154). As I mentioned in the previous chapter, Adorno calls this reversal of fortune, outlined by determinate negation, the dialectic of progress.

Adorno also applies determinate negation to exchange relations under capitalism. Capitalism must be superseded because the ubiquitous exchange principle on which it rests has always been a lie; its "doctrine of like-for-like" is contradicted by the fact that "the societally more powerful contracting party receives more than the other". But Adorno goes on to speculate that the "repeatedly broken exchange contract" would be satisfied if truly equal things were exchanged (P 159), or when exchange relations finally make good on the promise contained in the very idea of an exchange of *equivalents*. Acts of exchange will become more rational only when they satisfy the more emphatic notion of free and just exchange (*ND* 147). Since the abstract negation of exchange would only serve as an apology "for recidivism into ancient injustice" (*ND* 146), genuine progress "would not be merely an Other in relation to exchange, but rather exchange that has been brought to itself" (P 159). A society in which exchange were truly free and just would ultimately transcend exchange because no part of workers' labour would be withheld from them (*ND* 147). Adorno repeats this point when he remarks that, "in society as it ought to be, exchange would not just be abolished, but fulfilled: no individual would be shortchanged of the yield of her labor" (*ND* 296).

Like exchange, self-preservation is irrational because it benefits a few, while threatening the survival of both human and non-human nature. Our culture has failed because "it has clung to mere self-preservation and its various derivatives". However, Adorno also believes that it is now possible to orient productive forces towards the preservation of the species as a whole by satisfying the needs of everyone everywhere. And this can be done without forcing human beings to spend the greater part of their lives in dehumanizing, reifying and alienating labour. Indeed, Adorno alleges that we have outgrown the principle of self-preservation because we are "no longer confined by direct necessity to compulsive self-preservation, and ... no longer compelled to extend the principle of mastery over nature, both inner and outer nature, into the indefinite future" (*MCP* 129).

To be sure, self-preservation was "precarious and difficult for eons". This is why "the power of its instrument, the ego drives, remains all but irresistible". Today, however, technology "has virtually made self-preservation easy". Our situation has become objectively irrational because our exertions as members of the labour force have been made "superfluous by the state of the productive forces" (*ND* 349). If the separation of mental from manual labour has always been illusory (because the ability to perform mental labour presupposes that basic needs have been satisfied with the products of manual labour), the fact that some individuals live without having to perform manual labour indicates that this possibility exists for everyone. Although this possibility has always existed,[10] the prospect of living lives that are no longer devoted primarily to self-preservation is all the more viable today because "the technical forces of production are at a stage that makes it possible to foresee the global dispensation from material labor, its reduction to a limiting value" (MTP 267).

But, if a more rationally organized society – where production and consumption no longer occupy the lion's share of human life – is currently within reach, our relation to nature could be utterly transformed. Our relation to nature in the labour process could be altered in such a way as to respect the independent purposiveness of natural things. Among other things, this might mean that some instrumental activities and behaviours would need to be modified, curtailed or prohibited (temporarily or permanently) to allow natural things to develop in accordance with their own ends.[11] Moreover, once labour is reduced to a minimum, nature could become something other than a mere means to the end of our survival: we might acquire the capacity for a more complete aesthetic experience of nature, an experience that is now denied us because even those experiences of nature that are not geared to domination are, owing to their very opposition to society's exploitative practices, "integrated into the reified world" that they oppose (*AT* 68). Individuals who cannot distinguish nature "from objects to be acted upon – the distinction that constitutes the aesthetic – are incapable of aesthetic experience" (*AT* 274), but they may develop the capacity for it when they are no longer obliged to spend most of their lives in largely adversarial relationships with nature.

Although it is impossible to determine in advance the precise character of this radically altered relation to nature, Zuidervaart contends that art – itself a kind of labour – can "fan the flames of liberation" by modelling non-instrumental, non-hierarchical relationships (1991: 119). In recent work, he makes an even stronger claim: "modern art making can model how all labor could be transformed, from a condition of alienation from nature and of economic exploitation to one of disalienation and social solidarity" (2007: 36). However, Zuidervaart seems to overlook the pivotal role that Adorno gives to philosophy in outlining more rational relationships to nature. In addition, he should have acknowledged that art (like philosophy) can, at best, provide only an indirect glimpse of improved relationships with nature, rather than offering fully positive models. For artistic activity is as compromised as any other activity. Art should not be romanticized; it is not a panacea. If art has the capacity to point the way forwards, that capacity is a function of art's own "determinate negation of the existing order of the world" (*AT* 89).[12] As such, its emancipatory potential is also limited by its complicity in the conditions that prevent reconciliation.

For his part, Hammer believes that, in a reconciled condition, the use-value of objects would supersede their exchange value. But this claim is equally problematic. In response to Hammer, one could argue that, even if use-value were to supersede exchange value, nature would continue to be seen primarily in terms of its value for the satisfaction of human needs – that is, its instrumental value – and this is precisely what Adorno rejects. But Adorno would also reject the supposition on which Hammer bases this claim, namely that use-value can be construed as "a cipher for everything that can possibly contain a utopian promise: difference and heterogeneity, otherness, the qualitative, the radically new, the corporeal, in short … 'the non-identical'" (2006: 31).[13] Although production can (and should) be geared immediately to the satisfaction of needs, use-value cannot serve as a cipher for the non-identical because the non-identical is just what escapes mediation, including its mediation by use-value.

Of course, Adorno did not completely reject an assessment of nature in terms of its use-value, or the value that nature has for the satisfaction of human needs of whatever kind (whether needs of the stomach or of the imagination; Marx 1976a: 125). A more rational society would be one in which production is directed to the satisfaction of the needs of all, even as labour is reduced to a minimum and human beings are no longer obliged to struggle against the pleasure principle for the sake of self-preservation (MTP 262). In his early essay on needs, Adorno also speculated that needs themselves would be fundamentally altered: if production were "*forthwith unconditionally and unrestrainedly reorganized for the satisfaction of needs–even and especially for those needs produced by capitalism–needs themselves would be decisively transformed*" (1972d: 394).[14] "For the first time", Adorno remarked at the end of this essay, "production would act on need in a true, not distorted, sense: not because unsatisfied need is allayed by something useless, but because the allayed need can relate to the world without damaging it through universal utility" (*ibid.*: 396).[15]

If the production process were to satisfy human needs without damaging nature, it would finally become rational in Adorno's sense of that term. This helps to explain why Adorno states that his materialism agrees with theology: the great desire of both is the resurrection of the flesh. From a materialist perspective, however, the flesh will be resurrected only when individuals are no longer obliged to devote their entire lives to ensuring their material survival. To return to an earlier point, the sublation of materialism – and, by extension, of a history that has been more or less blindly impelled by survival instincts – will occur when human beings are emancipated "from the primacy of material needs in their state of fulfillment" (ND 207). With the resurrection of the flesh, moreover, materialism itself will be superseded in an emancipatory inversion similar to those that may liberate self-preserving reason from its thraldom to nature and exchange from its reifying abstractions. The "realization of materialism would mean today the end of materialism, of the blind and degrading dependence of human beings upon material conditions" (1998o: 15).

However, this brief discussion of reconciliation should end with a cautionary note. Again, "[i]f the whole is the spell, if it is the negative", then "a negation of particularities – epitomized in that whole – remains negative" (ND 158). Criticism of the totally administered world is invariably tainted by it. As Bernstein puts it, there are no clean ideals. Even if ideals could be detached from the "material and temporal conditions of meaning", or purified of "their material anchor and temporal core", they would "lose their foothold in empirical experience" (2005: 308). But, since the "truth" of emphatic ideas is always "bound up with the possibility of their being wrong, the possibility of their failure" (MCP 144), critics must engage in self-criticism, recognizing that the preponderance of nature and history compromises their ability to depict "a correct state of things" (ND 352). Indeed, when he states that, in "the right condition, as in the Jewish *theologoumenon*, all things would differ only a little from the way they are", Adorno also warns that "not even the least of these things can be conceived now as it would be then" (ND 299).

TOWARDS A RATIONAL SOCIETY

Although there is no "idea of progress without the idea of humanity", Adorno endorses Marx's claim that humanity has not yet constituted itself. Since "no progress is to be assumed that would imply that humanity in general already existed and therefore could progress", genuine progress would consist in "the very establishment of humanity in the first place" (P 145). Humanity will be able to establish itself only when we have learned to reconcile ourselves with non-human nature, our own internal nature, and other human beings, overcoming the exploitation, repression and oppression that have characterized history thus far. Somewhat problematically, Adorno also believes that the progress that will bring humanity into being depends on the emergence of a global subject. He declares that "humanity's own global societal constitution threatens its life if a self-conscious global subject [*ein seiner selbst bewußtes Gesamtsubjekt*] does not develop and intervene" (P 144).

By global subject, Adorno does not mean "an all-embracing terrestrial organization" such as the United Nations, whose organizational structure actually runs the risk of impeding emancipation. Instead, he is referring to "a human race that possesses genuine control over its own destiny right down to the concrete details" (*HF* 143). Here again, he appears to agree with Marx who wanted to make human beings the subjects of their own history, and believed that this would occur only in a worldwide attempt to abolish the exploitative economic conditions that continue to cause such widespread misery. On Adorno's view, it is not the task of the individual to abolish suffering; the abolition of suffering can be accomplished solely by the species "to which the individual belongs even where she subjectively renounces it and is objectively thrust into the absolute loneliness of a helpless object" (*ND* 203).

Since the emergence of a global subject is a necessary condition for progress, "[e]verything else involving progress must crystallize around it" (P 144). Today, however, self-preservation appears to be "doomed to remain irrational" because "the development of a rational collective subject, of a unified humanity, [has] failed to materialize – a situation with which, in turn, each individual must contend" (1967e: 78). The class consciousness that might have oriented self-preservation towards more universal and rational ends has been obstructed. Self-preservation is now firmly harnessed to the particular interests of the owners of the means of production, that is, to interests that attempt to pass themselves off as universal because they enable individuals in the West to preserve themselves, albeit only nominally. Moreover, as noted earlier, reification and narcissism undermine the very solidarity that is needed to overcome them.

For these reasons, then, the practice that might bring about a radical transformation of society has been undermined. But Adorno further argues that praxis "would inevitably eternalize precisely the present state of the world, the very critique of which is the concern of philosophy". Praxis will perpetuate irrational conditions until it "has a theory that can think the totality in its untruth", a theory that will also enable it to foster "a rationally and politically mature humanity". Although Adorno concedes that praxis risks reproducing damaged life only "at this historical moment" (1998o: 14), his lifelong concern about the oppression and exploitation of individuals in the name of the prevailing social order – in the former Soviet Union, for example, which he accused of betraying socialism by demanding the individual's complete submission to society (*ND* 284) – still resonates today. Indeed, the dictatorial leadership of the old Soviet bloc has a Western counterpart in hierarchically organized groups led by charismatic or authoritarian leaders.

Alluding to Habermas's *The Structural Transformation of the Public Sphere* in "Marginalia to Theory and Praxis", Adorno observed that discussions in activist groups are frequently corrupted by strategic manoeuvres. In principle, of course, all members of a group should be given a fair hearing and contribute equally to decision-making. However, group discussions are often manipulative, directed simply towards scoring points for particular positions. Opposing views are "hardly perceived and then only so that formulaic clichés can be served up in response". Opponents are turned into something "useable by means of engineered discussion and coerced solidarity"; but they may also be discredited, or "speechified out the window for the sake of publicity", or for narcissistic "self-advertisement". It is the force of a group member (or members), rather than the force of the better argument, that often prevails. Underlying group discussion is an "authoritarian principle: the dissenter must adopt the group's opinion" (MTP 269). In this case too, collective practice merely mimics existing conditions.[16]

Adorno did comment favourably on protest movements in the 1960s when he asserted that, even in the face of the disintegration of the individual, "traces of a countervailing trend [have] become visible among various sections of the younger generation: resistance to blind conformism, the freedom to choose rational goals, disgust with the world's deceptions and illusions, the awareness of the possibility of change". Still, only time would tell "how significant a movement this is, or whether society's collective drive to self-destruct will triumph nevertheless" (2003a: 123–4). Concerned about our narcissistic tendency to submerge ourselves in organizations or groups led by authoritarian leaders, Adorno appears to flout Marx in his search for an Archimedian point to ground a non-repressive praxis that would allow individuals to flourish within groups rather than being suppressed by them. Without presuming to have discovered this point, Adorno also contends that, if it exists, only theory can find it (MTP 274).

By "theory", Adorno obviously meant critical theory. In the opening section of *Negative Dialectics*, he warned that those who abandon the attempt to understand the world critically will succumb to the "defeatism of reason after the attempt to change the world miscarried" (*ND* 3). But critical

114

theorists find themselves in an impasse because they face a situation in which political practice is urgently needed but must be deferred. While imperative, practice should be temporarily postponed because individuals can do nothing today "that will not threaten to turn out for the worst even if meant for the best" (*ND* 245). Motives of self-preservation now compel even "conscious individuals, capable of criticizing the whole, to do things and to take attitudes which blindly help maintain the universal even though their consciousness is opposed to it" (*ND* 311). It is this very situation that should serve as the springboard for critical thought: "Paradoxically, it is the desperate fact that the practice that would matter is barred which grants to thought a breathing space that it would be practically criminal not to use" (*ND* 245).

Despite the debilitating effects of narcissism and reification, some individuals can play an important role in initiating change. But their resistance will be effective only when it includes critical reflection on the natural and social forces that now limit their own capacity to think and behave autonomously. Once again, the precondition for radical change is the sustained, self-critical spirit of reason (*ND* 29). Indeed, Adorno objects to Marx's dictum that the point is to change the world rather than to interpret it when he quips that "*one* reason why the world was not changed was probably the fact that it was too little interpreted" (2008: 58).[17] In contrast to Marx, he also insists that sustained criticism of our current predicament is itself "a comportment, a form of praxis". Today, critical thought is "more akin to transformative praxis than a comportment that is compliant for the sake of praxis" precisely because it is a force of resistance (1998l: 293).[18]

Since existing forms of collective action only reward the activist's leap into practice with "the grace of being chosen, of belonging", responsibility for initiating change now falls on critical, and self-critical, individuals (1998h: 122). This point is made frequently: "In contrast to the collective powers that usurp the world spirit in the contemporary world, the universal and rational can hibernate better in the isolated individual than in the stronger battalions that have obediently abandoned the universality of reason". A thousand eyes do not necessarily see better than two. In fact, Adorno describes Brecht's phrase as "the exact expression of that fetishizing of the collectivity and organisation which knowledge of society has the supreme duty to break through" (1972b: 455).[19] Repudiating the claim that, "by abandoning one's own reason and judgment one is blessed with a higher, that is, collective reason", Adorno counters that "to know the truth one needs that irreducibly individual reason that is ... supposedly obsolete" (MTP 276).

By pinning his hope on individual thinkers, Adorno simply underscores his lifelong concern "with the utopian particular that has been buried beneath the universal – with that nonidentity which would not come into being until realized reason has left the particular reason of the universal behind" (*ND* 318). As damaged as everyone else, those who denounce the status quo with the aim of changing it exhibit the "need to lend a voice to suffering", a need that Adorno describes as "a condition of all truth". Since so much human suffering has been caused by the preponderance of society over individuals, critical thinkers who lend a voice to suffering also reveal "the objectivity that weighs upon the subject". When they speak for those who are exploited and oppressed, whose instincts and needs are manipulated and controlled to benefit a few profiteers, whose infrequent and often ineffective attempts to improve their situation are met with harassment, tear gas, tasers, arbitrary arrests or torture, critical theorists may objectively convey the individual's most subjective experience (*ND* 17–18).

Commenting on this passage, Zuidervaart objects that Adorno regards expressions of suffering as self-authenticating. However, Zuidervaart (2007: 68) bases his objection on a misinterpretation of Adorno when he claims that Adorno describes the need to express suffering as a self-evident condition for truth.[20] To be sure, critical theorists are burdened with the task of lending their voices to the suffering of others – of making the "moral and, as it were, representative effort" of saying what those for whom they say it do not acknowledge, or "to do justice to reality", will not allow themselves to acknowledge (*ND* 41). They play an important mediating role in their attempts to understand the conditions that give rise to suffering because not all suffering is socially conditioned or, when socially conditioned, it is not always experienced as suffering (in neuroses, for example) or, where suffering is experienced as such, its sources may be misunderstood. However, their expressions of suffering are neither self-evident nor self-authenticating: Adorno constantly stresses the fallibility of criticism, and insists that critics must be self-critical as well, precisely because they can be mistaken.

Of course, even the most resolutely critical thinkers cannot bring about by themselves the changes needed to abolish unnecessary suffering. These changes can be made successfully only by a socially solidary, global subject. Still, those individuals who, by "a stroke of undeserved luck", have "not quite adjusted to the prevailing norms" can, at the very least, initiate change (*ND* 41). Adorno modelled his idea of a future humanity on those who resist society's norms and institutions by submitting them to sustained critique.[21] Critical, self-reflective thinkers are the forerunners of humanity because their concerted attempts to think for themselves, as they reveal and contest the conditions that adversely affect their own capacity for independent thought and action, make them more autonomous than those who simply adapt and conform to these conditions. The more advanced form of autonomous individuality – which each critic exemplifies to a greater or lesser degree – serves as the placeholder for humanity because humanity "can be thought only through this extreme form of differentiation, individuation, not as a comprehensive generic concept" (P 151).

Critical thinkers channel their aggression into resistance to the status quo. Theirs is "the happiness of humanity" because "[t]hought is happiness, even where it defines unhappiness: by enunciating it" (Adorno 1998l: 293). At the same time, Adorno recognizes that general and sustained human happiness – the prolonged happiness of humanity – depends, at least in part, on reconciling society with the individuals it comprises. This task of reconciliation is all the more urgent today because society has become as antagonistic towards the individuals who make up its substance as it is to non-human nature. The preponderance of the object in its social form must be attenuated by abolishing society's oppression and exploitation of individuals, along with its constant demands to defer, delay or renounce instinctual gratification.

Determinate negation can be used to depict more mutually beneficial relationships between the individual and society. Since the coercive superego consists in internalized social norms, individuals' moral conscience is derived from the "objectivity of society, ... the objectivity in and by which [they] live and which extends to the core of their individualization". However, antagonistic moments rend this objectivity: along with moments of "heteronomous coercion", one can also find "the idea of a solidarity transcending divergent individual interests". Just as freedom is the inverted image of existing forms of unfreedom, so too the social solidarity needed for the emergence of a global subject is the inverted image of the pressurized adaptation and conformity that now foster damaged forms of collectivity. After arguing that "it takes the repressive form of conscience to develop the form of solidarity in which the repressive one will be voided" (*ND* 282), Adorno ends by endorsing Kant's *Metaphysics of Morals*. In Kant's idea that "everyone's freedom need be curtailed only insofar as it impairs someone else's is a reconciled condition". This condition would not only supersede "the bad universal, the coercive social mechanism", but also transcend "the obdurate individual who is a microcosmic copy of that mechanism" (*ND* 283).

Adorno wants to extend the non-dualistic and non-reductive relationship between nature and history, matter and mind, to the relationship between the individual and society as well. On the one hand, individuals will always be socially determined because "not only particularity but the particular itself are unthinkable without the moment of the universal which differentiates the particular, puts its imprint on it, and in a sense is needed to make a particular of it". On the other hand, the fact that individuals are shaped and conditioned by society by no means authorizes their reduction to social constructs (*ND* 328). As Whitebook observes in his defence of Adorno against Habermas, the individual is shaped by the intersubjective social world, but it cannot be drawn into that world "without a residuum of private in-itselfness – without which we would all be precoordinated clones" (1995: 194).

In fact, Adorno suggests that individuals would play a far more active and participatory role in a rational society than they currently do in our irrational one. For there is "no available model of freedom save one: that consciousness as it intervenes in the total social constitution [*Gesamtverfassung*] will through that constitution intervene in the complexion of the individual" (*ND* 265). In other words, a rational society would be one in which society and the individual mutually condition one another. Rather than being mere pawns of socioeconomic forces that make a mockery of their individuality, individuals would finally be free to shape the institutions that in turn shape them. This is the social dimension of reconciliation, or the communication between what has been differentiated (SO 247).

Nevertheless, individuals in a more rational society will not resemble individuals today because they will no longer "frantically be guarding the old particularity" (*ND* 283). Given the adverse effects of narcissism and reification on individuals, the "old particularity" is largely a sham. Here Adorno sounds a Hegelian note when he objects that "the fixation on one's own need and one's own longing mars the idea of a happiness that will not arise until the category of the individual ceases to be self-seclusive" (*ND* 352). Conversely, a rational society would no longer "agree with the present concept of collectivity" because that concept is as shambolic as the concept of the individual (*ND* 284). In *History and Freedom*, Adorno declares: "Just as individuals have not existed hitherto, so too there has been no global subject; the two are corollaries to one another" (*HF* 118).

Human happiness depends on the uncompromising critique of our current predicament, a solid theoretical basis for the practical activity that will be needed to attenuate the preponderance of society over individuals, but it also requires the development of non-repressive forms of social solidarity, which can accommodate differences between individuals as they pursue common goals. Moreover, happiness requires the realization of free and just exchange, the reorientation of the production process towards the preservation and flourishing of both human and non-human nature, and global dispensation from dehumanizing and superfluous labour. So, despite Postone's objection that Adorno cannot account for the possibility of historical transformation – an objection that fails to recognize that he adopts many of Marx's ideas about the prospects for, and the nature of, this transformation[22] –much of his description of Marx applies to Adorno as well.

Like Marx, Adorno points "in the direction of the possible creation of modes of individual labor that, freed from the constraints of the detailed division of labor, could be fuller and richer", and also more varied, because "people would not necessarily be tied to one sort of labor for most of their adult lives". To overcome the "antagonistic opposition of individuals and society", labour must be also restructured in such a way that "the wealth of society and the 'wealth-creating' possibility of labor for the individual are parallel, not opposed". This restructuring would allow "productive capacities that had been constituted in alienated form" to be "reappropriated and reflexively utilized on the sphere of production itself". Moreover, labour in a free society would be reduced to a minimum, and our metabolism with nature would be regulated rationally. In other words, prospects for creating a truly free society depend on "the historical *negation* of that socially constituting role played by labor in capitalism" (Postone 1993: 363).

It is, perhaps, the prospect of life without reifying, dehumanizing labour that prompts Adorno to describe utopia as a condition in which "'being, nothing else, without any further definition and fulfilment', might take the place of process, act, satisfaction". The concept closest to fulfilled utopia is that of eternal peace (*MM* 157).[23] Adorno contends that, "even epistemologically, the relationship of subject and object would lie in a peace achieved between human beings as well as between them and their Other". Peace is a "state of differentiation without domination, with the differentiated participating in each other" (SO 247). In this state, the individual's cognitive activity, instinctual life, social relations and interaction with nature, would all be liberated "as an I reconciled with the non-I". Reconciled with their "Other", individuals would "also be above freedom" because freedom is now in league "with its counterpart, repression" (*ND* 283).

The reconciliation of the individual with society is of a piece with the reconciliation of labouring individuals with their Other – nature. In labour as well, workers would, at one and the same time, grant proximity to natural things and allow these things to remain "distant and different, beyond the heterogeneous and beyond that which is their own" (*ND* 191). Here too Adorno champions mindfulness of nature in the self: by acknowledging that they are always also part of nature, workers may eventually improve their metabolism with nature. However, since the determinate negation of our antagonistic relation to nature can do little more than intimate what a reconciled condition would look like, Adorno does not describe this condition in any detail or depth. This paucity of detail may disappoint, but it is consistent with Adorno's cautionary remarks about the limits to determinate negation. If determinate negation outlines "the only permissible figure of the Other" (1992: 18, cited in Pritchard 2004: 193), that Other will never be fully and positively visible.

In "Notes on Kafka", Adorno again commends the power of determination negation when he praises Kafka for seeking "salvation in the incorporation of the powers of the adversary". Like Kafka, Adorno wants "to beat the world at its own game" by making "the moribund become the harbinger of Sabbath rest" (1967d: 270). Thought may have inherited its critical character as an act of negation, of resistance, from its prototype, the relationship between labour and its material, nature (*ND* 19), but Adorno also suggests that a more resolutely critical, and self-critical, mode of thought may in turn foreshadow the Sabbath rest in which labour and nature are reconciled. Seeking to redress the damage we have inflicted on the natural world, critical, resistive thought may provide a glimpse of mutually beneficial relationships between individuals and the beautiful alien – nature – if only a glimpse that is refracted through the dark lens of determinate negation.

CHAPTER FIVE

ADORNO AND RADICAL ECOLOGY

Adorno recognizes that the damage we have inflicted on nature has been extensive, and predicts that it could assume catastrophic proportions if we continue to behave as we do now: as rapaciously acquisitive creatures whose survival instincts are veering so far out of control that we are now destroying not just what we are trying to preserve but need to survive. What we call progress is forcing hundreds of millions of people to renounce the satisfaction of their needs to the point where they suffer horribly from malnutrition, starvation and preventable diseases. In less severe cases, we are forfeiting far richer, more materially and spiritually fulfilling, lives because mere survival remains our primary goal. For its part, non-human nature lies in ruins because we have imposed goals and purposes on it that are far different from those that it would adopt independently. We have ignored and suppressed nature's autotelic powers.

The looming prospect of environmental catastrophe – the extinction of all life on this planet – now acts as a powerful stimulus to thinking about the changes that must be implemented to ensure the survival of human and non-human nature. As Adorno argues throughout his work, our current idea of progress – the progressive domination of nature – is incompatible with a more emancipated form of progress in which human beings would reconcile themselves with nature (*HF* 151). Since the clash between these contrary ideas of progress has become acute under late capitalism, emancipation "calls for a critical confrontation with society as it actually exists" (*HF* 150). On an optimistic note, Adorno states that "progress can begin at any moment". In a graphic metaphor, he compares a truly progressive humanity to a giant who, "after sleeping from time immemorial, slowly stirs himself awake and then storms forth and tramples everything that gets in his way". Conceding that this awakening may seem rude or unwieldy, Adorno also contends that it is the only way to achieve political maturity.

A politically mature humanity would ensure that its own tenacious nature does not have the last word (P 150; see also *HF* 151).

This chapter explores the paths that a more mature humanity might take by examining the work of representatives of three major trends in radical ecology: Arne Naess's deep ecology, Murray Bookchin's social ecology and Carolyn Merchant's ecofeminism. In Adornian terms, each of these ecologists is impelled by survival instincts to search for ways to repair the damage inflicted on human and non-human nature by the unfettered sway of these same instincts. Although their conceptions of nature differ, these ecologists are also prepared to endorse the injunction that we become conscious of nature in ourselves. Like Adorno, they claim that emancipation depends, in part, on acknowledging our own affinity with nature, while echoing Adorno's insistence on the urgent need for radical social change to avert catastrophe.

This comparative discussion will also show that Adorno tackles important issues in environmental philosophy, including anthropomorphism, speciesism, the claim that nature has intrinsic value, the idea of "good" nature and the origin of domination. Yet one of the main points that will emerge from this comparison is the need to reconsider the principle of unity in diversity because Naess, Bookchin and Merchant adopt this principle (albeit in different ways), and end by championing holistic accounts of nature. But, apart from problematizing the holistic principle of unity in diversity, this chapter also stresses a related issue: the need to rethink and reform environmental activism itself. Since Adorno's critical concept of natural history makes visible both the damage done to natural things when we treat them as mere instances of more general kinds and the impediments to social solidarity and collective action today, I argue that his work has a great deal to offer the environmental movement.

ARNE NAESS AND DEEP ECOLOGY

Naess claims that many different, even conflicting, philosophical principles are compatible with radically altered and more mutually beneficial relationships to non-human nature. Since ecologists need not adhere to the same principles, Naess is prepared to accommodate a wide variety of philosophical positions, understanding philosophy in the broadest sense to include religious and other viewpoints, as well as more strictly philosophical views (1999b: 199). However, he also insists that these viewpoints agree with his eight-point Deep Ecology Platform, which provides a general orientation for action that aims to initiate change rather than formulating specific precepts for action. It is therefore more important to determine whether Adorno's philosophy of nature is compatible with Naess's eight points than to compare their respective philosophies.

Nevertheless, as his interest in ecology grew during the 1960s and 1970s, Naess began to develop a philosophy of nature, a philosophy influenced, in particular, by Spinoza's *Ethics* and the Advaita Vedanta. He called his philosophy Ecosophy T. Unlike ecological philosophy (or ecophilosophy), which examines problems common to ecology and philosophy, an ecosophy is "a kind of total view which you feel at home with, 'where you philosophically belong'" (Naess 1989: 37). Among its more important features, Ecosophy T promotes self-realization, where the self that is realized is far more comprehensive than the egocentric self because it extends to all nature. Before I begin to discuss the Deep Ecology Platform, I shall look briefly at these ideas about self-realization, but readers should bear in mind that Naess denies that objections to Ecosophy T will fatally undermine his proposals for improving our relation to nature.

Naess postulates the fundamental unity of everything that exists. In a fascinating debate with A. J. Ayer, televised in the Netherlands in 1971, he stated simply: "All living beings are ultimately one" (Naess *et al.* 1999: 15). His belief in the unity of all things under the sun underlies his account of self-realization: a process in which individuals actualize themselves by identifying with other individuals, including individual animals, insects and plants, as well as individual parts of inorganic nature (mountains, rivers and so on). Recalling Adorno's concern for the particular, Naess develops his ecosophical outlook through an identification with individual beings that is so profound or "deep" that the self "is no longer adequately delimited by the personal ego or the organism". Through identification, which is based more on feelings such as compassion and empathy than on a rational acknowledgement of our place in the natural world, one experiences oneself to be a genuine part of all life (1989: 174).

This assertion about the unity of all things is obviously at odds with Adorno's claims about non-identity. Even, and especially, as part of nature, our species has evolved in such a way that it has acquired the – as yet only partially actualized – capacity to differentiate itself from nature. Radical changes in our relation to nature presuppose the further development of this capacity, not its dissolution. Adorno would therefore reject Naess's quasi-mystical[1] expansion of the individual to embrace all nature, even as he stresses our affinity with it. If he inflicts a narcissistic wound on our self-understanding when he argues that reason is just an organ of adaptation to the environing world, Adorno also denies that becoming conscious of nature in ourselves requires blind identification with nature.

On this point, an objection might be raised because Adorno is sometimes said to advocate mimetic interaction with nature. Speaking of our
first attempts to create images of nature, Adorno asserts that they must have
been "preceded by a mimetic comportment", which he describes as "the
assimilation of the self to its other" (*AT* 329). On the surface, this description accords with Naess's idea of identification as a "spontaneous, non-
rational, but not irrational, process through which *the interest or interests
of another being are reacted to as our own interest or interests*" (1988b: 261).
At issue, however, are both the character of mimesis and the role it plays in
Adorno's work. Mimesis is doubtless central to Adorno's aesthetics: art is
the "indigeneous domain of mimesis" (Huhn 2004b: 11, citing *AT* 41). But
artistic mimesis does not involve the assimilation of self to other as it did
in human prehistory (or, indeed, as it does in childhood). Rather, mimesis in artworks consists in their "resemblance to themselves" (*AT* 104).[2] At
their best, artworks have a proleptic orientation: they can be said to reflect
"being-in-itself" only to the extent that they anticipate "a being-in-itself
that does not yet exist, … an unknown that – by way of the subject – is self-
determining" (*AT* 77).[3] On Tom Huhn's provocative reading of this often
touted but largely misunderstood concept, mimesis provides a model for
becoming, transience; it shows "how to forestall becoming fixed and fixated, rigid and further bound up" (2004b: 8).

More to the point, when Bernstein observes that "the meaning deficit
caused by the disenchantment of the world is … a rationality deficit", he
rightly notes that Adorno wants to expand reason by means of a reinscrip-
tion of conceptuality, not to displace reason with aesthetic praxis (Bernstein
2001: 4). Non-identity thinking can certainly learn from art because the
mimetic vestige in art is "the plenipotentiary of an undamaged life in the
midst of mutilated life" (*AT* 117). But such thinking is not as dependent
on art as art is on it, because art requires philosophy to give its truth content conceptual form.[4] Where Naess seeks to erase "the experience of a
distinction between *ego* and *alter*, between me and the sufferer" (1988b:
261), Adorno would counter that the awareness of our affinity with nature
becomes untrue when it is posited as something positive because it leads to
the "false conclusion that the object is the subject" (*ND* 150). As a corrective, the subject should use concepts in such a way as to "make up for what
it has done to nonidentity" (*ND* 145).

Although Naess adopts diversity and ecological complexity as normative
values (1989: 46) that serve as guidelines for decision-making about environmental issues (*ibid.*: 42), he also claims that the "earth is *an integrated
process*" (1988a: 128). If we can debate the nature and limitation of this
unity, it is nonetheless a basic tenet of Ecosophy T that life is fundamentally

one. Self-realization involves the "mature experience of oneness in diversity" as "*inspired* by, but not conforming to, Gandhi's interpretation of the *Bhagavadgita*" (1988a: 128). In fact, Naess alleges that the diversity of life on earth only extends and heightens identity: the "greater the diversity …, the greater the Self-realization" (Naess & Bodian 1995: 30). Given this stress on identity, then, Adorno would probably be more inclined to agree with ecofeminist Val Plumwood, who underlined the importance of "relational dynamics, the precarious balance of sameness and difference, of self and other involved in experiencing sameness without obliterating difference" (1999: 209).

More germane to this discussion is the question of the extent to which Adorno would agree with the Deep Ecology Platform, which Naess first developed with George Sessions in 1984.[5] Very generally, the platform consists in key terms and phrases that are "tentatively proposed as basic to deep ecology" (Naess 1995b: 67). Although these terms admit a variety of interpretations, and are not meant to be taken dogmatically, Naess states that those who completely dismiss any one of the eight points cannot be considered supporters of deep ecology (*ibid.*: 68). Yet Naess later cautions against viewing the points as either "*the* philosophy characteristic of the Deep Ecology movement, or even *the* principles of Deep Ecology". Here the eight points seem to have a more heuristic status: they "*only* present an attempt to formulate what *might be* accepted by the great majority of the supporters of the movement at a fairly general and abstract level". Moreover, deep ecologists in less industrialized parts of the world will need different sets of formulations to express something similar to the eight points because the points "are in a sense provincial – adapted primarily to discussions among formally well-educated people in rich countries" (1995a: 220).

Each point in the Deep Ecology Platform is open to interpretation. This is especially obvious in the controversy that was sparked by the original formulation of the first point: "The flourishing of human and nonhuman life on earth has intrinsic value. The value of nonhuman life forms is independent of the usefulness these may have for narrow human purposes" (1999a: 8). Since critics objected to the idea that nature (or its flourishing) has an intrinsic value, Naess accepted Jon Wetlesen's proposal to use the phrase "value in itself" as a generic term, with "intrinsic value" or "inherent value" serving as "specifications" (Wetlesen 1999: 406; see also Naess 1999c: 418–19). Point 1 was revised to read: "The well-being and flourishing of human and non-human life on Earth have value in themselves (synonyms: intrinsic value, inherent worth). These values are independent of the usefulness of the non-human world for human purposes" (1995b: 68).

In defence of Naess, Andrew McLaughlin writes that the first point in the platform essentially targets anthropocentrism; it does not imply a commitment to any philosophically precise theory about intrinsic or inherent value. Rather than trying to "construct a formal ethical theory", Naess is using a language that can communicate in popular contexts. He wants to say that "we *can* care for the rest of nature for reasons which have nothing to do with whether or not it has intrinsic, inherent, or whatever sort of value" (McLaughlin 1995: 86–7). Ecologist Per Ariansen notes that a less confusing term, which Naess used "in his work on the history of philosophy, is *autotelic value*, the value something has in being sought as an end, not as a means" (1999: 423). In fact, Naess also used this phrase when he argued that the radical shift that accompanies more mutually beneficial relationships to nature will require recognition of the autotelic value of every living being (1988b: 266), a recognition that identification allegedly makes possible (1986: 506).

For his part, Adorno acknowledged the autotelic powers – rather than value – of non-human nature when he referred to nature's independent purposiveness. Naess acknowledges these powers as well when he states that self-realization can be rendered in the phrase "realizing inherent potentialities". The questions addressed by deep ecology are: "'What are the inherent potentialities of the beings of species X?' and 'What are the inherent potentialities of this specimen X of the species Y?'" (1995f: 229). For Naess, moreover, the "mature human individual, with a widened self, acknowledges a right to self-realization that is universal, and seeks a social order, or rather a biospherical order, which maximizes the potential for self-realization of all kinds of beings" (1995d: 257).

With some qualifications, Adorno would accept the second point in the Deep Ecology Platform: "Richness and diversity of life forms contribute to the realization of these values [the well-being and flourishing of human and non-human life] and are also values in themselves" (1995b: 68). But Adorno did not consider the richness and diversity of life forms to be inherent or intrinsic values. Instead, when he stated that the "matters of true philosophical interest at this point in history" are "nonconceptuality, individuality, and particularity" (*ND* 8), he suggested that diversity, the limitless profusion of individuated things, is philosophically interesting because it continues to elude us in our cognitive pursuit of unity, identity and permanence, thereby ensuring that we remain ignorant about natural things and ourselves.

To be sure, Adorno did hold as values, in the broadest sense of that word, the well-being and flourishing of both human and non-human life. His proleptic apprehension of the potential inherent in things seeks to evoke

126

conditions under which human and non-human nature would thrive. Moreover, his new categorical imperative – that nothing like Auschwitz should happen again – is a response to a situation in which human and non-human nature have been reduced to so many commensurable units of value, to lifeless, reified objects, and are either literally destroyed or damaged to the point where it can plausibly be said that they no longer live because they are prevented from developing freely. This new imperative is experienced somatically; it is "a bodily sensation of the moral addendum – bodily because it is now the practical abhorrence of the unbearable physical agony to which individuals are exposed" (*ND* 365).

For Naess, suffering is "perhaps the most potent source of identification" because most people find it difficult to inhibit their spontaneous aversion to it. However, Naess also criticizes Kant's "strange doctrine" that we should abstain from maltreating animals only because we are averse to suffering, while noting with approval that Kant would consider the spontaneous urge to eliminate suffering to be beautiful, and encouraging beautiful action (1988b: 264).[6] In his own gloss on Kant, Adorno observes that Kantian ethics accords affection, not respect, to other animals (*ND* 299). Praising the philosophy of Arnold Schopenhauer, with its compassion for non-human animals, Adorno (*PMP* 145) contends that our exploitation and maltreatment of animals are the most tangible and obvious expression of our blind domination of nature.[7] In *Dialectic of Enlightenment*, moreover, he was particularly critical of animal experimentation (*DE* C:245–6, J:204).

Since domination must end, the only remaining "social morality" is to abolish the "vicious system of compensatory exchange". As for individuals, they are left with "no more than the morality for which Kantian ethics … can muster only disdain: to try to live so that one may believe oneself to have been a good animal" (*ND* 299). Commenting on Adorno's idea about living life as a good animal, Fabian Freyenhagen interprets it to mean that we should "show solidarity with the tormentable body" (2008: 108; *ND* 285). Although he mistakenly thinks that solidarity should be based on identification, Freyenhagen rightly observes that solidarity "arises out of the abhorrence of physical suffering, which has direct motivational force for human animals and for other animals as well in so far as Adorno situates this abhorrence within the context of natural evolution" (2008: 108). This abhorrence is instinctive, impulsive. In fact, Adorno insists that "there can be no room for freedom and humanity" without the kind of impulsive action that Nietzsche is said (perhaps apocryphally) to have exhibited in response to the maltreatment of a horse. For Adorno, the "true primal phenomenon of moral behaviour … occurs when the element of impulse joins forces with the element of consciousness to bring about a spontaneous act" (*HF* 239–40 *passim*).[8]

Given the intrinsic value of diversity, Point 3 in the Deep Ecology Platform states that we "have no right to reduce … richness and diversity except to satisfy vital needs" (1995b: 68). Here, Naess is deliberately leaving the term "vital needs" vague to allow for "considerable latitude in judgment" owing to differences in "climate and related factors, together with differences in the structures of societies as they now exist" (*ibid.*: 69). But the vagueness of this term does not make it any easier to determine whether Adorno would agree. Even assuming that Adorno would limit vital needs to food, clothing and shelter (he was concerned about starvation in particular: "there is tenderness only in the coarsest demand: that no one shall go hungry any more" [*MM* 156]), much remains to be determined – how much food? of what kind? – as Naess himself admits.

Adorno also stressed the difficulty in distinguishing between true and false, primary and secondary, needs.[9] Yet he never suggested that the satisfaction of needs could be traded off against reductions in richness and diversity. Perhaps naively, he seemed at times to believe that such trade-offs would not be necessary. A society that has rid itself of "the irrationality in which production for profit is entangled" is one in which production "would act on need in a true, not distorted, sense: not because unsatisfied need is allayed by something useless, but because the allayed need relates to the world without damaging it through universal utility" (1972d: 396). So, while Adorno envisaged a society in which human needs would be met without damaging non-human nature, the extent to which he would accept that vital needs may trump diversity is moot.

Trade-offs between the satisfaction of vital human needs and the diversity of non-human nature might well be less frequent and problematic if the human population were smaller. Point 4 reads: "The flourishing of human life and cultures is compatible with a substantially smaller human population. The flourishing of non-human life *requires* a smaller human population" (Naess 1995b: 68). Although the stabilization and reduction of the human population will take centuries to achieve, without them, "substantial decreases in richness and diversity are liable to occur: the rate of extinction of species will be ten to one hundred or more times greater than in any other short period of earth history" (*ibid.*: 69). Unfortunately, Adorno never directly addressed this pressing (and controversial) issue. But it could be argued that his goal of satisfying the needs of all the living could be met far more easily if there were fewer human needs to satisfy. A smaller human population might also place fewer demands on the natural world, potentially freeing more of nature from exploitation.

There is no doubt that Adorno would adopt Point 5: "Present human interference with the non-human world is excessive, and the situation is rapidly worsening" (*ibid.*: 68). This point should be read in conjunction with Point 6: "Policies must therefore be changed. These policies affect basic economic, technological, and ideological structures. The resulting state of affairs will be deeply different from the present" (*ibid.*). Indeed, Naess criticizes those factions of "the new green wave" in philosophy and religion that fail to acknowledge the need for *"substantial change"* (1995c: 211). Since economic growth, as "conceived and implemented today by the industrial states, is incompatible" with the first five points (1995b: 69), Naess targets capitalism, noting that the "most forceful and systematic critique of capitalism is to be found in socialist literature". Although some socialist goals, such as centralizing and maximizing production, are not compatible with deep ecology, many are: "no excessive aggressive individualism .... Community, production for use, low income differentials, local production for local needs, participative involvement, solidarity" (1989: 157).

Deep ecology also seeks to realize the goals of global peace, social justice and *"long-range, local, district, regional, national, and global wide ecological sustainability"* (1995e: 447). On this point too, Naess is deliberately vague: by "ecological sustainability", for example, he means "protecting the full richness and diversity of Life on Earth" (1995a: 219). The platform provides no more than a general orientation; individuals and groups in different regions and countries must decide for themselves how to make ecological sustainability a reality. Concrete decisions about how to establish more mutually beneficial relationships between human and non-human nature are left to those who are carrying them out in practice (although, with his Gandhian adherence to non-violence, Naess seems to envisage incremental change).

Adorno too refuses to offer specific proposals for change. Philosophy is needed "only as critique, as resistance" (1998o: 10); it wants to know, not *how* the world should be changed, but "why the world – which could be paradise here and now – can become hell itself tomorrow" (*ibid.*: 14). In fact, Adorno charged that socialist proposals for change were often barbaric because they endorsed the constant revolutionizing of relations of production that characterizes capitalism, namely "unfettered activity, … uninterrupted procreation, … chubby insatiability, … freedom as frantic bustle". They also fed on the "bourgeois concept of nature that has always served solely to proclaim social violence as unchangeable, a piece of healthy eternity". By contrast, a more rational society would free itself from production for production's sake and unfettered economic growth: "Perhaps the true society will grow tired of development and, out of freedom, leave possibilities unused, instead of storming under a confused compulsion to the conquest of strange stars" (*MM* 156).

The policy changes mentioned in Point 6 will affect what Naess calls ideological structures. Point 7 explains how these structures may be improved:

> The ideological change will be mainly that of appreciating life quality (dwelling in situations of inherent value) rather than adhering to a constantly rising standard of living. There will be a profound awareness of the difference between bigness and greatness. (Naess 1995b: 68)

Against aggressive, acquisitive individualism, Naess advocates the peaceful coexistence of human and non-human nature in societies that allow each individual life form to develop its potentialities to the fullest. On his view, moreover, self-preservation requires "self-expression or realisation", or "life-unfolding", "life-expansion" (1989: 85). Today, however, self-realization is impeded by a crisis of consumption; this crisis points to our "inability to question deeply what is and is not worthwhile in life", and underscores the need for dramatic changes in our lifestyles. Such changes will occur only when we engage in activities that satisfy our whole being, living lives that are "simple in means and rich in ends" (Naess & Bogdian 1995: 30).

Of course, Adorno also condemns the vicious cycle of unrestrained production and torpid consumption. However, much of his work is devoted to understanding why monopoly capitalism has so far met with little effective resistance. Needs are now hammered into psychologically weak individuals by the increasingly sophisticated psychotechnology of the culture industry. Dependency on, and conformity to, the existing system are constantly reinforced. The affirmative refrain of the prevailing ideology – that is just the way things are; things are like this – implies that nothing can change, while suggesting that what exists *should* exist simply because it exists.

Given this situation, there are serious obstacles to meaningful change, including changes in lifestyle. Indeed, Adorno is arguably more realistic than Naess. The environmental policies adopted by governments over the past few decades have been completely watered down, and even these diluted targets have not been met. Furthermore, while the call to reduce consumption would almost certainly have far-reaching consequences if answered immediately by everyone everywhere, the kind of changes Naess advocates will not be achieved if (as is more likely) a few individuals adopt "green" lifestyles in a society that successfully commodifies lifestyle choices, including green ones. Radical change presupposes a critical understanding

130

of the tendencies and behaviours that now thwart effective political action; it requires a better understanding of our current predicament, a predicament in which the most well-meaning individuals often sustain the very system they oppose, even in their resistance to it. If resistance is ever to be anything other than futile, the forces that now weaken it must be thoroughly plumbed.

Change that affects not just economic, technological and ideological structures, but political organizations, social interaction, psychological make-up and cognitive "structures", ultimately requires the emergence of a global subject. However, since the solidarity in which a global subject would take shape is now blocked by reification and pathologies such as narcissism, Adorno calls for an uncompromising critique of impediments to solidarity, while outlining alternative forms that would sublate divergent individual interests (*ND* 282). For his part, Naess agrees that reification is pervasive because Western technology "reduces everything to mere objects of manipulation", treating human and non-human animals as "mere factors – mostly causing trouble – in the production process" (Naess 1989: 172 *passim*).[10] Yet, in contrast to Adorno, Naess believes that reification can be overcome, and solidarity achieved, by means of identification.

Naess also alleges that the solidarity generated by identification will not exclude diversity: the "widening and deepening of individual selves" through identification "*somehow* never makes them into one 'mass'" (*ibid.*: 172–3). At the same time, he admits that he does not know how to articulate the relationship between unity and diversity: "'In unity diversity!', yes, but how? As a vague postulate it has a specific function within a total view, however imperfectly" (*ibid.*: 173). Naess raises an important issue here: how to appreciate and foster diversity in both human beings and non-human nature. How can solidarity be achieved among disparate individuals such that they are capable of working together effectively to promote change without being subsumed completely under an organization, institution or party? How might human beings relate to non-human nature such that nature can thrive in all its diversity?

Although Adorno would reject identification as a viable solution to these problems, he need not endorse identification because it is not a plank in the platform but an ecosophical postulate. As I shall continue to argue in my discussion of Bookchin and Merchant, Adorno's attempts to square the circle of identity and difference – attempts outlined in the previous chapters – contribute to both the theory and the future practice of radical ecology because they address a crucial issue in environmental philosophy as a whole. According to Adorno, reconciliation between human beings and non-human nature does not require "the identity of all as subsumed beneath a totality, a concept, an integrated society". Rather, a truly achieved identity requires "the consciousness of *non-identity*", and "the creation of a reconciled non-identity" (*HF* 55).

To return to an earlier point, Adorno thinks we must defer the action urgently needed to effect radical change because we can do nothing today "that will not threaten to turn out for the worst even if meant for the best" (*ND* 245). Yet his insistence on the prior need for an uncompromisingly critical understanding of our current predicament is compatible with Point 8 of Naess's platform: "Those who subscribe to the foregoing points have an obligation directly or indirectly to try to implement the necessary changes" (1995b: 68). Again, Adorno claims that critical thought is itself a force of resistance, a comportment, a form of practice (1998l: 293).[11] Critical theory plumbs our natural history, examining the tendencies and trends that now undermine effective practice – including practices geared to solving environmental problems – while pointing towards a society that would negate "the physical suffering of even the least of its members", along with the "internal reflexive forms of that suffering". Agreeing with Naess about the importance of solidarity, Adorno writes: "By now, this negation in the interest of all can be realized only in a solidarity that is transparent to itself and all the living" (*ND* 204).

MURRAY BOOKCHIN AND SOCIAL ECOLOGY

A social ecologist for more than fifty years, Bookchin engaged polemically with many different figures, including Naess and Adorno. Suggesting, often without naming him directly, that Naess succumbed to mysticism, Bookchin (1990: 10) lambasts – to the point of ridicule at times – Naess's stress on unity, even as he adopts unity in diversity as one of the central principles of his social ecology. Bookchin is critical of Adorno as well. Much like Habermas, he considers Adorno to be too pessimistic, and points to counter-tendencies in existing social arrangements that may foster change. Yet he also believes that his social ecology keeps faith with the promise of critical theory:

> that humanity could have found its sense of self-identity and individuation through ecological differentiation rather than hierarchical opposition; that the "I" could have formed itself around mutuality, with its wealth of uniqueness, rather than around the commanding "lordship", with all its reversals, of Hegel's "master– slave" relationship. (*Ibid.*: 87–8 *passim*)

Bookchin devoted one of his major works, *The Ecology of Freedom*, to exploring the origin and historical trajectory of domination in the West. In human prehistory, Bookchin alleges, societies were not riven by distinctions between old and young, men and women, or by blood and family ties. Rather, they "visualized people, things, and relations in terms of their uniqueness". People and things were neither ranked nor rated; they were simply viewed as dissimilar (1991a: 44). Equally important, the feeling of unity, of profound social solidarity, that bound people together in these "organic" societies also generated a feeling of unity between human beings and the environing world, precluding the domination of nature. According to Bookchin, the "notion that man is destined to dominate nature ... is almost completely alien to the outlook of so-called primitive or preliterate communities" (*ibid.*: 43) because the non-hierarchical, harmonious coexistence of individuals in organic societies fostered non-hierarchical, harmonious relations with nature.

Bookchin criticizes the "traditional left" generally for assuming that "the 'domination of man by man' ... was, an historically unavoidable evil that emerged directly out of the objective human need to 'dominate nature'" (1991b: 56). He claims that our antagonistic relation to nature developed only after human beings began to dominate other human beings in gerontocracies. Gerontocracy is "hierarchy in its most nascent form: hierarchy embedded in the matrix of equality" (1991a: 83). Moreover, on this account, gerontocracies effectively precipitated our fall from a state of grace, a state of virtually complete social harmony, where "differences between individuals, age groups, sexes – and between humanity and the natural manifold of living and nonliving phenomena – were seen (to use Hegel's superb phrase) as a 'unity of differences' or 'unity of diversity', not as hierarchies" (*ibid.*: 5).

Basing this account of human prehistory on the work of anthropologists Dorothy Lee[12] and Paul Radin, *inter alia*, Bookchin contends that "otherness" originally took "the form of *differentiation*, of *articulation*, of *complementarity*". Prehistorical societies exhibited features such as:

> complete parity or equality ...; usufruct, and later reciprocity; the avoidance of coercion in dealing with internal affairs; and finally, ... the "inalienable right" ... of every individual in the community "to food, shelter and clothing" irrespective of the amount of work contributed by the individual to the acquisition of the means of life. (1991a: 56)

Although "the 'otherness' of complementarity was often subverted by emerging status groups, and slowly gave way to 'otherness' based on domination" (*ibid.*: xlvii), complementary forms of otherness persist. Human evolution has unfolded equivocally, and continues to offer alternatives to domination.

Adorno would counter that Bookchin romanticizes our prehistory by accepting the myth of the Golden Age. According to Adorno, the origin of domination cannot be settled with facts because these "fade away in the mists of primitive history" (*ND* 321). Still, Adorno does speculate about the origin of domination when he comments on Marx and Engels's claim that domination originated in stratified class relations. Noting that this claim was motivated by a rejection of anarchism, Adorno would agree with Bookchin – a self-professed anarchist – to the extent that the former Soviet Union showed that domination may outlast the planned economy (*ND* 322). Here, however, Adorno also conjectures that our domination of nature may have originated in a catastrophic event, while denying that the domination of human beings by human beings is more primordial than the domination of nature.[13] He would also contest Bookchin's belief that the establishment of non-hierarchical social relations will put an end to our domination of nature because it is entirely uncertain that harmonious social relations will necessarily lead (or necessarily led in human prehistory) to harmonious relations with non-human nature.

Where Adorno places great emphasis on humanity's underground instinctual history, Bookchin's view of the role of survival instincts in human history is somewhat ambivalent. At times, he warns against "placing the capabilities of human beings and their intellectuality on a par with animal skills for survival" because this would denigrate human beings (1991a: xxxvi). Once we began to distinguish ourselves from the natural world, we were no longer "limited to the bedrock existence of seeking mere survival" (*ibid.*: xlv). At other times, however, Bookchin sounds much like Adorno. For example, he remarks in *Post-Scarcity Anarchism* that the "great historic splits that destroyed early organic societies, dividing man from nature and man from man, had their origins in the problems of survival, in problems that involved the mere maintenance of human existence" (1986: 11). In *The Ecology of Freedom*, he maintains that survival instincts gave rise to our "capacities to think conceptually, to create extrabiological tools and machines, and to do this with a high degree of collective organization and intentionality". A product of natural evolution, these cognitive capacities in turn enabled us "to evolve along *social* lines and produce a second nature that profoundly affects the evolution and life-forms of first nature" (1991a: xxx).

This distinction between natural evolution and social evolution is equally problematic.[14] Again, for Adorno, human beings remain all too natural, and nature has become all too human. But Bookchin adopts Marx's goal in the

Economic and Philosophic Manuscripts when he calls for a new sensibility that would foster the humanization of nature and the naturalization of humanity (1986: 70). According to Bookchin, "[t]o recover human nature is to 'renature' it, to restore its continuity with the creative process of natural evolution, its freedom and participation in that evolution conceived as a realm of incipient freedom and as a participatory process" (1990: 118). Conversely, non-human nature is given a human face when we recognize that we evolved from nature and that human beings are not wholly Other than nature. Since "humanity's vast capacities to alter 'first nature' are themselves a product of natural evolution", they reveal "the thrust of natural evolution toward organic complexity and subjectivity – the potentiality of 'first nature' to actualize itself in self-conscious intellectuality" (*ibid*.: 42–3). Nature can be humanized "by seeing in human consciousness a natural world rendered self-conscious and self-active" (1980b: 70).

Where Adorno thinks our species has not yet distinguished itself fully from nature by becoming aware of its own natural history, Bookchin could be accused of "speciesism" because he regards human beings as the *apogée* of natural evolution. Although he denies that our place in the evolutionary chain makes us superior to nature, Bookchin believes that human beings are more advanced than other animals,[15] and that nature expresses itself most completely in human consciousness and reason. Reason subtends nature "as the self-organizing attributes of substance"; it "is the latent subjectivity in the inorganic and organic levels of reality that reveal an inherent striving toward consciousness" (1991a: 11). In other words, this latent subjectivity "ultimately yields mind, will, and the capacity for freedom" (1990: 172–3). To defend this claim, Bookchin argues (invalidly, in my view) that, "[t]o deny the existence of subjectivity in nonhuman nature, is to deny that it can exist either in its given human form or in any form at all" (1991a: 236).

Effectively subsuming nature under mind, Bookchin espouses Hegel's view of mind as the absolute *prius*. He identifies nature with reason such that human beings are natural only because nature is implicitly rational, because nature harbours reason within itself. This subsumption of nature under reason simplifies Bookchin's goal of humanizing nature and naturalizing humanity. Since nature and mind are ultimately identical, since both converge in reason, humanizing nature and naturalizing the human involves showing that reason underlies both. In fact, Bookchin would like to see human sociality conform to a much greater degree to its more rational, "organic", origins in a kind of return to nature, which effectively amounts to a return to reason.

Interestingly, Bookchin sometimes dismisses teleological accounts of natural history. In the introduction to *The Ecology of Freedom*, for example, he denies "that there are predetermined ends or a *telos* in natural evolution that guides life's development inexorably toward consciousness and freedom". Instead, we can say only that "the *potentiality* for achieving consciousness and freedom does exist" (1991a: xxviii). However, towards the end of *The Ecology of Freedom*, Bookchin complains that we "have lost sight of the *telos* that renders us an aspect of nature" (*ibid.*: 315). Later still, he writes:

> [F]rom the ever-greater complexity and variety that raises subatomic particles through the course of evolution to those conscious, self-reflexive life forms we call human beings, we cannot help but speculate about the existence of a broadly conceived *telos* and a latent subjectivity in substance itself that eventually leads to mind and intellectuality.   (*Ibid.*: 364)

Bookchin would like to recover the "notion of an immanent world reason, albeit without the archaic, quasi-theological trappings". But when he attributes this goal to Adorno (*ibid.*: 10), Bookchin fails to see that Adorno unequivocally rejected Hegel's view of mind or spirit as the immanent telos of all nature. To be sure, Adorno recognized that reason was once believed to be immanent in reality, but he did not adopt this belief himself. In fact, Adorno was highly critical of teleological accounts of history, even the dystopian one that is sometimes attributed to him. If he would agree that "[t]he history of 'civilization' has been a steady process of estrangement from nature that has increasingly developed into outright antagonism" (*ibid.*: 315), he nonetheless insisted that change can begin at any moment. Giving the lie to the tired charge of pessimism levelled by Bookchin and others, Adorno remarked that "the critical yardstick that … compels and obliges reason to oppose the superior strength of the course of the world is always the fact that in every situation there is a concrete possibility of doing things differently" (*HF* 68).

Bookchin also revises Darwin's theory of evolution on the grounds that Darwinians and neo-Darwinians tend to regard life forms "as 'objects' of selective forces exogenous to them". He adopts a participatory account of evolution (1990: 108), which reveals that "mutual cooperation–symbiosis – is as important in evolution as the so-called 'struggle' for survival" (*ibid.*: 78). In this account, the concept of matter must also be revised because life and all its attributes are already latent in matter. In other words, "what we call 'matter' may more properly be characterized as active substance" (*ibid.*: 79). By extension, "nature" refers to "an *evolutionary development* … that should be conceived as an aeons-long process of ever-greater differentiation" (1991a: xx).

Bookchin wants to foster a new sensibility, which is informed by what he calls "libertarian reason" with its symbiotic relation to nature. The germinal conditions for this sensibility lie in the early formative process that introduces the newborn child to culture (*ibid.*: 304). In maternal care, "human 'second nature' ... is structured around nurture, support, and a deobjectified world of experience rather than a world guided by domination, self-interest, and exploitation" (*ibid.*: 307). Although history has been blighted by our attempts to extirpate the seeds of libertarian reason, it continues to harbour these seeds. In libertarian terms, human nature is defined as "a biologically rooted process of consociation, a process in which cooperation, mutual support, and love are natural as well as cultural attributes" (*ibid.*: 317). Since it exhibits these quintessentially human traits, maternal care reveals "the enduring features of a subterranean libertarian realm that has lived in cunning accommodation with the prevailing order of domination" (*ibid.*: 318).

It is in this context that Bookchin endorses an ethics of complementarity. Imbued with the values of mutualism, subjectivity and freedom, it was this ethics that informed prehistorical organic societies. Although we cannot return to these societies because our "values and practices now demand a degree of consciousness and intellectual sophistication that early bands, clans, and tribes never required to maintain their freedom as a lived phenomenon", Bookchin also believes that "organic societies spontaneously evolved values that we rarely can improve" (*ibid.*: 319). Oriented towards freedom, his ethics aims to accommodate difference much as organic societies once did (and maternal care allegedly still does) by making "every effort to compensate for the unavoidable inequalities in physical differences, degrees of intellectuality, and needs among individual human beings" (*ibid.*: lii).

Against this Adorno argued, not just that we can know little about our prehistory, but that the idea of an originally good nature is a mere "phantasm". Acknowledging that this idea is seductive, Adorno also objected that the concept of origin is both a category of domination and an ideological principle because "it confirms that a man ranks first because he was there first; it confirms the autochthon against the newcomer, the settler against the migrant" (*ND* 155). In a criticism that can be levelled against Bookchin as well, Adorno challenged Hegel's philosophy of origins. With its "return to the starting point of the motion", Hegelian philosophy ends by positing the continuous identity of subject and object (*ND* 156). By contrast, the task of Adorno's negative dialectics is "to break the compulsion to achieve identity, and to break it by means of the energy stored up in that compulsion and congealed in its objectifications" (*ND* 157).

Of course, Adorno also objected to Hegel's progressive subsumption of matter under mind. But if he tried to counter Hegel's idealism with his non-reductive and non-dualistic conception of nature and history, Bookchin occasionally seems to do something similar. Although we are distinct from non-human nature because human reason is the more advanced form of reason, Bookchin nonetheless rejects dualism when he asserts that "human history can never disengage itself or disembed itself from nature" (1991a: 34). Dualism is illusory; it is an outgrowth of our problematic social evolution with its increasingly antagonistic stance towards nature. Concealed by our dualist conception of nature and mind is a more complementary relationship, a more "natural" relation to otherness, that we ought to revive.

On this point, however, Adorno would also disagree: a more complementary relation to nature is something that has yet to be achieved, rather than something we can potentially (or will eventually) recuperate. Humanity too has yet to come into being. This is precisely why Adorno states that nothing is original except the goal. Bookchin's ideologically suspect return to origins is especially obvious in his view that maternal care continues to exhibit values that can serve as an antidote to our antagonism towards nature. For he implies that women are immune to the vicissitudes of history. Against this, one could simply point out that maternal care is neither an ahistorical phenomenon, nor an activity completely devoid of domination, self-interest and exploitation. Indeed, this uncritical view of mother love seems remarkably naive and is arguably sexist because it regards women as placeholders for nature.

Bookchin rejects reductionism as well. Like Adorno, he maintains that our capacity for thought distinguishes us from non-human nature because it enables us to think beyond the given state of affairs, thereby distancing us, in potentially emancipatory ways, from "an imperturbable existence that consists of eating, digesting, and defecating". Implicitly targeting Naess, he contends that "the danger that confronts ecological thinking is less a matter of a dualistic sensibility" than of "*reductionism*, an intellectual dissolution of *all* difference into an undefinable 'Oneness' that excludes the possibility of creativity and turns a concept like 'interconnectedness' into the bonds of a mental and emotional straightjacket" (*ibid.*: xlv–xlvi).

Nevertheless, it should already be clear that Bookchin does not avoid reductionism. Attempting to embrace otherness, his ethics effectively sublates otherness into sameness in Hegelian fashion. Bookchin's remarks on unity in diversity – a central principle in his ethics – illustrate this. Unity in diversity means that "nature is conceived not merely as a constellation of ecosystems but also as a meaningful natural *history*, a developing, creative, and fecund nature that yields an increasing complexity of forms and interrelationships" (*ibid.*: 274). And, developing, creative, fecund nature is fundamentally One: its unity takes the form of an "ineffable *sensibilité* that

138

is a function of increasingly complex patterns of integration". Again, for Bookchin, nature as a whole is a subjectivity that "expresses itself in various gradations, not only as the mentalism of reason, but also as the interactivity, reactivity, and the *growing purposive activity of forms*". This subjectivity "*is* the history of reason – or, more precisely, of a slowly forming mentality that exists on a wider terrain of reality than human cerebral activity". Substance is subject because substance "*actively* functions to maintain its identity, equilibrium, fecundity, and place in a given constellation of phenomena" (*ibid*.: 275).

This stress on unity is also apparent when Bookchin champions the fusion of natural and social evolution "in a new transcendence such that all the splits that separate us from the biological world will be sublated into a rational society" because humanity would finally live "in harmony with itself". To facilitate this harmonious fusion, however, Bookchin adopts his own version of the injunction that nature should become conscious of itself: humanity should become "natural evolution rendered self-conscious, guided by a humanistic ethics of complementarity" (1995: 9). Attributing this phrase to Johann Fichte in *Die Bestimmung des Menschen*, Bookchin observes that the idea of nature becoming conscious of itself appeared much earlier in the Presocratic concept of *nous*, or mind, a concept that, "in Fichte's stirring prose, envisions consciousness 'no longer as that stranger in Nature whose connection and existence is so incomprehensible'". Rather than seeing nature as alien, humanity must understand that it is part of nature as "'one of its necessary manifestations'" (1980c: 110).

To be sure, we are not yet fully conscious of nature in ourselves. Mistakenly charging that Adorno despaired of reason, Bookchin actually seems to follow his lead when he insists that reason alone will enable us to play the pivotal role of self-conscious nature, thereby facilitating our reconciliation with nature. But if the dialectical reason he endorses systematically explores "processes of change" to discover "how a living entity is so constructed as a *potentiality* to phase from one stage of its development into another" (1990: 14), Bookchin ultimately ontologizes reason and succumbs to the fallacy of constitutive subjectivity. Like Hegel, he believes that our human, all-too-human, categories are "the truth, objectivity, and actual being of … things themselves" (Hegel 1970, cited in Stone 2008: 49).

Nevertheless, Bookchin does share Adorno's goal of fostering the rational potential in society (1990: 32). He too stresses the urgent need for radical social change: our world "will either undergo revolutionary changes so far-reaching in character that humanity will totally transform its social relations and its very conception of life, or it will suffer an apocalypse that may well end humanity's tenure on the planet" (1991a: 18). Although the abolition of capitalism will not, by itself, abolish hierarchical social relations, Bookchin denounces capitalism because it has subverted the integrity of the human community (*ibid.*: 260). Like Adorno, he recognizes that capitalism has become far more than an economic system because it now affects society as a whole. He emphatically rejects capitalism's emphasis on economic growth for its own sake, and is equally critical of consumerism and the pernicious role that the media play in fostering consumption.

Bookchin also thinks that we can now provide adequately for everyone on earth. One of the central tasks of his social ecology is to dispel the illusion, propagated under capitalism, that resources are scarce and sacrifices must continue to be made. Given advances in technology, we can satisfy the reasonable needs of everyone everywhere. In *Post-Scarcity Anarchism*, for example, he declares: "for the first time in history we stand on the threshold of a post-scarcity society". Technology already enables us "to provide food, shelter, garments, and a broad spectrum of luxuries without devouring the precious time of humanity and without dissipating its invaluable reservoir of creative energy in mindless labor" (1986: 12). But since capitalism thwarts the better potential of technology, and justifies its exploitation of nature on the largely specious grounds of scarcity, its "systems of production, distribution, and promotion of goods and needs are not just grossly irrational but antiecological" (1991a: 262).

The transformation of our death-oriented society into a life-oriented one demands "a revolution in all areas of life – social as well as natural, political as well as personal, economic as well as cultural" (1991c: 76). (Like Naess, Bookchin warns that, if ecologists are not sufficiently radical, the ecology movement will "gradually degenerate into a safety valve for the established order" [*ibid.*].) Moreover, ecologist Janet Biehl remarks that Bookchin looks to grass-roots politics to promote change. Characterized by "the popular self-management of the community by free citizens", grass-roots politics represents the democratic dimension of anarchism because it "seeks to create a vital public sphere based on cooperation and community". Today, the urban neighbourhood is the privileged site for grass-roots activity with radical potential. In local assemblies, for example, individuals can become active citizens who "recreate the public sphere, democratically making decisions on matters that affect their common life". Optimally, they will not only "'municipalize' the economy, managing their community's economic life", but abolish private property, and distribute goods according to need. At the root of this transformation are post-scarcity technologies that can "minimize the time consumed by labor, making possible broad political participation" (Biehl 1997: 172).

140

Adorno shares some of Bookchin's optimism about the emancipatory potential of technology. Although there are serious psychological, social, political and economic impediments to the realization of more substantively democratic polities, Adorno is not entirely without hope. On the one hand, individuals "are continuously molded from above" in order to maintain "the over-all economic pattern". On the other hand, "the amount of energy that goes into this process bears a direct relation to the amount of potential, residing within people, for moving in a different direction" (Adorno *et al.* 1982: 480). This countervailing potential is linked to our capacity for self-criticism. To become more autonomous, individuals must recognize the extent to which their own ideas, beliefs, attitudes and behaviours have been shaped and conditioned by both socioeconomic institutions and their instincts and needs. Such critical self-awareness is the precondition for more genuinely democratic forms of government because it fosters the capacity to think for oneself rather than merely parroting others, to form ideas and opinions independently of prevailing opinion and the influence of authorities. In short, critical self-reflection engenders a form of political maturity that is essential for democracy (1998b: 281).

Where Bookchin seems to believe that it is now possible to create a viable and vibrant public sphere, Adorno maintains that economic conditions are such that they severely impair the interpersonal relations required to sustain it. Although the public sphere is "the most important medium of all politically effective criticism", it has become so commodified that it "works against the critical principle in order to better market itself" (*ibid.*: 283). In fact, Adorno decries the absence of an independent sphere in which citizens could form opinions about what lies in the general interest. Relying in part on his empirical analyses of the role of the privately owned media in forming public opinion, he claims that what passes for public opinion today has been imposed on people "by the overall structure of society and hence by relations of domination" (1998h: 121), thereby making a mockery of the liberal ideal of autonomous opinion-formation. The dominant opinion disseminated by the culture industry merely reflects the opinion of the economic and political elite; it is entangled in particular interests in profit and power that try to pass themselves off as universal (*ibid.*: 117).

Adorno did say that public opinion could play a positive role by averting "the worst in an antagonistic society". It had already done so during the Dreyfus affair, and when students in Göttingen forced a Nazi sympathizer to resign from his government post (*ibid.*).[16] Hence, the concept of public opinion should be respected. Today, however, public opinion often takes a pathological form: the form of collective narcissism that gives "individuals some of the self-esteem the same collective strips from them and that they hope to fully recover through their delusive identification with it". This is why public opinion must also be disdained (*ibid.*: 118). Independent opinion- and will-formation are possible only in a society of free, equal and emancipated people. But "society's actual organization hinders all of that and produces and reproduces a condition of permanent regression among its subjects" (*ibid.*: 119). This point is also made in "Kann das Publikum Wollen?" The public wills only "what has already been imposed upon it". Its identification with what perpetuates its political immaturity must "be broken, and the weak ego ... built up" before opinion- and will-formation become autonomous (1986: 343).

Bookchin's claims about the prospects for establishing a viable public sphere seem unwarranted. For on his own account, capitalism, with its distinctive and deeply embedded "cultural, traditional and psychological systems of obedience and command" (1991a: 4), must first be dismantled before the public sphere is able to accommodate the "equality of unequals" (*ibid.*: 167). To establish a freer and more rational society, in which each individual participates "directly in the formulation of social policy", we must confront and eradicate "the psychic problems of hierarchy as well as social problems of domination" (*ibid.*: 340–41). Yet Bookchin has no solutions to these crippling psychological and social problems. And, as long as these problems persist, they will undermine environmental movements and compromise grass-roots politics. Adorno's assessment of the impediments to radical change may appear bleak at times, but it does have the merit of recognizing the gravity of our predicament. By becoming more fully aware of our own natural history, we may finally transform those attitudes, behaviours, ideas and goals that have led, either directly or indirectly, to our destructive and self-destructive domination of human and non-human nature. In the final analysis, Bookchin's optimism is tied to his teleological view of history, but his idealist account of natural history, with its return to an originally "good" nature, is far too tendentious to support a positive outlook on our future prospects.

CAROLYN MERCHANT AND ECOFEMINISM

Merchant examines the narratives that have helped to shape our relationships to nature. Her first book, *The Death of Nature*, explores the cultural impact and the historical trajectory of narratives that have gendered nature as female. Living for millennia "in daily, immediate, organic relation with the natural order for their sustenance", human beings once regarded nature as a benign and beneficent earth mother. Although an opposing conception saw female nature as wild, disorderly and uncontrolled (Merchant 1980: 1), it would only supersede the view of nature as earth mother in the seventeenth century when the "organically oriented mentality in which female principles played an important role was undermined and replaced by a mechanically oriented mentality" (*ibid.*: 2). The replacement of one mentality by the other marks the transition from feudalism to capitalism.

This account differs from Adorno's in at least one important respect. To be sure, both Merchant and Adorno observe that nature was once thought to possess immanent powers or hidden properties. They also agree that nature was gendered as female. On Adorno's account, however, the animistic worldview resembles the enlightenment view that succeeded it because both portray nature as a hostile force. Indeed, Merchant indirectly challenges Adorno with her claims about the prevailing conception of nature prior to the seventeenth century. For she contends that animism was far less pernicious to both nature and women than the mechanistic view that succeeded it. A projection of the ways that people experienced nature in their daily lives, animism saw female nature as "God's involuntary agent, a benevolent teacher of the hidden pattern and values that God employed in creating the visible cosmos (*natura naturata*, the natural creation)" (*ibid.*: 7).

In *Earthcare* and *Reinventing Eden*, Merchant covers new ground when she examines the "recovery narratives" that aim to restore the earthly paradise we supposedly lost when we fell from grace. Here too, nature is gendered: it is identified specifically with the figure of Eve, and seen either as an untamed, virgin wilderness to be ravished and conquered, or as a "powerful female to be revered" (2003: 118).[17] The first image of nature informs "progressive" stories about recovering Eden, while the second has been a feature of the "declensionist" narratives that only began to emerge in the nineteenth century. Nevertheless, both narratives share the aim of recovering nature. Whether recovery involves the progressive ascent from untamed wilderness to a domesticated garden of Eden, or the reversal of a decline from Edenic nature and an egalitarian society (as in Bookchin, for example [*ibid.*: 192]), the recovery narrative is "perhaps the most important mythology humans have developed to make sense of their relationship to the earth" (*ibid.*: 2).

The Death of Nature describes conflicting conceptions of female nature in the West: nature is a living organism that nurtures humankind, or a passive, atomistic, machine. However, Merchant seems to have revised her views about the predominance of the first conception in *Earthcare* and *Reinventing Eden* where Christianity plays a more central role in her account of Western history. The story of our fall from grace and banishment from Eden has shaped Western culture from its "earliest times". In this narrative, which was secularized when it "merged with science, technology, and capitalism to form the mainstream Recovery Narrative" (*ibid.*: 11), nature is seen as wild, unpredictable and savage. It is this progressive recovery narrative, with its "ideology of domination over nature and other people" (*ibid.*: 36), that has predominated in the West, becoming even more pronounced after the seventeenth century.

By shaping our perceptions of nature, narratives like these have also affected our interaction with it. According to Merchant, every narrative "contains an ethic and the ethic gives permission to act in a particular way toward nature and other people" (*ibid.*: 37). In turn, however, ethically informed narratives are themselves shaped by prevailing socioeconomic conditions. Although Merchant denies that the economic base completely determines the cultural superstructure (1989: 4), she also argues that narratives are not just "socially constructed from a real, material world by real bodies", but "mediated through modes of production and reproduction" (1995: xxi). Subordinate to both production (where "human actions have their most direct and immediate impact on nonhuman nature") and reproduction, narratives are "[t]wo steps removed from the immediate impact on the habitat", and "must be translated into social and economic actions ... to affect the nonhuman world" (1989: 5).

Throughout her work, Merchant explores the radical changes in production and reproduction – the ecological revolution – that accompanied the rise of capitalism and the birth of modern mechanistic science. She also shows that the prevailing modes of production and human reproduction interact dialectically (*ibid.*: 11). In *Ecological Revolutions*, she studies the connections between the capitalist mode of production and patriarchal relations of reproduction, remarking, *inter alia*, that the transition from subsistence farming to industrial production "split production and reproduction into two separate spheres": production was a male prerogative, and reproduction (biological, social and material – the reproduction of everyday life) was women's work. More controversially, Merchant maintains that this "structural split between productive and reproductive spheres was necessary for the maintenance of the market economy" (*ibid.*: 233).

Merchant is justifiably critical of the division between male and female, public and private labour that accompanied capitalism and persists to this day. Like other radical ecologists, she targets capitalism's relentless pursuit of economic growth. However she does so, not just because of its harmful effects on non-human nature, but because it has had a direct, and profoundly negative, impact on women and human reproduction generally.[18] She hopes that we will "move toward a stable no- or low-growth economy as population growth slows and standards of living rise". We should substitute for capitalism's "obsession with growth" an ecologically responsible "obsession with conservation" (1992: 38). Arguing that "growth is not necessary to the economy", Merchant champions socialism because socialism would bring "human production and reproduction into balance with nature's production and reproduction" (1995: 16). Under socialism, "many of the problems that promote exponential growth, unlimited economic expansion, and environmental degradation would wither away" (*ibid*.: 224).

Given the serious environmental problems caused by our exploitation of nature under capitalism, Merchant advocates a fundamental transformation in our relation to nature. This transformation would require a "*global social and economic revolution*". In fact, this revolution may already be occurring, prompted by a "global ecological crisis that transcends national boundaries" – a crisis that may "trigger a transition to a sustainable earth" (1989: 264, emphasis added). Despite her abiding interest in our conceptions of nature, Merchant certainly realizes that a symbolic revolution will not succeed "without a simultaneous revolution in the social, sexual, and economic structures that exploit both women and Nature" (1995: 142). On her view, "[e]nvironmental, technological, social, and linguistic revolutions" must all take place at the same time if we are to have any chance at all of ensuring "the future of life on Earth" (*ibid*.: 166).

In *Earthcare* and later work, Merchant offers a glimpse of the direction this radical transformation might take when she advances a partnership ethic of earthcare. This ethic holds "*that the greatest good for the human and nonhuman communities is in their mutual living interdependence*" (2003: 223). The four precepts that guide her partnership ethic in *Earthcare* are: equity between the human and non-human communities; moral consideration for humans and non-human nature; respect for cultural diversity and biodiversity; and inclusion of women, minorities and non-human nature in the code of ethical accountability (1995: 217). In *Reinventing Eden*, however, the second precept is revised to read "moral consideration for both humans and other species", and a fifth is added: "an ecologically sound management that is consistent with the continued health of both the human and nonhuman communities" (2003: 224; cf. 1989: 263).

The goal of partnership ethics – the mutual living interdependence of human and non-human communities – is somewhat vague. Among other things, it could be objected that human and non-human nature are already mutually interdependent. On a more charitable reading, however, Merchant is gesturing towards improved relations between them. Grounded in the concept of relation, her partnership ethic is "an ethic of the connections between a human and a nonhuman community". These connections have

145

both local and global dimensions. In the first instance, the relationship between human and non-human nature is "situational and contextual within the local community". For its part, however, the community is "embedded in and connected to the wider earth, especially national and global economies" (1995: 217). We should begin by building and expanding on local environmental concerns, while working to establish a new global balance between ourselves and nature, a balance that will make us "equal partners, neither having the upper hand, yet cooperating with each other" (*ibid.*: 218).

Since she views both non-human nature and human beings as active agents, Merchant wants to give equal consideration to "the needs of nature to continue to exist and the basic needs of human beings" (*ibid.*). But while she proposes an equal partnership between human and non-human nature, she never clarifies what precise form equality would take. This problem is especially vexing because Merchant is keen to avoid the "ecocentric dilemma" in which some deep ecologists find themselves, namely that humans are only "one of many equal parts of an ecological web and therefore morally equivalent to a bacterium or a mosquito" (*ibid.*: 8). She also rejects the claim that "all nonhuman organisms have moral consideration equal to human beings" because it "undercuts the real struggles of the poor and of disadvantaged minorities for a better life" (2003: 217).

The problem of equality takes on a different cast when seen in light of Adorno's criticisms of equality as the ideological counterpart of the exchange principle. In law, for example, "the formal principle of equivalence becomes the norm; everyone is treated alike". Since differences are obscured in equality, equality "secretly serves to promote inequality" (*ND* 309). On the one hand, the norms and procedures employed by bureaucratic organizations (such as welfare agencies) enable these organizations to "deal with every case automatically and 'without consideration for the person'". They do promise an element of justice to the extent they guarantee that "arbitrariness, accident, and nepotism do not rule people's destiny". On the other hand, bureaucratic norms and procedures lead to depersonalization and reification (Adorno 1972b: 447) because they treat everyone and everything as "the same" without regard for their particular and concrete circumstances. Moreover, Adorno criticizes the appeal to equity as a corrective to injustice because this appeal is easily "knocked down by the rational legal system as favoritism, as inequitable privilege". Rather than treating people fairly and impartially *qua* individual, the legal system must first reduce their interests "to the common denominator of a totality" (*ND* 311).

But if viewing human and non-human nature as equal partners is problematic in a society based on exchange where equality tends to level all differences, problems also arise with the second and fourth precepts, which give moral consideration to other species and include nature in ethical accountability. In so doing, the fourth precept implies that nature can and should be seen as ethically accountable in a completely unspecified sense, and the second precept presupposes that other species have an intrinsic value that makes them worthy of moral consideration. This presupposition is all the more striking because Merchant acknowledges that the search for "a philosophically adequate justification for the intrinsic value of non-human beings has been called by some environmental philosophers the central axiological problem of environmental ethics" (1992: 78). In fact, Soper has argued that we need to reflect further on this problem: the insistence of some ecologists on the intrinsic value of nature should "invite us to think more seriously about how nature may be said to have value, and about the incoherence of attempting to speak for this except by reference to human utilitarianism, moral or aesthetic interests and predispositions" (1995: 257).

Nevertheless, Bernstein has argued that it is not incoherent to speak about the intrinsic value of natural things. Although it is trivially true that an object cannot be "accepted as having worth, unless it is recognized as having worth", Bernstein claims that it does not follow logically from this "that its worth is *constituted*, conferred upon the object through our activities" (2001: 248). In other words, the fact that we alone give value to things does not preclude things having value in themselves. But when Bernstein interprets Adorno as a moral realist, he ignores Adorno's stress on the non-identity of concepts and objects: conceptual mediation does not invariably distort objects, but it always remains a block to objectivity because it "fails to absorb entity [*Seiendes*], which objectivity is in essence" (*ND* 185). As I have already argued, the emphatic concepts that Adorno deploys in his critique of late capitalism derive their critical force from their non-identity with existing states of affairs. Moreover, Bernstein's argument can be reversed: although moral values may be significantly object-dependent (Bernstein 2001: 35)[19] – because they are derived from the negation of the negative conditions that cause suffering – moral realism does not follow logically from this object-dependency.

If Adorno would question Merchant's second and fourth precepts, he does share the general concern expressed in the third: respect for cultural diversity and biodiversity. However, his conception of diversity is far more radical than that of many ecologists, including Merchant's. Non-identity thinking involves a profound regard for an infinitely variegated "otherness" that is not predetermined by any conceptual schema (*ND* 13). Hence, respect for otherness goes well beyond respecting the otherness of age, sex, gender, race or species (indeed, it is telling that we tend to conceptualize difference in abstract categories like these). For the "Other" is uniquely individuated. If reification turns individuals into lifeless equivalents, suggesting invariant concepts of both human and non-human nature (*ND* 96), humanity – and, by extension, nature – should be conceived only through the most "extreme form of differentiation, individuation", not subordinated to and identified with, "comprehensive generic" concepts (P 151). Reconciliation will take place, not between generically conceived "human beings" and "nature", or "women" and "men", but between highly individuated persons and things.

Adorno would endorse Merchant's fifth precept: ecologically sound management consistent with the continued health of both human and non-human nature. With some qualifications, he would also agree that the "health" of human and non-human nature requires that the current relationship between the process of production and the reproduction of human and non-human life be reversed. Production should serve human and non-human reproduction in all senses of that term: biological, social and material (Merchant 1995: 17). Referring to self-preservation – rather than to reproduction – Adorno insists that a more rational society would make self-preservation its primary goal (MTP 272–3). And, since the "self" that is preserved is always also part of nature, self-preservation requires that we improve the metabolism between our species and the natural world.

With its five precepts, Merchant's partnership ethics outlines a major transformation in our interaction with nature. Underlying this ethic is a view of nature as process (1995: xxii). Merchant associates this view with holistic philosophies of nature in *The Death of Nature* and *Ecological Revolutions* (1980: 293; 1989: 263), but she later rejects holism on the grounds that chaos and complexity theories "undercut assumptions of a stable, harmonious nature and question holism as a foundation for ecology" (2003: 216). At the same time, she continues to approve of David Bohm's non-mechanistic process physics because it "starts with undivided, multidirectional wholeness (a flow of energy called the 'holomovement') and derives the three-dimensional world of classical mechanics as a secondary phenomenon" (*ibid.*: 209). To this endorsement of Bohm, however, one could offer the obvious objection that his physics is a type of holism, as the very word "holomovement" implies. In fact, Merchant herself described Bohm's physics as a theory of holism in *Radical Ecology* (1992: 59). And, of course, in a holistic conception of nature, unity ultimately trumps diversity.

When she champions chaos and complexity theories as an antidote to mechanistic science, Merchant argues that these theories are:

> based on a different set of assumptions about the nature of reality than mechanism: wholeness rather than atomistic units, pro-

cess rather than the rearrangement of parts, internal rather than external relations, the nonlinearity and unpredictability of fundamental change, and pluralism rather than reductionism.

(2003: 220)

She even goes so far as to say that these new theories may herald "the breakdown of modernism, mechanism, and, potentially, capitalism", making possible "a new birth, a new world, a new millennium" (1995: 53) because they "challenge humanity to rethink its ethical relationship to nature" by suggesting that we "should consider ourselves as partners with the nonhuman world" (2003: 6).

However, Merchant's enthusiasm seems misplaced: while it is doubtless the case that chaos and complexity theories mark a change in our conception of nature, it is far less clear that this change is as radical and salutary as she believes. For these sciences continue to identify nature with mathematical constructs and see it as causally determined. Their aim is to find the laws governing irregularities in nature, the hidden structures in apparently random systems, and underlying deterministic causes. Furthermore, they do so to facilitate the domination of nature. As one theorist quips: "we seek not to destroy chaos but to tame it" (Stewart 1989: 1). If chaos theory has displaced mechanistic science, and makes it more difficult to predict the precise behaviour of some natural phenomena – while simultaneously making it easier to predict chaotic events – it abandons neither the goal of prediction nor "the hubris of dominating nature" (Merchant 2003: 206).

Criticizing mechanistic conceptions of nature, Merchant effectively revives the Weberian thesis that is central to *Dialectic of Enlightenment*: capitalism and modern science disenchanted the world.[20] And, whether disenchantment consists in displacing an organic worldview, or in secularizing the Christian narrative of our fall from grace, Merchant often echoes Marx's critique of the fetish character of commodities in her discussion of it. Capitalism converts "living nature into dead matter", while "changing inert metals into living money" (Merchant 1995: 49). It became second nature (a phrase Merchant eschews) when "animate nature died" and "dead inanimate money was endowed with life". Substituting themselves for nature, "capital and the market would assume the organic attributes of growth, strength, activity, pregnancy, weakness, decay, and collapse, obscuring and mystifying the new underlying social relations of production and reproduction that make economic growth and progress possible". Echoing Adorno, Merchant adds: "Perhaps the ultimate irony in these transformations was the new name given them: rationality" (1980: 288).

When Merchant criticizes the disenchantment of nature, she also appears to retain the hope for some sort of re-enchantment of it. Earlier, she seemed to advocate a return to origins in the form of a partial revival of the animistic, organic worldview (Eckersley 1998). Yet re-enchantment takes a somewhat different form in her partnership ethic where "nature becomes a subject". Human beings should communicate with nature on a more equal footing, thereby opening up "the possibility of nondominating, nonhierarchical modes of interaction". Both human and non-human nature have "voices", and it is imperative that these voices be heard (Merchant 2003: 229). Here Merchant could be said to promote re-enchantment by viewing nature as a speaking, active subject in its own right.

Although Merchant cites Horkheimer's *Eclipse of Reason* when she refers to nature's voice (*ibid.*: 227; see also 1995: 265), Horkheimer did not anthropomorphize nature in the passage Merchant quotes. Instead, he complained that "nature's tongue is taken away" when philosophers and artists, who formerly served as the voice of nature, are turned into technicians of language in the service of industry (Horkheimer 1974: 101). Nor can Adorno be accused of anthropomorphism, as I argued in Chapter 2 when I criticized Bernstein's claim that Adorno wants "to resurrect … an anthropomorphic nature that is somewhere between the mythic extremes of myth … and enlightenment" (2001: 196–7). If Merchant seems to agree with Adorno when she acknowledges that nature remains wholly other than our ideas of it, her appeal to nature's voice risks "resurrecting" an anthropomorphic nature.[21]

Nevertheless, when attempts to "re-enchant" nature more modestly stress the importance of recognizing nature's autotelic powers, they can avoid anthropomorphism. At times, Bernstein himself appears to modify his views about resurrecting anthropomorphic nature when he limits the project of re-enchanting nature to regarding things as having ends for themselves. Bernstein calls this view the "nonprojective core of animism". On his reading, Adorno relates "the excess beyond phenomenal appearing" to "what has *powers* of resistance to the subject and its own ends, possesses a 'life' of its own" (Bernstein 2001: 192–3).[22] For her part, Merchant occasionally limits re-enchantment in a similar fashion. Although she does not use the word "reification", she objects in all her work to the suppression of nature when it is treated instrumentally as an object of exchange, or reduced to numerical equations, on the grounds that nature should be respected as a power or force in its own right.

To claim that non-human organisms exhibit autotelic powers or forces is not necessarily tantamount to resurrecting an anthropomorphic nature, as Bernstein suggests on more than one occasion. Similarly, to assert that non-human organisms have their own powers of growth, responsiveness or even reflexivity, is not to endorse Merchant's view that nature is "a free autonomous actor, just as humans are free, autonomous agents" (2003: 220). For this is an anthropomorphic projection of human traits (or values) on to non-human nature. It fails to respect nature as something other, non-identical. Moreover, where animism projected human powers on to nature, seeing the forces of nature as divine or quasi-divine, as manifestations of gods or spirits, Adorno's claim that natural things must be distinguished from our concepts of them is explicitly intended to avoid anthropomorphism, or the fallacy of constitutive subjectivity.

Merchant also runs the risk of anthropomorphism when she constructs nature as an equal partner, albeit a genderless one, in new stories or narratives (1995: 8). Rather than rejecting anthropomorphic constructs, she seems to want to exchange one such construct for another. More generally, however, Adorno might agree with Merchant's view that our narratives about nature should be altered because they adversely affect our relation to it. As we have seen, imprisonment is one of his central metaphors, including our imprisonment in prevailing forms of objectivity or thought. Since Merchant effectively believes that we are "imprisoned" in our narratives, she devotes her work to examining the stories that have shaped our acquisitive and rapacious interaction with nature, while searching for new narratives that may help to foster more beneficial relationships. When she points to the ideological dimension in existing stories, she also contends that, by rewriting them, "we can challenge the structures of power". Indeed, while we cannot dispense with them, "all stories can and should be challenged" (*ibid.*: 55).

Insisting on the need to rewrite the stories we tell about nature, Merchant also responds to the pressing issue of how to implement a partnership ethic when she recommends that all parties in, and representatives of, the human and non-human biotic community should sit "as partners at the same table", including "individuals, corporate and tribal representatives, foresters, dam builders, conservation trusts, scientists, community representatives, and spokespersons for wetlands, mountain lions, and gnatcatchers". In their discussions, full recognition would be given to the needs of other species and complex environmental systems. Such partnerships already exist today in "resource advisory committees, watershed councils, self-governing democratic councils, collaborative processes, and cooperative management plans" (2003: 238–9).

So, where Horkheimer lamented that philosophers and artists no longer play a significant role as the voice of nature, Merchant claims that various groups and individuals can, and do, speak on nature's behalf, voicing its concerns. In *Earthcare*, for example, she documents women's groups that have spoken out on behalf of nature in the United States, Sweden and Australia (see Merchant 1995: chs 7–9). Here she also comments favourably on the Code of Environmental Ethics and Accountability developed at the 1992 Earth Summit in Rio de Janeiro, claiming that it exemplifies a partnership ethic of earthcare. Partnership between the human and non-human communities is featured in Article 7 of the Rio Declaration, which calls on nations to "cooperate in a spirit of global partnership to conserve, protect, and restore the health of the Earth's Ecosystem". Partnership is also invoked in the title of a Miami-based group, the Global Assembly of Women and the Environment – Partners in Life (*ibid.*: 218–19).

At the same time, Merchant admits that "the implementation of partnership ethic is not easy". In *Reinventing Eden*, she describes three major obstacles to the implementation of a partnership ethic. The greatest challenge comes from "the free-market economy's growth-oriented ethic, which uses both natural and human resources inequitably to create profits". But a partnership ethic also faces resistance from "the property rights movement, which in many ways is a backlash against both environmentalism and ecology". Finally, there are "deep, long-standing, cultural differences among environmental advocates, corporate interests, and community governments". These differences "may be intractable because of historically bitter debates or the continuing presence of uncompromising personalities" (2003: 239–40).

Unfortunately, Merchant does not respond to the question of how to stem capitalism's calamitous pursuit of growth; nor does she have any suggestions for dealing with "cultural differences" between groups that represent divergent – if not completely incompatible – interests. Instead, she simply seems to hope that solutions to these problems will be found as we confront a global environmental crisis. Equally important, Merchant does not explain how non-human nature can play the role of an equal partner when it cannot express its concerns and interests (assuming it can be said to have them). Indeed, this anthropomorphic conception of nature as a partner obscures nature when it offers the thin and easily defeasible reassurance that nature is just like us: we are all "the same". Much like self-realization in Naess's and Bookchin's ethics of complementarity, Merchant's partnership ethic tends to stress unity over diversity, a problem to which I shall return in the Conclusion. To end this chapter, however, I shall take up some of the points I have raised about political action today. In order to have a significant impact on the development and implementation of environmental policies, radical ecologists must first consider how to make themselves and their organizations more socially solidary, democratic and politically efficacious.

PROBLEMS WITH PRAXIS

I said earlier that if resistance is ever to be anything other than futile, the forces that now weaken it must be thoroughly understood. On Adorno's view, socioeconomic conditions either stultify political action, making it largely impotent, or suppress it completely. In response to those who accuse Adorno of being too pessimistic, I would counter that his so-called pessimism about prospects for radical social change is well grounded in arguments culled from decades of both theoretical and empirical research on the character and limits of collective action in the twentieth century. Like Marcuse, Adorno thought long and hard about the myriad ways in which individuals, groups and organizations are "contained", and resistance thwarted, under capitalism. They agreed that "we cannot think any more as Marx thought, namely that the revolution was immanent" because, at the time Marx wrote, "the proletariat was not integrated into bourgeois society and, … bourgeois society did not yet possess the vast instruments of power, both actual physical instruments of power and also psychological instruments in the broadest sense, that it now has" (Adorno 2008: 45). Rather than simply dismissing Adorno with the claim that he "overlooks … collective practices and institutions" (Zuidervaart 2007: 161),[23] or rejecting his views about the viability of political action today as too pessimistic, critics must address these views directly. They need to look critically and self-critically at the factors that foil prospects for truly radical change.

Political activism now confronts an impasse. On the one hand, to speak of a "we" with whom one identifies "already implies complicity with what is wrong". Speaking of a "we" implies complicity because it subsumes individuals without remainder under a collective, summarily identifying them with it. It also fosters the "illusion that goodwill and a readiness to engage in communal action can achieve something" under conditions in which "every will is powerless". On the other hand, a "purist attitude that refrains from intervening likewise reinforces that from which it timorously recoils". Doing nothing allows an already bad situation to grow worse. Attributing this impasse to the "constitution of reality", Adorno thought that it lent some credence to "paltry reforms" which may now "presume more right than they are in fact due" (1998a: 4). On his view, then, those who seek radical change must chart a difficult course between the Scylla of quietistic withdrawal and the Charybdis of pathological forms of collective action.

To make the transition from what is to what ought to be, difference must be accommodated within collectivities rather than suppressed by them. Adorno's global subject is an internally differentiated one, not a monolithic party with a univocal party line. In the final analysis, of course, what is needed are more robust forms of solidarity that extend universally to all, while respecting the singularity of each. And, to build solidarity, activists first need to think critically about the wide-ranging tendencies and trends that undermine solidarity today. Again, Adorno claims that the solidarity needed for the emergence of a global subject is the inverted image of the adaptation and conformity that now damage collectivities. The forces that promote adaptation and conformity must be understood; effective counters to them must be found. But if solidarity should be rethought and remodelled with a view to creating the conditions needed for the emergence of a socially solidary global subject, so too must individuality. A humanity that preserves the species in all its diversity by rising above the "bad universal" must also transcend the individual, its "microcosmic copy" (*ND* 283).

To prepare for the now-deferred transition from critical thought to practical action, Adorno endorsed consciousness-raising educational strategies in a number of essays (see e.g. Adorno 1998n: 69–70). More to the point, in "Education after Auschwitz", he declared that the "only education that has any sense at all is education toward critical self-reflection" (1998c: 193).[24] Yet Adorno realized that the road to a more humane and rational society is fraught with almost insurmountable obstacles, and he openly despaired on many occasions about the possibility of achieving this goal. Events over the past century have demonstrated that extremely destructive tendencies drive the socioeconomic order of late capitalism, hell-bent as it is on realizing its particular interests in profit and power no matter what the cost to life on this planet. Although he refused to capitulate to these tendencies, Adorno could scarcely ignore them. In an epigraph to part two of *Minima Moralia*, he defended his engagement with critical social theory in a phrase he borrowed from the English philosopher, F. H. Bradley: "Where everything is bad, it must be good to know the worst".

CONCLUSION

> In the end, hope, wrested from reality by negating it, is the only form in which truth appears. Without hope, the idea of truth would be scarcely even thinkable, and it is the cardinal untruth, having recognized existence to be bad, to present it as truth simply because it has been recognized.
>
> Theodor W. Adorno (*MM* 98)

The radical ecologists discussed in Chapter 5 emphasize the unity of nature to the detriment of its diversity. Naess may have conceded that we can debate the nature and limits of the unity of life on this planet, but it is a central tenet of Ecosophy T that life is fundamentally one (1989: 166). Bookchin stressed the unity of nature as well; he gave this idea a Hegelian twist when he argued that nature's unity takes the form of a latent subjectivity that "expresses itself in various gradations, not only as the mentalism of reason, but also as the interactivity, reactivity, and the *growing purposive activity of forms*" (1991a: 275). And, while Merchant claims that her ethics recognizes both the continuities and the differences between human beings and the rest of the natural world (2003: 217), she views human and non-human nature as identical when she treats them as partners. When she endorses Bohm's process physics, which grounds animate and inanimate matter in the holomovement (*ibid.*: 209), Merchant again champions unity over diversity.

For these ecologists, nature is one in an ontological sense: all is substantively, inherently One. This idea has a long history, extending as far back as Presocratic philosophy, when philosophers began to search for a single principle underlying all things. Even Heraclitus, who is perhaps better known for the view that nothing remains the same, postulated the unity of things. In one of the remaining fragments of his thought, Heraclitus urged: "It is wise to hearken, not to me, but to my Word, and to confess that all

155

things are one" (fr. 50). This oneness or unity is alleged to be real. Nor does unity exclude diversity. To cite Frederick Copleston, "it is essential to the being and existence of the One that it should be one and many at the same time, that it should be Identity in Difference" (1962: 56–7). Of course, Parmenides laid even greater stress on unity. Consigning difference or otherness to the realm of non-being, Parmenides asserted that only Being – the One – exists.

In "The Unity of Reason in the Diversity of its Voices", Habermas offered an important psychological gloss on this perennial theme of the One and the Many. Describing Parmenides as an idealist, Habermas noted in an explicitly Adornian vein that, with his abstract conception of a "universal, eternal, and necessary being", Parmenides tried to break the "spell of mythological powers and the enchantment of demons". With Parmenides, the "fear of uncontrolled dangers that displayed itself in myths and magical practices now lodges within the controlling concepts of metaphysics itself". But the dangers that Being was meant to avert also expressed themselves in "deep-seated fears of death and frailty, of isolation and separation, of opposition and contradiction, of surprise and novelty". By reducing the Many to "mere *images*" of the One, Parmenides not only demoted diverse particulars to the realm of appearance, he considered them to be reassuringly "univocal, the surveyable parts of a harmonic order" (Habermas 1992: 120).

Three problems beset this conception of the unity of all things. First, how can the One be everything if the universe is composed of many different things? Second, how can justice be done to the uniqueness and individuality of things if all is ultimately One? And third, how should matter be conceived (*ibid.*: 120–23 *passim*)? While the first two questions concerning the priority of the One over the Many interested Adorno, the third preoccupied Schelling. However, Habermas claims that Schelling marked a breakthrough in the conception of the One, Being or unity. If the unity of all things was regarded for millennia as an ontological postulate, Schelling broke with this tradition when he denied that "the unity of the many" is "an objective whole prior to the human mind". Rather than existing objectively, unity is "the result of a synthesis executed by the mind itself". In fact, Habermas alleges that Schelling revolutionized "the basic concepts of metaphysics". Making reason "the source of *world-constituting* ideas", and regarding history as "the medium through which mind carries out its synthesis", Schelling formulated problems that would eventually "set postmetaphysical thinking in motion" (*ibid.*: 124).

For his part, Adorno maintains that Schelling succumbed to identity thinking. Yet he follows Schelling to the extent that he too regards the postulate of unity as a function of thought. In thought, we try to range natural phenomena under abstract universals even as we confront a world that literally teems with particular things. Ignoring the concrete singularity of human and non-human particulars, thought, in its abstract generality, is animated by a unifying, totalizing impulse. In fear of the powers of nature, thought reassures itself that all is one, that unity triumphs over diversity, that there is nothing new under the sun. Although the unity of nature is also something "real" because natural things have now been pressed into the mould of universal laws, totalizing conceptual schema and homogenizing exchange relations, Adorno objects that the stress on unity at the expense of diversity has subverted our practical relations with nature, while compromising our cognitive grasp of natural things and depriving us of a more complete aesthetic appreciation of them.

When he criticizes the unifying impetus of thought, Adorno also asks why unity has superseded diversity. He raises this question in his lectures on the *Critique of Pure Reason* when he observes that, for Kant, the concept of unity is "the canon by which everything else can be judged". The idea that the one has primacy over the many is the unquestioned "metaphysical premise" that Kant shared with "the Enlightenment in the broadest sense, as … with early Greek thought and with Christianity in its entirety". For Adorno, moreover, this premise is not "a mere homogenization that results from depriving a mass of diverse varied things of their differentiating features, while retaining the one thing they have in common". Instead, it is derived from the unity of consciousness itself. As a result, the emphasis on unity at the expense of diversity is not "so much the product of knowledge, as its essence" (*KCPR* 196–7).

The cognitive ascent from the many to the one, from particulars to unifying principles and laws, obscures the differences between things because it fails to do justice to their qualitative moments. We have equated reason "*more mathematico* with the faculty of quantification" for centuries, ignoring the fact that mathematics actually presupposes the capacity to make qualitative distinctions. In the absence of this capacity, Adorno contends, "the synthetic function of thought – abstract unification – would not be possible" (*ND* 43). At the same time, Adorno observes that our capacity to discriminate between things has atrophied. Today, thought continues to perpetuate its bondage to nature by compulsively imposing unity on the qualitatively diverse. Since thought remains "blinded to the point of madness by whatever would elude its rule", Adorno describes reason as pathic and declares that "nothing but to cure ourselves of it would be rational" (*ND* 172).

Of course, non-identity thinking is meant to provide a counterweight to thought's impetus towards unity. The programme of Adorno's negative dialectics consists, in part, in reflecting on the process that led Western philosophy to deal almost exclusively with abstract universals, while attempting to revise and reverse this process "in so far as this can be achieved with conceptual methods". Praising Freud's interest in "'the dregs of the phenomenal world'", Adorno wants philosophy to focus on what it generally tends to neglect: "the dregs of the concept" or "what is not itself concept". Negative dialectics tries to disentangle the conceptual from the non-conceptual to disclose the lack of identity between universal and particular, concept and object, even as it reveals their affinity. Through the "critical self-reflection of the concept", non-identity thinking hopes to penetrate "the wall that the concept erects around itself and its concerns by virtue of its own conceptual nature" (2008: 62–3).

Negative dialectics is "suspicious of all identity"; its logic "is one of disintegration: a disintegration of the prepared and objectified form of the concepts which the cognitive subject finds immediately to hand". But if concepts obscure the *individuum ineffabile* (*ND* 145), the subject cannot simply dispense with them. Adorno refuses to abandon reason by resorting to a mystical intuition of things, attempting instead to make cognition more rational. As I also argued in Chapter 3, non-identity thinking uses concepts emphatically in order to judge, not just whether concepts do justice to particulars, but the extent to which particular things realize their existing potential. In fact, Adorno takes up Marx's claim that what currently exists "already contains within itself what 'ought' to be as a possibility". Like Marx, he focuses on "the very form of existing actuality" to develop out of it ideas about "true actuality as its 'ought' and its 'goal'".[1]

With its dual orientation towards things, non-identity thinking represents Adorno's attempt to address the cognitive dimension of the problem of the One and the Many. But I have shown that this problem has a social dimension as well: how can society accommodate itself to the diverse individuals it comprises? Chapter 4 revealed that the two dimensions of this problem are linked because late capitalist society and identity thinking are akin: they converge in "exchange, in something subjectively thought and at the same time objectively valid, in which the objectivity of the universal and the concrete definition of the individual subjects oppose each other, unreconciled, precisely by coming to be commensurable" (*ND* 316). Society may owe its unity to the "particularities it covers" in so far as it "synthesizes them", but that unity currently takes shape "in ruthless disregard of those particularities". Now that all individuals – be they individual persons, animals or inanimate things – have become mere appendages of society, "the One takes precedence as the identity of the system that leaves nothing at large" (*ND* 315).

If Adorno appears to be championing nominalism when he asserts that the "matters of true philosophical concern at this point in history are ... nonconceptuality, individuality, and particularity" (*ND* 8), he charges that nominalism "denies society in its concepts by degrading it into an abbreviation for the individual" (SO 258). In so doing, nominalism becomes ideology (*ND* 49 n.). Against nominalism, Adorno avers that the more particular things are socialized, turned into conceptual constructs or instances of exchange value, "the greater ... the tendency of individual facts to be direct transparencies of their universals" (*ND* 83). Philosophical materialism is sympathetic to nominalism, but this sympathy has historically been problematic because the "thesis that individuality and individuals alone are the true reality is incompatible with Marx's Hegelian theory of the law of value which capitalism realizes over people's heads" (*ND* 199).[2]

Now transmuted into exchange value, "private life drags on only as an appendage of the social process" (Adorno 1967c: 30). Life under late capitalism does not live. Complaining that "[a]nything that is not reified, cannot be counted and measured, ceases to exist" (*MM* 47), Adorno also contends that, by turning individuals into lifeless objects of exchange, reification is already tantamount to "permanent death" (*ND* 370). Nature too has been reduced to "a residual *caput mortuum*" (*HF* 151). This is the situation that Bookchin condemns when he rails against our death-oriented society, and that Merchant encapsulates in the phrase "the death of nature". Like these ecologists, Adorno is concerned that the primacy of the capitalist process of production, on which our lives now completely depend, will lead, quite literally, to the annihilation of all life on the planet because that process shackles us to our socially determined interest in our own individual survival in complete disregard of the more rational interests of our species. In *Negative Dialectics*, Adorno speaks of "a universal feeling, a universal fear, that our progress in controlling nature may increasingly help to weave the very catastrophe from which it was supposed to protect us" (*ND* 67).

Just as thought dismisses whatever fails to fit within its conceptual schema, Western societies repudiate Otherness. And, as Adorno frequently observes, nature remains the primary placeholder for Otherness. To return to a point raised in Chapter 2, nature has almost invariably been conceived as the complete opposite of what we understand ourselves to be: if humanity sees itself as mind or spirit, nature is demoted to the status of mere matter; if human beings are free, nature is something lesser by virtue of being determined. As opposed to our exalted conception of ourselves as rational, nature is merely animal, irrational and instinctual; it is unconscious and reflexive rather than conscious and self-determining. Nature's radical Otherness has prompted our coercive and self-vitiating efforts to dominate it, to categorize all natural things in order to control and manipulate them. In fact, the differences imposed by "nature" have become a "key stimulus to aggression" (*DE* C:248, J: 206).

It is not just our capacity to make qualitative distinctions – the font of all thought – that has atrophied; late capitalist society too atrophies when it reduces human and non-human nature to their value in the capitalist marketplace, flattening out all "qualitative moments" in the "universal exchange relationship" (*ND* 88). In each case, the universal is "working against itself, for its substance is the life of the particular; without the particular, the universal declines to an abstract, separate, eradicable form". Late capitalism's dissociation from the lives of particulars unleashes aggression, which "accumulates in an openly destructive drive" towards what is different, Other, revealing that total socialization turns "objectively" into its opposite. Unable to predict whether the reversal of total socialization will be a disaster or a liberation, Adorno nonetheless speculates that the spell cast by reifying exchange relations may dissipate precisely because late capitalist society has dissociated itself from the individuals who sustain it, even as it perpetuates the illusion of its identity with them (*ND* 346).

Prospects for emancipation remain open. Although we will continue to behave like other animals as long as survival instincts shape our behaviour, we can deliberately alter this behaviour because we have acquired the as yet undeveloped capacity to distinguish ourselves from nature by becoming aware of our own natural history. Since self-reflection, which reveals that we are inextricably entwined with nature, also marks our specific difference from other animals, we can differentiate ourselves from the ostensible unity of nature precisely by recognizing its preponderance over us. More fully aware of the extent to which we are part of nature, we may one day cease to oppose ourselves destructively and self-destructively to it. We may also begin to enjoy freedom: freedom from our blind compulsion to dominate nature, and freedom to pose ends for ourselves that supersede the end of mere biological survival. Rather than being led blindly by instinct, we would channel our instincts consciously in ways that ensure the preservation and enhancement of both non-human nature and ourselves.

Radical change that benefits both human and non-human nature requires that we strike a blow for freedom: we must break out of the prison of survival imperatives, and escape the subjective prison of cognition by "de-reifying", as Asher Horowitz puts it, "the ability to discriminate, the ability without which reason cannot exist" (2007: 212). Equally important, we must free ourselves from the "objective context of delusion" promoted by identitarian exchange relations because this context serves as "the authority for a doctrine of adjustment" (*ND* 148). With their homogeniz-

160

ing and levelling tendencies, exchange relations promote the conformity to which they reduce living things anyway when they make all things identical and commensurable. Reinforced by the mass media, conformity to existing norms of behaviour (such as consumerism and status-seeking) and adaptation to a society that makes a mockery of each of us *qua* individual, are powerful impediments to change.

Given the "overwhelming power of ... the static, rigid categories of the universal", even the most resolute critics of late capitalism unconsciously assume something of this rigidity "if only so as to describe [these categories] in the course of asserting their own position". Since society "has penetrated into the darkest recesses of our souls", we "remain the children of the condition that we oppose, and carry endless baggage around with us which we then reproduce, all unbeknownst to ourselves" (*HF* 56–7, trans. mod.). In response to a situation where those who resist exploitation, oppression and renunciation unwittingly perpetuate damaged life, Adorno imbues the Socratic maxim "Know thyself" with psychological, social and moral force when he insists that the key to initiating transformative change is critical self-awareness. Critics of existing institutions and practices must first transform themselves by becoming cognizant of the preponderance of nature and history on their own behaviour and thought.

Nevertheless, even the most self-critical individuals cannot bring about the changes needed for reconciliation. For reconciliation to occur, we must all abandon that stubborn attachment to our egocentric interests that is fostered under late capitalism because this attachment has become, not just damaging to nature, but self-vitiating. Paradoxically, perhaps, it is no longer in our interest to be self-interested. Our interest in our own survival would be better served if we were to embrace the interests of the species as a whole. Adorno is not reviving the crude rhetoric of self-sacrifice here; he endorses the goal that all rational human beings seek – self-preservation. At the same time, he recognizes that the survival of individuals – not to speak of their flourishing as individuals – requires that they develop a far more profound sense of solidarity with all other individuals on this planet. Survival depends on sympathy with the human, with embodied and finite individuals whose diverse needs and interests make them all too vulnerable to the pain and suffering they must now endure.

Reconciliation would finally enable communication to take place between nature, the socioeconomic order and the human and non-human particulars over whom nature and society will always preponderate. Concepts would reach beyond themselves to grasp the qualitative differences that individuate natural things. Establishing freer intercourse between mind and body, ego and instinct, human beings would also improve the metabolism between themselves and the environing natural world. Socially, individuals would shape the institutions and practices that in turn shape them. They would learn to respect and appreciate difference, not primarily in the generic straitjackets of age, sex and race, but in the form of the diverse, the many, the diffuse and ambiguous (*KCPR* 196). New forms of solidarity might emerge that accommodate differences between individuals, even as they pursue common goals. In short, reconciliation would release the non-identical; it would disclose the multiplicity of different things (*ND* 6) by substituting "for the principle of unity and the primacy of the superordinated concept the idea of what would lie outside the spell of such unity" (*ND* xx). Adorno aims to foster reconciliation by overcoming the tyranny of the One to reveal the astounding profusion of the Many.

NOTES

INTRODUCTION

1. Robert Hullot-Kentor notes that Adorno examined the role that the concepts of nature and history played in Freud's work as early as his 1927 *Habilitationsschrift*, "Der Begriff des Unbewußtsein in der transcendentalen Seelenlehre" (The concept of the unconscious in transcendental psychology): "[P]sychoanalytic research presents this antithesis [of nature and history] with full clarity in the distinction between archaic symbols, to which no associations may attach themselves, and intersubjective, dynamic, inner-historical symbols, which can all be eliminated and transformed into psychical actuality and present knowledge" (Hullot-Kentor 2006: 251).
2. Ashton's translation of *Negative Dialectics* (1973c) may be modified throughout.
3. References to the *Dialectic of Enlightenment* give the page reference to Cumming's translation (Horkheimer & Adorno 1972) first, followed by the page reference to Jephcott's translation (Horkheimer & Adorno 2002). In the quotations I choose the translation I consider the more accurate, or modify the translation.
4. The full passage reads: determinate negation "is a methodological principle if I may speak of such a principle for once without your pouncing on me like vultures and claiming that I do have a general methodological principle after all; the issue is not whether one has any fixed or universal principles, but the standing, the function of such principles in the context of a philosophy" (Adorno 2008: 28).

1. CRITICAL MATERIALISM

1. For a Nietzschean reading of Adorno, see Bauer (1999); for a reading influenced by Max Weber, see Bernstein (2001); for an idealist reading, see Sherratt (2002); and for a Marxist reading, see Jameson (1990).
2. The insertion is from Adorno (1973b).
3. See also: "The organic nature of capitalist society is both an actuality *and* at the same time a socially necessary illusion. The illusion signifies that within this society laws can be implemented as natural processes over people's heads, while their validity

arises from the form of the relations of production within which production takes place" (Adorno 2006a: 118).

4. Brian O'Connor (2004: 56) also borrows this phrase from Strawson.

5. I explore Adorno's ideas about mediation at greater length in Chapter 2.

6. The German text is unclear: "In ihm [dem Begriff] überlebt sein Vermitteltsein durchs Nichtbegriffliche vermöge seiner Bedeutung, die ihrerseits sein Begriffsein begründet" (see *ND* 24). Here "*seiner Bedeutung*" may refer to the concept's meaning, in which its mediation by the non-conceptual survives, or to the "meaning" of the non-conceptual. One of these, in turn, grounds the concept as a concept. I endorse the first interpretation.

In *Adorno's Negative Dialectic*, O'Connor states that objects can be "coherently understood as determining the *content* of *experience*" by virtue of their "meaning-bearing properties" (2004: 56). For his part, J. M. Bernstein also speaks of the "structures of meaningfulness that animate objects possess" (2001: 306). It is unclear, however, whether Adorno thinks objects have such properties, and further, if they do, whether these properties determine the content of experience. For if meaning were a property of objects, and experience consisted in being determined by it, then our apprehension of objects would be more passive than active. But Adorno denies both that experience discloses things-in-themselves and that experience is largely passive. On this point, moreover, O'Connor (2004: 20) is inconsistent because – as I show later in this chapter – he also denies that the subject passively receives meaning from objects.

7. Pickford's translation of "On Subject and Object" (1998m) may be modified throughout.

8. In *Social Philosophy after Adorno*, Lambert Zuidervaart claims that Adorno's concept of domination refers to "three forms of violence in Western societies". First, the "control of nature becomes violent when it does not promote the interconnected flourishing of all creatures but promotes human flourishing at the expense of all other creatures". Second, the "formation of the self becomes violent when it represses urges and desires that would lead to the satisfaction of basic needs". Third, "the social distribution of power becomes exploitative, and therefore illegitimate and destructive, when it persistently promotes the … flourishing of one group at the expense of another" (2007: 124).

9. See also: "To experience that objectivity, which ranks ahead of the individual and his consciousness, is to experience the unity of totally socialized society. Its closest kin in the sense of tolerating nothing outside of it is the philosophical ideal of absolute identity" (*ND* 314).

10. More positively, however, Adorno argues that the "universality" and "all-encompassing totality" of this subject would be possessed only by the as yet non-existent "global social subject". Kant's transcendental subject "points beyond the merely contingent nature of individual existence and, ultimately, even beyond the conditioned and ephemeral form that a society possesses at certain stages in its history". It becomes the very *logos* of society because it represents "the overall social rationality in which the utopia of a rationally organized society is already implicit" (*KCPR* 172–3 *passim*).

11. Livingstone's translation of "Reflections on Class Theory" (2003) may be modified throughout.

12. Jephcott's translation of *Minima Moralia* (1974a) may be modified throughout.
13. Carolyn Merchant has an equally insightful gloss on capitalism as second nature, which I discuss in Chapter 5.
14. See also: "The realm of freedom only begins … where that labour which is determined by need and external purposes ceases; it is therefore, by its very nature, outside the sphere of material production proper" (Marx 1976b: 873).
15. I discuss Adorno's critique of science in Chapter 3.
16. Moreover, I question whether this proposition can be rendered in the way Bernstein proposes, namely that "philosophy, as the domain of the presumptively autonomous concept, and art, as the practice that preserves the materiality of the sign, are one" (2004: 20). As I point out in Chapter 3, Bernstein himself warns against conflating art and philosophy.
17. Cited in Schmidt (1971: 49). For the English translation, see Marx & Engels (1970: 62–3). Interestingly, Adorno does not cite Marx in his essay on natural history. Yet Susan Buck-Morss notes that Adorno was aware of Marx's use of the term "natural history" as early as 1932. In the *Economic and Philosophic Manuscripts of 1844*, to which Adorno had access even before their publication in Germany, Marx stated "that 'history is an actual part of *natural history*';" he "used the terms 'nature' and 'history' as critical, intercorrective concepts in much the same manner as Adorno, and attacked Hegelian idealism because it subsumed nature within the historical unfolding of absolute spirit" (Buck-Morss 1977: 62).
18. Buck-Morss also notes here that the concept of *Einmaligkeit* was borrowed from Georg Simmel.
19. See also *HF* 125, where Adorno refers to the following passage in *The Origin of German Tragic Drama*: "The allegorical physiognomy of the nature-history is put on stage in the *Trauerspiel* is present in reality in the form of the ruin. In the ruin history has physically merged in the setting. And in this guise history does not assume the form of the process of an eternal life so much as that of irresistible decay" (Benjamin 1977: 177–8).
20. See: "Division of labour only becomes truly such from the moment when a division of material and mental labour appears. (The first form of ideologists, *priests*, is concurrent.) From this moment onwards consciousness *can* really flatter itself that it is something other than consciousness of existing practice, that it *really* represents something without representing something real; from now on consciousness is in a position to emancipate itself from the world and to proceed to the formation of 'pure' theory, theology, philosophy, ethics, etc." (Marx & Engels 1970: 51–2).
21. See Chapter 4 for a more detailed account of the process of individuation.
22. However, Whitebook also remarks that, in *The Future of an Illusion*, Freud was aware of the "difficulty of justifying his adherence to the scientific *Weltanschauung* – of justifying his faith in reason, as it were, after access to the Absolute has been foreclosed" (1995: 98).
23. See also: "Material needs should be respected even in their wrong form, the form caused by repression" (*ND* 92).
24. Zuidervaart is right to say that Adorno did not adopt Marx's proposal in the *Economic and Philosophic Manuscripts of 1844* to naturalize humanity and humanize nature, but I disagree with his claim that "Adorno's recollection of the early Marx is largely ironic" (1991: 165). As I have shown here, Adorno borrowed a great deal

from Marx's dialectical account of the relation between nature and history, and especially from his early work, *The German Ideology*.

25. In a long section of the second chapter, Schmidt describes the historical development and significance of the term "*Stoffwechsel*". However, Foster takes issue with Schmidt's account, claiming that this term was in widespread use from the 1840s, and that Marx was influenced more by Justus von Liebig's use of the word in *Agricultural Chemistry* than by Jakob Moleschott's: "Although Marx was aware of Moleschott's work …, and this may have played into his use of the term, there is no evidence that he took it particularly seriously. In contrast, Marx studied Liebig closely, and was undoubtedly familiar with his earlier, more influential use of the concept. Moreover, in his use of the concept in *Capital* Marx always stayed close to Liebig's argument, and generally did so within a context that included direct allusions to Liebig's work" (Foster 2000: 161).

26. Adorno's lecture "Die Revidierte Psychoanalyse", delivered in San Francisco in 1946 under the title "Social Science and Sociological Tendencies in Psychoanalysis", first appeared in *Psyche* **6**(1) (1952). It was later translated into German by Rainer Koehne and published in 1962 in *Sociologica* 2 as "Die Revidierte Psychoanalyse". (In Adorno, *Letters to his Parents 1939–1951* [2006c: 254 n.1], the editors supply the English title of this lecture, and the reference to its first German publication.) In "On the Question: What is German?" (1998j: 211), Adorno complained that the editors of *Psyche* "disfigured" this essay "beyond recognition". Remarking on this complaint in a footnote to "On the Question: What is German?", translator Henry W. Pickford mistakenly states that "Social Science and Sociological Tendencies in Psychoanalysis" was first published in 1946 (see *ibid*.: 367 n.10).

27. To support this point, Alfred Schmidt (1971: 84) cites Marx's *Grundrisse der Kritik der politischen Ökonomie* (1957: 157).

28. This passage from Marx's *Grundrisse* appears as an epigraph to a chapter in Leiss (1994: 73).

29. Comparisons have also been made between Adorno and John McDowell. For example, Italo Testa compares McDowell's non-foundational philosophy of nature to Adorno's, arguing that they both wanted to go beyond the "dualistic conception of nature and history, nature and reason, to work out a notion of natural history or of dialectical nature as a concrete unity of the *relata*: not, that is, as an abstract, foundationalist identity, which founds the terms – understood in isolation – on one another, but rather as a concrete unity of terms among which an inner relation subsists, and which are therefore [both] identical and nonidentical" (2007: 476). For further comparisons of Adorno and McDowell, see Bernstein (2001, 2002). See also Jonathan Short's (2007) comparison. Espen Hammer (2000) also compared the two philosophers.

30. Unfortunately, Adorno used this word himself. O'Connor cites Adorno's claim that subject and object "constitute [*konstituieren*] one another" (2004: 48). See also *ND* 174.

31. See also Adorno's discussion of the problem of genesis and validity in *HF* 258–9. Here Adorno criticizes his own study of Edmund Husserl in *Against Epistemology* when he admits that he placed too much emphasis on the genesis of logic to the detriment of its objective validity. However, he also observes that "we have accustomed ourselves … to thinking of validity and genesis as absolutely distinct, as a *choris*,

and in the process have fallen victim to a false consciousness; and perhaps, once we admit that these two elements are not mutually exclusive and irreconcilable, we shall be able to see how a mediation may be brought about between objective validity ... and an ontic state of having developed, a genesis" (*HF* 258–9).

32. To be sure, Adorno is targeting the claim that we are socially determined here. However, he implicitly rejects physical determinism in his account of the genesis of reason and consciousness. For a more robust refutation of determinism, see Searle (1992, 2007).

2. NATURE, RED IN TOOTH AND CLAW

1. Adorno tells his students that by "first" or "primary" nature, he means "in the first instance no more than the elements, the objective elements that the experiencing consciousness encounters without ... experiencing them as things he has himself mediated" (*HF* 122).

2. Cf. "It lies in the definition of negative dialectics that it will not come to rest in itself, as if it were total. This is its form of hope. Kant registered some of this in his doctrine of the transcendent thing-in-itself, beyond the mechanisms of identification". But if, by "defining the thing-in-itself as the intelligible being", Kant "conceived transcendence as nonidentical", it is also the case that by "equating it with the absolute subject he ... bowed to the identity principle after all. The cognitive process that is supposed to bring us asymptotically close to the transcendent thing is pushing that thing ahead of it, so to speak, and removing it from our consciousness" (*ND* 406–7).

3. Adorno may be thinking of Kant's gloss on the fourth paralogism: "Neither the *transcendental object* which underlies outer appearances nor that which underlies inner intuition, is in itself either matter or a thinking being, but a ground (to us unknown) of the appearances which supply to us the empirical concept of the former as well as of the latter mode of existence" (1929: 352).

4. The full sentence reads: "As pure antitheses, however, each refers to the other: nature to the experience of a mediated and objectified world, the artwork to nature as the mediated plenipotentiary of immediacy".

5. In more recent work, Steven Vogel states that a non-alienated relation to nature would involve recognizing that nature is a social construct. But, while Adorno concedes that nature is always also socially constructed, he constantly criticizes the fallacy of constitutive subjectivity, arguing that to identify nature with our concepts of it is "the primal form of ideology" (*ND* 148).

6. This is how Adorno describes the prevailing conception of immediacy. Jephcott's translation of *Metaphysics: Concepts and Problems* (2001b) may be modified throughout.

7. I return to this issue in my discussion of Carolyn Merchant in Chapter 5.

8. In *Minimal Theologies: Critiques of Secular Reason in Adorno and Levinas*, Hent de Vries also conflates the non-identical with nature: "the nonidentical stands for 'nature' and the transience (*Vergänglichkeit*) of 'natural history'" (2005: 37).

9. When he criticizes Marx's equation of the non-identical with nature in *Negative Dialectics*, Adorno cites Alfred Schmidt's *The Concept of Nature in Marx* (1971: 27).

10. Adorno insists on the lack of identity between concept and object. However, he generally uses the term "non-identity" to refer to the *relation* between concepts and objects, rather than to non-conceptual objects alone. In the relational sense of non-identity, the concept can equally well be described as the non-identical: it is non-identical with respect to objects, just as objects are non-identical *vis à vis* concepts.

11. Pickford's translation of "Progress" (1998i) may be modified throughout.

12. Indeed, Adorno does not appear to take this passage into account when (see Chapter 1) he claims that the truth content in Marx's idea of natural history consists in his recognition that human history, "the history of the progressive mastery of nature, continues the unconscious history of nature, of devouring and being devoured" (*ND* 355).

13. See also: "In its commonest and most fundamental sense, the term 'nature' refers to everything which is not human and distinguished from the work of humanity. Thus 'nature' is opposed to culture, to history, to convention, to what is artificially worked or produced, in short, to everything which is defining of the order of humanity. I speak of this conception of nature as 'otherness' to humanity as fundamental because, although many would question whether we can in fact draw any such rigid divide, the conceptual distinction remains indispensable. Whether, for example, it is claimed that 'nature' and 'culture' are clearly differentiated realms or that no hard and fast delineation can be made between them, all such thinking is tacitly reliant on the humanity-nature antithesis itself and would have no purchase on our understanding without it" (Soper 1995: 15).

14. See also: "by situating the sublime in overpowering grandeur and setting up the antithesis of power and powerlessness, Kant directly affirmed his unquestioning complicity with domination" (*AT* 199). See also: "Kant had noted, in one of the profoundest passages in the 'aesthetics of the sublime', that what a common-or-garden [variety] aesthetics customarily thinks of as aesthetic 'pleasure' is in reality a state in which the mind remains in control of itself in the face of the overwhelming power of nature, in the face of total transience" (*HF* 137).

15. See also: "At times subject, as unrestricted experience, will come closer to object than the [subjectless] residuum [of science] filtered and curtailed to suit the requirements of subjective reason" (SO 253).

16. Buck-Morss reports that Adorno regretted that he had overlooked the materialist moment in Freud's thought in his first *Habilitationsschrift*, "*Der Begriff des Unbewußtsein in der transcendentalen Seelenlehre*" (The concept of the unconscious in transcendental psychology) (1973a).

17. See also Adorno's "Theory of Pseudo-Culture" (1993b: 22–3). Conceding that there is "convincing empirical evidence to refute the thesis of the withering of culture" – the thesis advanced in "Theory of Pseudo-Culture" – Adorno insists that the thesis must not be rejected simply because it is exaggerated. If it is "simplistic and exaggerated" to describe pseudo-culture as universally pervasive, Adorno wants to retain the concept, and others like it, because what they purport to do is "not to include all peoples and classes indiscriminately but rather to give shape to a tendency, to sketch the physiognomy of a spirit which also determines the signature of an age even if its validity is limited both quantitatively and qualitatively".

18. Peter Sloterdijk makes a similar point: "Cure presupposes the recognition of the id

as the precondition and foundation of life for the mature ego. … The point is not that the ego should now become completely the 'master of its own house'; rather the point lies in the chance that the 'spirits of the house' learn to live together under one roof" (1987: 367).

19. See also "Sociology and Psychology" (1967e: 78), where Adorno argues that psychoanalysis promotes adjustment and conformity to existing conditions. Yet he also concedes in his lectures on moral philosophy that Freud's endorsement of renunciation was confined to his metapsychology; Freud allegedly offered a more critical account of renunciation in his "technical writings on psychoanalysis" (*PMP* 138, 208 n.7).

20. In "The Marriage of Marx and Freud" (2004a), Whitebook seems to contradict the view he advanced in *Perversion and Utopia* (1995: 133), namely that Adorno (and Jacques Lacan) thought the ego was a narcissistic, paranoid structure.

21. Adorno also objects to Freud's view of the ego as both "the opposite of repression *qua* consciousness, and the repressive agency *qua* unconscious". He remarks: "It is even questionable whether it is the ego that performs the function of repression, the chief of all the so-called defence mechanisms. Perhaps the repressive agency itself should be regarded as ego-oriented, narcissistic libido which has ricocheted back from its real goals and then fused with moments specific to the ego. In which case, 'social psychology' would not be, as people today would like to think, essentially ego-psychology, but libido psychology" (1968: 88).

22. See also *Problems of Moral Philosophy*, where Adorno notes that Freud distinguished between two types of renunciation: "On the one hand there is repression – this is a behaviour that refuses to look … renunciation in the eye, but instead shifts the instincts into the unconscious and produces in their place some kind of surrogate gratification of a precarious and problematic sort. Alternatively, there is the conscious renunciation of instinct, so that even our instinctual behaviour is placed under the supervision of reason" (*PMP* 137).

23. For Adorno's interpretation of this essay, see "Freudian Theory and the Pattern of Fascist Propaganda" (1978), and the chapter on anti-Semitism in *Dialectic of Enlightenment*. Herbert Marcuse also adopted some of Freud's views about aggression in a number of his books, and Horkheimer showed how National Socialists directed aggression towards Jews and other out-groups (as placeholders for nature) in *Eclipse of Reason* (1974).

24. Here Adorno cites Walter Benjamin's "Zum gegenwärtigen gesellschaftlichen Standort des französischen Schriftsteller" (On the current social situation of the French writer). This essay first appeared in the *Zeitschrift für Sozialforschung* (1934), and was later published in Benjamin's *Gesammelte Schriften*, vol. 2 (1972).

25. However, in "The *Urgeschichte* of Subjectivity Reconsidered", Whitebook claims that Horkheimer and Adorno rejected delayed gratification altogether in *Dialectic of Enlightenment*. Without providing textual support for this claim, he states that it follows from their arguments "that nothing short of remaining in or recapturing the original state and fulfilling 'the instinct for complete, universal, and undivided happiness' could prevent the dialectic of enlightenment from unfolding" (2004b: 94). Yet I have already shown that Adorno rejects the idea of an original state of nature to which we might return. There is no turning back; nor is there an originally "good" nature (*ND* 155).

26. See also: "Where the human being seeks to resemble nature, at the same time it hardens itself against it. Protection as petrified terror is a form of camouflage. These numb human reactions are archaic patterns of self-preservation: the tribute that life pays for its continued existence is adaptation to death" (*DE* C:180, J:148).

27. See also Adorno's remark that "the true primal phenomenon of moral behaviour … occurs when the element of impulse joins with the element of consciousness to bring about a spontaneous act" (*HF* 240).

28. For Adorno's criticisms of sublimation, see "Sociology and Psychology" (1968: 86–7). Here Adorno remarks on the inherent weakness of the Freudian ego, adding that there are no adequate criteria for distinguishing positive ego functions from negative ones. As a result, it is not possible fully to distinguish sublimation from repression. See also: "In renouncing the goal of instinct, [artists] remain faithful to it, and unmask the socially desirable activity naively glorified by Freud as sublimation–which probably does not exist" (*MM* 214).

29. Sublimation is one way to avoid suffering. However, Freud argues that the "weak point" in the displacement of instinctual aims through sublimation is that it is "not applicable generally: it is accessible to only a few people. It presupposes the possession of special dispositions and gifts which are far from being common to any practical degree" (1975a: 17).

30. Citing "The Ego and the Id", Sara Beardsworth acknowledges that Freud speculated that the ego might reconcile itself with the id by means of sublimation in work that he wrote before he advanced his hypothesis about the life and death instincts.

31. Hence, I disagree with Seyla Benhabib in *Critique, Norm, and Utopia: A Study of the Foundations of Critical Theory*. For Benhabib contends that, in contrast to Horkheimer who "acknowledges that reason had an emancipatory force", Adorno views reason as "*inherently* an instrument of domination" (1986: 164).

32. For my response to this claim see "Staying Alive: Adorno and Habermas on Self-Preservation under Late Capitalism" (2006).

33. In a recent paper, "Science, Normativity, and Skill: Reviewing and Renewing the Anthropological Basis of Critical Theory", Lenny Moss suggests that Freud's concept of instinct should be viewed as a "placeholder for a biologically-based anthropology of compensatory need rooted in human detachment". Moss praises the ambiguous status of instinct as both biological and psychological because it allows instinct to serve as "an intermediate concept that brings nature into culture and society and brings culture and society into nature. It is a medium for the dialectical interplay between the human body and passions and socio-historical worlds of power and domination" (2010).

3. THOUGHT THINKING ITSELF

1. Adorno also notes here that the *intentio obliqua* did not appear as such in Aristotle's work; Aristotle merely anticipated it.

2. "What Adorno wanted to comprehend was the capacity of thought – of identity itself – to cause reality to break in on the mind that masters it" (Hullot-Kentor 2006: 15).

3. After citing this passage, Hent de Vries inexplicably argues that *Dialectic of Enlight-*

enment "can no longer be understood as 'a chapter in speculative naturalism'", but rather as "a philosophy of ab-soluteness–and absolution? – of a 'good nature' whose referent and telos are never given or attainable as such" (2005: 216). For a careful and evocative reading of Kraus's epigram as a leitmotif in Adorno's work, see Hullot-Kentor's "Introduction: Origin is the Goal" (2006: 1–22).

4. Although Cumming first translated *Seitensprung* as "chance phenomenon", he translated this word as "sideward movement" two paragraphs later. In his translation, Edmund Jephcott renders both occurrences of *Seitensprung* as "freak event (*DE* C:222–3, J: 184–5). However, I believe that Horkheimer and Adorno were referring to the theory of spontaneous generation.

5. Nevertheless, I noted in Chapter 2 (see note 21) that Adorno also points to problems with Freud's view that the ego acts as the repressing agent.

6. "First nature is understood as the objectified domain of processes that have to be made intelligible insofar as they are subject to mere legality …. This, in fact, is a strictly Galilean conception and it is in this light that we have to read McDowell's opposition to the identification of the logical space of natural science with the logical space of causality …. [A]n identification of the realm of law with causality runs the risk of proposing an obsolete view of science" (Testa 2007: 480). For further comparisons between Adorno and McDowell, see Chapter 1, note 29.

7. Although McDowell (1994: 117–18) endorses Marx's account of a truly free human life, he does not fully grasp the critical import of Marx's claims about life under capitalism because Marx believes that capitalism prevents us from fully developing our humanity or, in McDowell's terms, our second nature.

8. See McDowell's reply to Robert Pippin in *Reading McDowell on Mind and World*: "Pippin is also surely right that Hegel's thought tends toward ultimately leaving nature behind. It is only his overestimate of the role nature needs to play for me that makes him think this marks a contrast with me. Once my reminder of second nature has done its work, nature can drop out of the picture too" (Smith 2002: 277). In fact, McDowell also seems to adopt Hegel's view that the real is already rational, and the rational real.

9. Here I am revising and expanding my criticisms of Bernstein in *Adorno, Habermas, and the Search for a Rational Society* (2004a: 115–17), and "From the Actual to the Possible: Nonidentity Thinking" (2005).

10. I make similar, but less well-developed, points in "Adorno, Ideology, and Ideology Critique" (2001); "Critical Stratagems in Adorno and Habermas: Theories of Ideology and the Ideology of Theory" (2000); and "The Rhetoric of Protest: Adorno on the Liberal Democratic Tradition" (1996–7).

11. See Chapter 1, note 6, for criticism of the claim that animate objects possess structures of meaningfulness. Bernstein also relies in his construction of an Adornian ethics on the questionable assertion that Adorno's model of concepts "appears to project … a heterodoxical and utopian form of particularistic moral realism" (2001: 35). Bernstein's view of Adorno as a moral realist is discussed in Chapter 5.

12. Cf. Adorno on longing in art in *Aesthetic Theory*: "Artworks would be powerless if they were no more than longing, though there is no valid artwork without longing. That by which they transcend longing, however, is the neediness inscribed as a figure in the historically existing. By retracing this figure, they are not only more than what simply exists but participate in objective truth to the extent that what is in need

summons its fulfillment and change. Not for-itself, with regard to consciousness, but in-itself, what is wants the other; the artwork is the language of this wanting, and the artwork's content [*Gehalt*] is as substantial as this wanting. The elements of this other are present in reality and they require only the most minute displacement into a new constellation to find their right position. Rather than imitating reality, artworks demonstrate this displacement to reality. Ultimately, the doctrine of imitation should be reversed; in a sublimated sense, reality should imitate the artworks. However, the fact that artworks exist signals the possibility of the nonexisting. The reality of artworks testifies to the possibility of the possible" (1997: 132).

13. Cf. Anke Thyen: non-identity thinking "identifies the object *as* something", rather than simply "identifying the object *with* something" (2007: 205).

14. "According to Adorno, there are three ways of thinking: identity thinking, non-identity thinking, and rational identity thinking ... . [C]oncepts also refer to their objects, and by this he means the conditions of their ideal existence. This is the *utopian* aspect of identifying. For the concept to identify its object in this sense the particular object would have to have all the properties of its ideal state. Adorno called this condition *rational identity* (*rationale Identität*)" (Rose 1978: 44). See also: "If no man had part of his labor withheld from him any more, rational identity would be a fact, and society would have transcended the identifying mode of thinking" (*ND* 147).

15. "The universalistic ideals of equality and liberty are in part *formed* through the appreciation of the awfulness of slavery; finding slavery awful, intolerable, by slaves themselves and the opponents of slavery gives a sense to what *we mean* by liberty and equality that they would not possess without it" (Bernstein 2001: 341).

16. The last two sentences of this paragraph appear in my "Response to [Gordon] Finlayson" (2003: 192).

17. See also: "[W]e might perhaps say (this is a formula I have already tried out on earlier occasions) that the Spinozist proposition, one very characteristic of identity philosophy, that *verum index sui et falsi*, in other words, that the true and the false can both be read directly off from the truth, is a proposition whose validity we cannot accept; but that the false, that which should not be the case, is *in fact* the standard of itself: that the false, namely that which is not itself in the first instance – i.e. not itself in the sense that it is not what it claims to be – that this falseness proclaims itself in what we might call a certain immediacy, and this immediacy of the false, this *falsum*, is the *index sui atque veri*. So here then, ... is a certain pointer to what I consider 'right thinking'" (2008: 28–9). Adorno also praises Kafka for recognizing that falsehood serves as an index of truth in "Notes on Kafka" (1967d: 247).

18. Indeed, Pritchard insists (2004: 205 n.2) that the *Bilderverbot* should not be confused with negative theology's view of the divine as unknowable because the ban on images only forbids making and worshipping images. She also notes that Adorno described his own work as an *inverse*, not a negative, theology.

19. This interpretation of Adorno refutes Gordon Finlayson's view that the attempt to derive ideas of the good from "the existing untruth of what ought not to be flatly contravenes Adorno's philosophical negativism, the ban on graven images" (Pritchard 2004: 223) . Indeed, Adorno actually rejects the ban on images in a 1964 radio talk with Ernst Bloch, "Etwas fehlt ... Über die Widersprüche der utopischen Sehnsucht" (Something is missing ... on the contradictions in utopian longing)

(1985): "if we are forbidden to generate images, something very bad happens: the more it becomes possible only to talk negatively about what should be, the less one can imagine anything definite about it. But then – and this is probably more disturbing still – this prohibition on concrete statements about utopia tends to denigrate utopian consciousness as such and to block what is really important, namely the will that things should be different .... If it is true that a free and happy life is possible today, then *one* theoretical form of utopia would involve saying concretely what would be possible given the current status of humanity's productive powers: this really can be said, without embellishment or arbitrariness. If it is not said, if this vision does not appear, I almost want to say tangibly, then basically one does not know what the point of it all is, why the whole mental apparatus is being set in motion. Forgive me if I adopt the unexpected point of view of the *positivist*, but I believe that without this factor a phenomenology of utopian consciousness would not be possible" (Schweppenhäuser 2009: 89, trans. mod., quoting Bloch 1985: 362ff.). Unfortunately, Rolleston refers neither to the book nor the page from which this citation (and many other citations) is taken. Schweppenhäuser provides the reference in the original; see *Theodor W. Adorno zur Einführung* (2003: 181 n.124).

20. See also "'No Individual Can Resist':" *Minima Moralia* as Critique of Forms of Life" (Jaeggi 2005), where Rahel Jaeggi argues against Martin Seel's claim (in *Adornos Philosophie der Kontemplation*) that Adorno's ethics surreptitiously takes its point of departure from radically positive experiences.

21. "[T]he rationality and logic invoked in the movement of thought and action is that *of* the given conditions to be transcended. The negation proceeds on empirical grounds; it is a historical project within and beyond an already [on-]going project, and its truth is a chance to be determined on these grounds" (Marcuse 1964: 223).

22. In *The Origin of Negative Dialectics*, Buck-Morss notes that Adorno described "philosophy's task as the construction of 'changing constellations'" as early as 1931 in his inaugural lecture "The Actuality of Philosophy". She also remarks that Adorno borrowed the term "constellation" from Benjamin's *The Origin of German Tragic Drama*. Through constellations, "the subject constituted 'ideas' whose structure was objective, determined by the phenomena themselves, by the 'elective affinities' of their elements, to use Goethe's term; in Adorno's language, by their 'inner logic'" (1977: 90–91).

23. Here Honneth quotes Weber's "Objectivity in Social Science and Social Policy" (1949: 90). Thyen also compares Adorno's constellations to Weber's ideal types in *Negative Dialektik und Erfahrung: Zur Rationalität des Nichtidentischen bei Adorno* (Negative dialectics and experience: On the rationality of the non-identical in Adorno) (1989).

24. According to Honneth, Adorno adopted Weber's methodology of ideal types in order to "adumbrate the idea of a materialist hermeneutic of the capitalist form of life". In "Objectivity in Social Science and Social Policy", Weber maintained that ideal types "'would accentuate certain individual concretely diverse traits of modern material and intellectual culture in its unique aspects into an ideal construct which from our point of view would be completely self-consistent. This would then be the delineation of an "*idea*" of *capitalist culture*'" (Honneth 2005: 53–4).

25. In this passage, Adorno justifies his adoption of Weber's procedure, arguing that the "real course of history" commends a constellative approach because society

becomes increasingly integrated as elements of capitalism "entwine into a more and more total context of functions". Consequently, asking about causes has become "more and more precarious" (*ND* 166).

26. For further references to art and determinate negation in *Aesthetic Theory*, see *AT* 35, 36, 68, 88, 93, 103, 129, 140, 226, 321. In fact, art resembles philosophy because art also offers a prospective apprehension of undamaged life. As I remark briefly in Chapter 5, this may be what Adorno meant by "mimesis".

27. Interestingly, Adorno also distinguishes philosophy from art when he calls art an *index veri et falsi* in *Aesthetic Theory* (*AT* 315).

28. See also the English translation, "Negativity in Adorno", in *Theodor Adorno: Critical Evaluations in Cultural Theory* (2007: 187).

29. See, for example, the fourth proposition in Kant's "Idea for a Universal History with a Cosmopolitan Purpose": "*The means which nature employs to bring about the development of innate capacities is that of antagonism within society, in so far as this antagonism becomes in the long run the cause of a law-governed social order*" (1971: 44). In *History and Freedom*, where he reprises large sections of "Progress", Adorno cites Kant's remarks on the fifth proposition: "*The greatest problem for the human species, the solution of which nature compels him to seek, is that of attaining a civil society which can administer justice universally*" (*HF* 144).

30. A more recent example can be found in Abu Ghraib prison where, among other things, American soldiers treated detainees like animals while attaching them to leashes, defecating and urinating on them, and raping them. See also Soper's *What is Nature? Culture, Politics and the Nonhuman*: "'Nature' may be viewed as a register of changing conceptions as to who qualifies, and why, for full membership of the human community; and thus also to some extent as a register of Western civilization's anxieties and divisions of opinion about its own qualities, activities and achievements". Barbarians, slaves, blacks, women, indigenous peoples, savages and witches are among those whom "Western culture has at various points in its development deemed 'inhuman' or less than properly human". These groups "have been associated with functions or attributes that place them nearer to nature and render them not quite fully human (they are lacking in reason; or bestial in their behaviour; or immersed in the body and reproductive activity; or untameable, and so on)" (1995: 74).

31. This passage was discussed at the end of Chapter 2.

32. Adorno borrows this phrase from Baron von Eichendorff. However the sentence referring to von Eichendorff is missing from the English translation. In German it reads: "Über die Romantik hinaus, die sich als Weltschmerz, Leiden an der Entfremdung fühlte, erhebt sich Eichendorffs Wort 'Schöne Fremde'". See *ND* 192. The sentence may be translated as follows: "Hovering over romanticism, which experienced the suffering caused by alienation as world-weariness, is Eichendorff's phrase: 'Beautiful Alien'".

4. ADORNO'S ENDGAME

1. See also: "To experience that objectivity, which ranks ahead of the individual and his consciousness, is to experience the unity of a totally socialized society. Its clos-

est kin, in the sense of tolerating nothing outside of it is the philosophical ideal of absolute identity" (*ND* 314).

2. Stefan Müller-Doohm (2005: 358) reports that, during a lunch with Beckett in 1959, Adorno discussed his view that "Hamm" is derived from "Hamlet". Beckett responded that he did not have Shakespeare in mind when he wrote his play.

3. For my analysis of the psychotechnologies employed by the culture industry and the industry's positivist ideology, see Chapters 3 and 4 in *The Culture Industry Revisited: Theodor W. Adorno on Mass Culture* (1996).

4. In "A Physiognomy of the Capitalist Form of Life: A Sketch of Adorno's Social Theory", Axel Honneth mistakenly states that reification "extinguishes our gift for imitation" (2005: 55). However, this chapter will take up a point raised in Chapter 2, namely that our "imitation" of reified conditions is more pronounced than it was in the past.

5. In the next few paragraphs, I am paraphrasing my article "*Ein Reaktionäres Schwein?* Political Activism and Prospects for Change in Adorno" (2004b: 51–3).

6. Like some other commentators, Andrew Biro seems to make cognition responsible for our current predicament: "We might say, then, that for Adorno, the domination of nature is rooted in the definition of nature" (2005: 130).

7. Consequently, when Moishe Postone (1993: 119) criticizes Adorno for grounding the reified character of bourgeois thought in the interaction of human beings with nature, he is telling only part of the story. For, like Marx, Adorno certainly recognized that our interaction with nature is shaped by prevailing modes and relations of production, or by both nature and history.

8. See also Sara Beardsworth, "From Nature to Love: The Problem of Subjectivity in Adorno and Freudian Psychoanalysis": the uncontrolled and uncritical mimetic response, which also characterizes myth, reappears today "as the mimesis of *death*" (2007: 373).

9. See also: Marx "holds that the negation of the negation does not immediately spell affirmation .... [T]he communist action of world-appropriation does not in itself bring man the affirmative consciousness of himself as man. [Marx] credits Feuerbach with showing that the destructive process of negation of the negation is not, *per se*, an affirmation. And he says that the affirmative stage of human self-realization lies beyond the immediate revolutionary action against private property .... The human negation of the negation produces only 'unthinking' or 'raw communism' (*der rohe Kommunismus*), in which man remains, for the moment, more than ever a negation of himself" (Tucker 1967: 154).

10. "I should add, very speculatively and perhaps rashly, that this possibility of making a leap forward, of doing things differently, always existed, even in periods when productivity was far less developed .... [I]n all probability the opportunity we see today of a sensible organization of humankind was *also* possible in less complicated times, when there were far fewer people and social conditions were incomparably more modest" (*HF* 67–8). See also: "I would almost go so far as to say that actually [freedom] has always been possible, that it has been possible at every moment" (*HF* 181).

11. However, allowing nature to pursue an independent course would not free nature from human control, as environmentalists such as Roderick Nash claim. Since human beings would effectively permit nature to develop in accordance with its own ends, nature would remain under human control, albeit a more benign form

of control. Indeed, Adorno's idea of natural history suggests that it is not possible for nature to develop outside the ambit of human history precisely because nature and history are inextricably entwined.

12. See Chapter 3, note 26, for further references to art and determinate negation.

13. Although Espen Hammer does not support this point with reference to Adorno's texts, he may be basing his interpretation on the following passage: "the ineffable part of utopia is that what defies subsumption under identity – the 'use value' in Marxist terminology – is necessary anyway if life is to go on at all" (*ND* 11). However, I would argue that, if what defies subsumption under identity in Marx is use-value, Adorno does not equate the non-identical with use-value. Indeed, when he objects (see Chapter 2) that Marx too crudely calls the non-identical "nature" (*ND* 178), Adorno could be interpreted as refusing the equation of the non-identical with use-value because the use-value of objects consists in those "natural", or physical, properties that satisfy human need. Indeed, in *Time, Labor, and Social Domination*, Postone speculates that use-value itself could be transformed with the determinate negation of capitalism. Since reappropriating the use-value dimension of labour "depends on the abolition of [exchange] value, this reappropriation implicitly presupposes a separation of the two dimensions of the basic social forms of capitalism; this, in turn implies a possible transformation of the elements of the use value dimension. In other words, ... if [exchange] value were abolished, what was constituted historically as the concrete dimension of capital ... could exist in another form" (1993: 364).

14. Adorno inserts, nearly verbatim, Thesis 5 (where this passage is found) and Thesis 8 into his essay on Aldous Huxley; see "Aldous Huxley and Utopia" (1967b: 109–10). Interestingly, Detlev Claussen (2008: 242–3) reports that in August 1942, Adorno hosted a seminar on needs during which Marcuse initiated a discussion of Huxley's *Brave New World*.

15. On the previous page, however, Adorno denied that a rational society would orient production *exclusively* to the satisfaction of need, while suggesting that scarcity might one day disappear, transforming the relationship between need and satisfaction. Referring to scarcity more than twenty years later, Adorno declares that the natural sciences have brought about the possibility "of worldwide freedom from scarcity" (*ND* 191–2).

16. See also: "in politics debate has long been supplanted by the assertion of power .... Speakers seek to pile up points: there is no conversation that is not infiltrated like a poison by an opportunity to compete. The emotions, which in conversation worthy of human beings were engaged in the subject discussed, are now harnessed to an obstinate insistence on being right, regardless of the relevance of what is said" (*MM* 137).

17. However, in "Critique", Adorno praised the early Marx for endorsing the "ruthless critique of everything existing" (1998b: 282). The translator, Henry Pickford, notes that Adorno was alluding to Marx's 1843 letter to Arnold Ruge: "If we have no business with the construction of the future or with organizing it for all time there can still be no doubt about the task confronting us at present. I mean the *ruthless critique of everything existing*, ruthless in that it will shrink neither from its own discoveries nor from conflict with the powers that be" (*ibid.*: 384 n.6).

18. Adorno argued in "Marginalia to Theory and Praxis" that thinking is already "a

doing", and theory "a form of praxis". Not only is thought always already practical, "an inalienably real mode of behavior in the midst of reality" because it is geared towards self-preservation, but the thinking subject itself is "already also practical" inasmuch as it is objective, embodied, and driven by survival instincts (MTP 261).

19. See also: "Solidarity was once intended to make the talk of brotherhood real .... It was seen in groups of people who together put their lives at stake, counting their own concerns as less important in the face of a tangible possibility, so that, without being possessed by an abstract idea, but also without individual hope, they were ready to sacrifice themselves for each other. The prerequisites for this waiving of self-preservation were knowledge and freedom of decision: if they are lacking, blind particular interest immediately reasserts itself. In the course of time, however, solidarity has turned into the confidence that the Party has a thousand eyes, into enrolment in workers' battalions – long since promoted into uniform – as the stronger side, into swimming with the tide of history" (*MM* 51).

20. Zuidervaart states that he originally made this point in *Adorno's Aesthetic Theory* (1991: 306).

21. In *Late Marxism*, Fredric Jameson wrongly states that Adorno wants to remove "the need for a survival instinct". But he also travesties Adorno's idea of an emancipated individual, claiming that Adorno promoted a utopia of "misfits and oddballs, in which the constraints for uniformization and conformity have been removed, and human beings grow wild like plants in a state of nature: not the beings of Thomas More, ... but rather those of the opening of Altman's *Popeye*, who, no longer fettered by the constraints of a now oppressive sociality, blossom into neurotics, compulsives, obsessives, paranoids, and schizophrenics whom our society considers sick but who, in a world of true freedom, may make up the flora and fauna of 'human nature' itself" (1990: 102). Among other things, Jameson ignores Adorno's desideratum in *Minima Moralia*: "And how comfortless is the thought that the sickness of the normal does not necessarily imply as its opposite the health of the sick, but that the latter usually only present, in a different way, the same disastrous pattern" (*MM* 60). In fact, Adorno's criticism of neuroses as the pillars of late capitalism also refutes Jameson's interpretation.

22. "The realm of freedom only begins ... where that labour which is determined by need and external purposes ceases; it is therefore, by its very nature, outside the sphere of material production proper. Just as the savage must wrestle with Nature in order to satisfy his wants, to maintain and reproduce his life, so also must civilized man, and he must do it in all forms of society and under any possible mode of production. With his development the realm of natural necessity expands because his wants increase; but at the same time the forces of production, by which these wants are satisfied, also increase. Freedom in this field cannot consist of anything else but the fact that socialized mankind, the associated producers, regulate their interchange with nature rationally, bring it under their common control, instead of being ruled by it as by some blind power, and accomplish their task with the least expenditure of energy and under such conditions as are proper and worthy for human beings. Nevertheless, this always remains a realm of necessity. Beyond it begins that other development of human potentiality for its own sake, the true realm of freedom, which however can only flourish upon that realm of necessity

as its basis. The shortening of the workday is its fundamental prerequisite" (Marx 1976b: 873).

23. However, Adorno later calls this image of reconciliation into question: "As long as the world is as it is, all pictures of reconciliation, peace and quiet resemble the picture of death" (*ND* 381). Claussen (2008: 258) also reports that, in a 1956 discussion with Horkheimer, Adorno rejected the idea expressed in *Minima Moralia* that utopia would consist in doing nothing, like other animals (see *MM* 157), claiming that this stage of our evolutionary development can "'no longer be retrieved'".

5. ADORNO AND RADICAL ECOLOGY

1. Naess rejects the terms "mystical union" and "mysticism" in "Identification as a Source of Deep Ecological Attitudes", where he also states that self-realization should "not necessarily be conceived as a mystical state" (1988b: 261). On the following page, however, Naess writes: "In certain forms of mysticism, there is an experience of identification with every life form, using this term in a wide sense. Within the deep ecological movement, poetical and philosophical expressions of such experiences are not uncommon" (*ibid.*: 262). In his "Response to Peder Anker", Naess (1999d: 447) admits that he was strongly influenced by nature mysticism. But in "The Deep Ecology 'Eight Points' Revisited" he adds that "'nature mysticism' (the ultimate unity of all living beings and similar Level I views) has no place among views which supporters may have *in common*" (1995a: 215). Finally, in "Deep Ecology and Ultimate Premises", Naess (1988a: 128) doubts he would be comfortable with philosophical and religious mysticism and denies that he is a mystic.

2. See also: "If mimetic comportment does not imitate something but rather makes itself like itself, this is precisely what artworks take it upon themselves to fulfill" (*AT* 111); and "Artworks are self-likeness freed from the compulsion of identity" (*AT* 125).

3. For Adorno's views on longing (*Sehnsucht*) in artworks, see Chapter 3, note 12.

4. See also: "To represent the mimesis it supplanted, the concept has no other way than to adopt something mimetic in its own comportment. The aesthetic moment is thus not accidental to philosophy ..., but it is no less incumbent upon philosophy to avoid its aestheticism, to sublimate the aesthetic into the real, by cogent insights. Cogency and play are the two poles of philosophy. Its affinity to art does not entitle it to borrow from art .... What the philosophical concept will not abandon is the longing that animates the nonconceptual side of art, and whose fulfillment shuns the immediate side of art as mere appearance" (*ND* 15).

5. Naess positions the eight points within a pyramidal "derivational system", where ecosophical principles, are situated at Level 1, and the points on Level 2. But there are two additional levels in the pyramid: Level 3 "consists of an extensive description of social states of affairs as viewed by environmental interests and represents subsequent concretizations of the principles of the platform in the form of general ... norms of action" (see Anker 1999: 434), and Level 4 comprises "concrete decisions in concrete situations which appear as conclusions from deliberations involving premises at levels 1 to 3" (see Naess 1995b: 78). Since "a decision is derived in

part from details of a particular situation", Level 4 "will always involve premises in addition to those of the upper levels" (see Naess 1988a: 131).

6. For further discussion of beautiful action, see Naess's "Beautiful Action: Its Function in the Ecological Crisis" (1993).

7. In *Theodor W. Adorno: One Last Genius*, Claussen cites a remark Adorno made in a discussion with Horkheimer on theory and praxis: "Philosophy actually exists in order to redeem what is to be found in the gaze of an animal" (2008: 255).

8. Adorno denies that the impulsive aspect of human action makes action irrational on the grounds that impulse ultimately "ends up in the service of the ego principle" (*HF* 237). Conversely, because the ego consists of "libidinous energy that has split off and turned to the testing of reality", it is "not absolutely alien to ... this impulse". For Adorno's reference to Nietzsche, see P 151.

9. "[T]he social aspect of need, as something secondary, may not be separated from the natural aspect of need, as something primary, in order to set up a ranked order of satisfactions. As a natural category, hunger can be allayed with grasshoppers and a meal of gnats which many wild animals consume. Part of the satisfaction of the concrete hunger of civilized people consists in the fact that they get something to eat which does not disgust them – all history is reflected in disgust and its opposite. This is the case with every need" (1972d: 392).

10. Interestingly, Naess claims that existing policies of economic growth do not "*prevent* the growth of identification", while conceding that they render identification "politically powerless". However, the solution for the political impotence of identification seems to involve more identification: identification needs to grow significantly "in the near future" (1988b: 269).

11. This point was made in Chapter 4.

12. In his review of Dorothy Lee's *Freedom and Culture*, published in *American Anthropologist*, David French criticized Lee: the reader has "no way of knowing whether a particular passage really contains a valid insight or not. To illustrate, in more than one paper, [Lee] describes certain non-European peoples as having a profound respect for the integrity or worth of every individual in their group. Consequently, one person does not impose his will upon another; even children are expected to make their own choices in their own way. How can we know, however, that the 'respect' for others is not simply *indifference* to their choices? The essays do not enable one to settle such a question" (1960: 1067–8).

13. Adorno states that Marx and Engels were, "rightly so no doubt", convinced of the "profound historical impotence of anarchism" (*HF* 54–5). However, he does not explain why they were right to consider anarchism impotent.

14. See Bookchin's discussion of this distinction in *From Urbanization to Cities: Toward a New Politics of Citizenship* (1995: 6–7).

15. "[N]owhere in any of my writings do I use the word *superior* to denote humans' relationship to nonhuman beings. That humans differ significantly from nonhuman beings, however, is a fact that even the most naïve mystics are obliged to acknowledge .... [S]ome species are more flexible than others in their ability to adapt and ... they possess more complex nervous systems that endow them with the capability to make more suitable choices from among evolutionary pathways that promote their survival and development. In short, they can be said to be more advanced in dealing with *new* situations than are other, less flexible and less neurologically

developed species. But in no sense does it follow that a more *advanced* life-form will or must *dominate* less advanced life-forms" (Bookchin 1991a: xxxii–xxxiii).

16. See also the translator's note (Adorno 1998a: 346 n.18). Nine years later, in "Critique", Adorno denied that he was "underestimating attempts at effective public critique in Germany". Here he cited again the "fall of a radical right-wing minister of culture" (Franz Leonard Schlüter), which was precipitated by the Göttingen Student Union, as an example of effective critique. He continued: "However, since that solidarity between students and professors does not exist anywhere now the way it did then in Göttingen, it is doubtful whether something similar could happen again today. It looks to me as though the spirit of public critique, after it was monopolized by political groups and thereby became publicly compromised, has suffered severe setbacks; I hope I am mistaken" (1998b: 287).

17. Merchant first discussed the recovery narrative in *Earthcare: Women and the Environment* (1995: 28–53).

18. See, for example, *Earthcare*, where Merchant criticizes "the assaults of production on biological and social reproduction" (1995: 187).

19. In *Adorno and the Political*, Hammer seems to agree with Bernstein, but his account is also problematic: Adorno's idea of intrinsic value does not "appeal to values existing independently of human beings". Rather, Adorno believes that a thing "can, when placed in a relationship of proximity to human beings possessed of a capacity for affection, itself *generate* an ethical demand" (2006: 175).

20. Interestingly, Merchant does not seem to have been aware of *Dialectic of Enlightenment* until 1995, when she cites it in *Earthcare*.

21. Adorno does refer to the language of nature when he writes: "With human means art wants to realize the language of what is not human". Yet, "the language of nature is mute", and art tries to make this muteness eloquent (*AT* 78). Moreover, the "true language of art" is itself "mute" (*AT* 112); this is why art requires philosophy.

22. See also my criticisms of Bernstein in Chapter 2.

23. Zuidervaart notes that the "standard defense of Adorno … is to recall the radicalness of his social critique: it is so radical that it must call into question all existing forms of collectivity and normativity" (2007: 162). Zuidervaart then states, without argument, that this defence cannot be correct. *Contra* Zuidervaart, however, Adorno's extensive empirical and theoretical examination of collective action – from fascism to the student movements of the 1960s – do support his view that we need radically to rethink political praxis. Rather than simply dismissing it, Zuidervaart must show *in what precise respects* Adorno's critique of narcissism and reification (along with other problems afflicting collective action) is mistaken.

24. Some would argue that Adorno is endorsing Hegel here. See, for example, John Russon's *Reading Hegel's Phenomenology*: "In the end the only adequate system of social relations is, on Hegel's account, the one that prescribes that the individual become self-conscious, … that is, conscious of oneself as founded in a 'real' self that is the system of social institutions itself, such that one sees that it is the social system that acts through the singular agents" (2004: 160). To this, however, Adorno would add that self-conscious individuals should alter the social system, making it more rational. To do this, they must act on ideas about what is right and better: ideas derived by negating the social system.

180

CONCLUSION

1. I am quoting Marx's 1843 letter to Arnold Ruge. As I remarked in Chapter 4, note 17, Adorno cites part of this letter in "Critique" (1998b: 282).
2. Adorno stated in a footnote to the section on existentialism in *Negative Dialectics* that "a genuinely critical philosophy's relationship to nominalism is not invariant; it changes historically with the function of skepticism" (*ND* 49 n.). This remark is followed in the German text by a reference to Horkheimer's "Montaigne and the Function of Skepticism" (Adorno 1973b: 59 n.). The English translation of Horkheimer's essay appears in *Between Philosophy and Social Science: Selected Early Writings* (1993).

BIBLIOGRAPHY

WORKS BY ADORNO

Adorno, T. W. 1967a. *Prisms*, S. Weber & S. Weber (trans.). Cambridge, MA: MIT Press.

Adorno, T. W. 1967b. "Aldous Huxley and Utopia". See Adorno (1967a), 95–117.

Adorno, T. W. 1967c. "Cultural Criticism and Society". See Adorno (1967a), 17–34.

Adorno, T. W. 1967d. "Notes on Kafka". See Adorno (1967a), 243–71.

Adorno, T. W. 1967e. "Sociology and Psychology", I. N. Wohlfarth (trans.). *New Left Review* **46**: 67–80.

Adorno, T. W. 1968. "Sociology and Psychology", I. N. Wohlfarth (trans.). *New Left Review* **47**: 79–97.

Adorno, T. W. 1969–70. "Society", F. Jameson (trans.). *Salmagundi* 3(10–11): 144–53.

Adorno, T. W. 1972a. *Soziologische Schriften I* (vol. 8 of *Gesammelte Schriften*). Frankfurt: Suhrkamp.

Adorno, T. W. 1972b. "Individuum und Organisation" [Individual and organization]. See Adorno (1972a), 440–56.

Adorno, T. W. 1972c. "Die Revidierte Psychoanalyse" [Revised psychoanalysis]. See Adorno (1972a), 20–41.

Adorno, T. W. 1972d. "Thesen über Bedürfnis" [Theses on need]. See Adorno (1972a), 392–6.

Adorno, T. W. 1973a. "Der Begriff des Unbewußtsein in der transcendentalen Seelenlehre" [The concept of the unconscious in transcendental psychology]. In *Philosophische Frühschriften* (vol. 1 of *Gesammelte Schriften*), 85–322. Frankfurt: Suhrkamp.

Adorno, T. W. 1973b. *Negative Dialektik*. Frankfurt: Suhrkamp.

Adorno, T. W. 1973c. *Negative Dialectics*, E. B. Ashton (trans.). New York: Continuum.

Adorno, T. W. 1974a. *Minima Moralia: Reflections from Damaged Life*, E. F. N. Jephcott (trans.). London: New Left Books.

Adorno, T. W. 1974b. *Philosophische Terminologie zur Einleitung* [Introduction to philosophical terminology], vol. 2. Frankfurt: Suhrkamp.

Adorno, T. W. *et al.* 1976. *The Positivist Dispute in German Sociology*, G. Adley & D. Frisby (trans.). London: Heinemann.

Adorno, T. W. 1977. "The Actuality of Philosophy", B. Snow (trans.). *Telos* 31: 120–33.

Adorno, T. W. 1978. "Freudian Theory and the Pattern of Fascist Propaganda". In *The Essential Frankfurt School Reader*, A. Arato & E. Gebhardt (trans.), 118–37. New York: Urizon Books.

Adorno, T. W., E. Frenkel-Brunswik, D. J. Levinson *et al*. 1982. *The Authoritarian Personality*, abridged edn. New York: W. W. Norton.

Adorno, T. W. 1986. "Kann das Publikum Wollen?" [Can the public will?]. In *Vermischte Schriften I* (vol. 20 of *Gesammelte Schriften*), 342–7. Frankfurt: Suhrkamp.

Adorno, T. W. 1991. "Trying to Understand *Endgame*". In *Notes to Literature*, vol. 1, S. Weber Nicholsen (trans.), 241–75. New York: Columbia University Press.

Adorno, T. W. 1992. "Toward a Portrait of Thomas Mann". In *Notes to Literature*, vol. 2, S. Weber Nicholsen (trans.), 12–19. New York: Columbia University Press.

Adorno, T. W. 1993a. *Hegel: Three Studies*, S. Weber Nicholsen (trans.). Cambridge, MA: MIT Press.

Adorno, T. W. 1993b. "Theory of Pseudo-Culture", D. Cook (trans.). *Telos* **95**: 15–38.

Adorno, T. W. 1997. *Aesthetic Theory*, R. Hullot-Kentor (trans.). Minneapolis, MN: University of Minnesota Press.

Adorno, T. W. 1998a. *Critical Models: Interventions and Catchwords*, H. W. Pickford (trans.). New York: Columbia University Press.

Adorno, T. W. 1998b. "Critique". See Adorno (1998a), 281–8.

Adorno, T. W. 1998c. "Education after Auschwitz". See Adorno (1998a), 191–204.

Adorno, T. W. 1998d. "Free Time". See Adorno (1998a), 167–75.

Adorno, T. W. 1998e. "Marginalia to Theory and Praxis". See Adorno (1998a), 259–78.

Adorno, T. W. 1998f. "The Meaning of Working Through the Past". See Adorno (1998a), 89–103.

Adorno, T. W. 1998g. "Notes on Philosophical Thinking". See Adorno (1998a), 127–34.

Adorno, T. W. 1998h. "Opinion Delusion Society". See Adorno (1998a), 105–22.

Adorno, T. W. 1998i. "Progress". See Adorno (1998a), 143–65.

Adorno, T. W. 1998j. "On the Question: What is German?" See Adorno (1998a), 205–14.

Adorno, T. W. 1998k. "Reason and Revelation". See Adorno (1998a), 135–42.

Adorno, T. W. 1998l. "Resignation". See Adorno (1998a), 289–93.

Adorno, T. W. 1998m. "On Subject and Object". See Adorno (1998a), 245–58.

Adorno, T. W. 1998n. "Television as Ideology". See Adorno (1998a), 59–70.

Adorno, T. W. 1998o. "Why Still Philosophy". See Adorno (1998a), 5–17.

Adorno, T. W. 2000. *Problems of Moral Philosophy*, R. Livingstone (trans.). Stanford, CA: Stanford University Press.

Adorno, T. W. 2001a. *Kant's "Critique of Pure Reason"*, R. Tiedemann (ed.), R. Livingstone (trans.). Stanford, CA: Stanford University Press.

Adorno, T. W. 2001b. *Metaphysics: Concept and Problems*, E. F. N. Jephcott (trans.). Stanford, CA: Stanford University Press.

Adorno, T. W. 2003a. "Late Capitalism or Industrial Society? The Fundamental Question of the Present Structure of Society", R. Livingstone (trans.). In *Can One Live After Auschwitz? A Philosophical Reader*, 111–25. Stanford, CA: Stanford University Press.

Adorno, T. W. 2003b. "Reflections on Class Theory", R. Livingstone (trans.). In *Can One Live After Auschwitz? A Philosophical Reader*, 93–110. Stanford, CA: Stanford University Press, 2003.

Adorno, T. W. 2006a. *History and Freedom: Lectures 1964–1965*, R. Livingstone (trans.). Cambridge: Polity.

Adorno, T. W. 2006b. "The Idea of Natural-History", R. Hullot-Kentor (trans.). In *Things Beyond Resemblance: Collected Essays on Theodor W. Adorno*, 252–69. New York: Columbia University Press.

Adorno, T. W. 2006c. *Letters to his Parents 1939–1951*, C. Gödde & H. Lonitz (eds), W. Hoban (trans.). Cambridge: Polity.

Adorno, T. W. 2008. *Lectures on "Negative Dialectics": Fragments of a Lecture Course 1965/1966*, R. Livingstone (trans.). Cambridge: Polity.

Horkheimer, M. & T. W. Adorno 1969. *Dialektik der Aufklärung* [Dialectic of Enlightenment]. Frankfurt: S. Fischer.

Horkheimer, M. & T. W. Adorno 1972. *Dialectic of Enlightenment*, J. Cumming (trans.). New York: Continuum.

Horkheimer, M. & T. W. Adorno 2002. *Dialectic of Enlightenment: Philosophical Fragments*, E. Jephcott (trans.). Stanford, CA: Stanford University Press.

SECONDARY WORKS

Anderson, P. 1976. *Considerations on Western Marxism*. London: New Left Books.

Anker, P. 1999. "From Skepticism to Dogmatism and Back: Remarks on the History of Deep Ecology". See Witoszek & Brennan (1999), 431–43.

Ariansen, P. 1999. "Platforms, Nature, and Obligational Values". See Witoszek & Brennan (1999), 420–28.

Bauer, K. 1999. *Adorno's Nietzschean Narratives: Critiques of Ideology, Readings of Wagner*. Albany, NY: SUNY Press.

Beardsworth, S. 2007. "From Nature to Love: The Problem of Subjectivity in Adorno and Freudian Psychoanalysis". *Continental Philosophy Review* **40**(4): 365–87.

Beckett, S. 1958. *Endgame: A Play in One Act*. London: Faber.

Benhabib, S. 1986. *Critique, Norm, and Utopia: A Study of the Foundations of Critical Theory*. New York: Columbia University Press.

Benjamin, W. 1972. "Zum gegenwärtigen gesellschaftlichen Standort des französischen Schriftsteller" [On the current social situation of the French writer]. In *Gesammelte Schriften*, vol. II.2, 776–803. Frankfurt: Suhrkamp Verlag. Originally published in *Zeitschrift für Sozialforschung* 3(1) (1934).

Benjamin, W. 1977. *The Origin of German Tragic Drama*, J. Osbourne (trans.). London: Verso.

Bernstein, J. M. 2001. *Adorno: Disenchantment and Ethics*. Cambridge: Cambridge University Press.

Bernstein, J. M. 2002. "Re-enchanting Nature". In *Reading McDowell on Mind and World*, N. H. Smith (ed.), 217–45. London: Routledge.

Bernstein, J. M. 2004. "Negative Dialectic as Fate: Adorno and Hegel". See Huhn (2004a), 19–50.

Bernstein, J. M. 2005. "Suffering Injustice: Misrecognition as Moral Injury in Critical Theory". *International Journal of Philosophical Studies* **13**(3): 303–24.

Biehl, J. 1997. "Introduction". In *The Murray Bookchin Reader*, J. Biehl (ed.), 172–6. London: Cassell.

Biro, A. 2005. *Denaturalizing Ecological Politics: Alienation From Nature From Rousseau to the Frankfurt School and Beyond*. Toronto: University of Toronto Press.

Bloch, E. 1985. "Etwas fehlt ... Über die Widersprüche der utopischen Sehnsucht" [Something is missing ... on the contradictions in utopian longing]. In *Tendenz-Latenz-Utopie, Ergänzungsband*, 350–68. Frankfurt: Suhrkamp.

Bookchin, M. 1980a. *Toward an Ecological Society*. Montreal: Black Rose Books.

Bookchin, M. 1980b. "The Concept of Ecotechnologies and Ecocommunities". In *Toward an Ecological Society*, 97–112. Montreal: Black Rose Books.

Bookchin, M. 1980c. "An Open Letter to the Ecology Movement". In *Toward an Ecological Society*, 73–83. Montreal: Black Rose Books.

Bookchin, M. 1986. *Post-Scarcity Anarchism*, 2nd edn. Montreal: Black Rose Books.

Bookchin, M. 1990. *The Philosophy of Social Ecology: Essays on Dialectical Materialism*. Montreal: Black Rose Books.

Bookchin, M. 1991a. *The Ecology of Freedom: The Emergence and Dissolution of Hierarchy*, rev. edn. Montreal: Black Rose Books.

Bookchin, M. 1991b. "Ecology and the Left". In *Defending the Earth: A Dialogue between Murray Bookchin and Dave Foreman*, S. Chase (ed.), 47–62. Cambridge, MA: South End Press.

Bookchin, M. 1991c. "Radical Visions and Strategies". In *Defending the Earth: A Dialogue between Murray Bookchin and Dave Foreman*, S. Chase (ed.), 68–86. Cambridge, MA: South End Press.

Bookchin, M. 1995. *From Urbanization to Cities: Toward a New Politics of Citizenship*, rev. edn. London: Cassell.

Bookchin M. 1997. *The Murray Bookchin Reader*, J. Biehl (ed.). London: Cassell.

Bronner, S. E. 1996. *Of Critical Theory and its Theorists*. Oxford: Blackwell.

Buck-Morss, S. 1977. *The Origin of Negative Dialectics: Theodor W. Adorno, Walter Benjamin, and the Frankfurt Institute*. London: Free Press.

Chase, S. (ed.) 1991. *Defending the Earth: A Dialogue between Murray Bookchin and Dave Foreman*. Cambridge, MA: South End Press.

Clark, J. 1993. "Marx's Inorganic Body". In *Environmental Philosophy: From Animal Rights to Radical Biology*, M. Zimmerman (ed.), 390–405. Englewood Cliffs, NJ: Prentice Hall.

Claussen, D. 2008. *Theodor W. Adorno: One Last Genius*, R. Livingstone (trans.). Cambridge, MA: Harvard University Press.

Cook, D. 1996. *The Culture Industry Revisited: Theodor W. Adorno on Mass Culture*. Lanham, MD: Rowman & Littlefield.

Cook, D. 1996–7. "The Rhetoric of Protest: Adorno on the Liberal Democratic Tradition". *Rethinking Marxism* **9**(1): 58–74.

Cook, D. 2000. "Critical Stratagems in Adorno and Habermas: Theories of Ideology and the Ideology of Theory". *Historical Materialism* **6**(1): 67–87.

Cook, D. 2001. "Adorno, Ideology, and Ideology Critique". *Philosophy and Social Criticism* **27**(1): 1–20.

Cook, D. 2003. "Response to [Gordon] Finlayson". *Historical Materialism* **11**(2): 189–98.

Cook, D. 2004a. *Adorno, Habermas, and the Search for a Rational Society*. London: Routledge.

Cook, D. 2004b. "*Ein Reaktionäres Schwein*? Political Activism and Prospects for Change in Adorno". *Revue internationale de Philosophie* **1**(227): 47–67.

Cook, D. 2005. "From the Actual to the Possible: Nonidentity Thinking". *Constellations* **12**(1): 21–35.

Cook, D. 2006. "Staying Alive: Adorno and Habermas on Self-Preservation under Late Capitalism". *Rethinking Marxism* **18**(3): 433–47.

Copleston, F. 1962. *A History of Philosophy, Vol. 1: Greece and Rome, Part 1*, rev. edn. New York: Doubleday.

De Vries, H. 2005. *Minimal Theologies: Critiques of Secular Reason in Adorno and Levinas*, G. Hale (trans.). Baltimore, MD: Johns Hopkins University Press.

Eckersley, R. 1998. "The Death of Nature and the Birth of Ecological Humanities". *Organization and Environment* **11**(2): 183–5.

Finke, S. 2004. "Concepts and Intuitions: Adorno after the Linguistic Turn". In *Theodor W. Adorno*, vol. 1, *Philosophy, Ethics and Critical Theory*, G. Delanty (ed.), 103–33. London: Sage.

Finlayson, G. 2004. "Adorno on the Ethical and the Ineffable". In *Theodor W. Adorno*, vol. 1, *Philosophy, Ethics and Critical Theory*, G. Delanty (ed.), 213–39. London: Sage.

Foster, J. B. 2000. *Marx's Ecology: Materialism and Nature*. New York: Monthly Review Press.

French, D. 1960. Review of Dorothy Lee, *Freedom and Culture*. *American Anthropologist* **62**(6): 1067–8.

Freud, S. 1960. *The Ego and the Id*, J. Riviere (trans.). New York: W. W. Norton.

Freud, S. 1975a. *Civilization and its Discontents*, J. Riviere (trans.). London: Hogarth Press.

Freud, S. 1975b. "Instincts and their Vicissitudes". In *Papers on Metapsychology and Other Works* (vol. 14 of the *Standard Edition of the Complete Works of Sigmund Freud*), J. Strachey (trans.), 111–40. London: Hogarth Press.

Freud, S. 1975c. *"New Introductory Lectures on Psycho-analysis" and Other Works* (vol. 22 of the *Standard Edition of the Complete Works of Sigmund Freud*), J. Strachey (trans.). London: Hogarth Press.

Freud, S. 1985a. "The Future of an Illusion". In *Civilization, Society and Religion* (vol. 12 of the *Penguin Freud Library*), A. Richards (trans.), 183–241. Harmondsworth: Penguin.

Freud, S. 1985b. "Group Psychology and the Analysis of the Ego". In *Civilization, Society and Religion* (vol. 12 of the *Penguin Freud Library*), A. Richards (trans.), 95–178. Harmondsworth: Penguin.

Freyenhagen, F. 2008. "Moral Philosophy". In *Theodor Adorno: Key Concepts*, D. Cook (ed.), 99–114. Stocksfield: Acumen.

Gandesha, S. 2004. "Writing and Judging: Adorno, Arendt and the Chiasmus of Natural History". *Philosophy and Social Criticism* **30**(4): 445–75.

Geuss, R. 2005. "Suffering and Knowledge in Adorno". *Constellations* **12**(1): 3–20.

Habermas, J. 1984. *The Theory of Communicative Action*, vol. 1, *Reason and the Rationalization of Society*, T. McCarthy (trans.). Boston, MA: Beacon Press.

Habermas, J. 1987. *The Philosophical Discourse of Modernity: Twelve Lectures*, F. Lawrence (trans.). Cambridge, MA: MIT Press.

Habermas, J. 1989. *The Structural Transformation of the Public Sphere: An Inquiry into a Category of Bourgeois Society*, T. Burger & F. Lawrence (trans.). Cambridge, MA: MIT Press.

Habermas, J. 1992. "The Unity of Reason in the Diversity of its Voices". In *Postmetaphysical Thinking: Philosophical Essays*, W. M. Hohengarten (trans.), 115–48. Cambridge, MA: MIT Press.

Hacking, I. 1999. *The Social Construction of* What? Cambridge, MA: Harvard University Press.

Hammer, E. 2000. "Minding the World: Adorno's Critique of Idealism". *Philosophy and Social Criticism* **26**(1): 71–92. Reprinted in *Theodor W. Adorno*, vol. 1, *Philosophy, Ethics and Critical Theory*, G. Delanty (ed.), 81–101 (London: Sage, 2004).

Hammer, E. 2006. *Adorno and the Political*. London: Routledge.

Hegel, G. W. F. 1969. *Hegel's Science of Logic*, A. V. Miller (trans.). London: Allen & Unwin.

Hegel, G. W. F. 1970. *Philosophy of Nature*, vol. 1. M. J. Petry (trans.). London: Allen & Unwin.

Hegel, G. W. F. 1971. *Philosophy of Mind*, W. Wallace & A. V. Miller (trans.). Oxford: Oxford University Press.

Hegel, G. W. F. 1977. *Phenomenology of Spirit*, A. V. Miller (trans.). Oxford: Oxford University Press.

Honneth, A. 2005. "A Physiognomy of the Capitalist Form of Life: A Sketch of Adorno's Social Theory", J. Ingram (trans.). *Constellations* **12**(1): 50–64.

Horkheimer, M. 1974. *Eclipse of Reason*. New York: Seabury Press.

Horkheimer, M. 1993. "Montaigne and the Function of Skepticism". In *Between Philosophy and Social Science: Selected Early Writings*, G. F. Hunter, M. S. Kramer, & J. Torpey (trans.), 265–311. Cambridge, MA: MIT Press.

Horowitz, A. 2007. "Mystical Kernels? Rational Shells? Habermas and Adorno on Reification and Re-enchantment". In *Adorno and the Need in Thinking: New Critical Essays*, D. A. Burke, C. J. Campbell, K. Kiloh, M. K. Palamarek & J. Short (eds), 203–17. Toronto: University of Toronto Press.

Huhn, T. (ed.) 2004a. *The Cambridge Companion to Adorno*. Cambridge: Cambridge University Press.

Huhn, T. 2004b. "Introduction: Thoughts Beside Themselves". See Huhn (2004a), 1–18.

Hullot-Kentor, R. 2006. *Things Beyond Resemblance: Collected Essays on Theodor W. Adorno*. New York: Columbia University Press.

Husserl, E. 1970. *The Crisis of European Sciences and Transcendental Phenomenology*, D. Carr (trans.). Evanston, IL: Northwestern University Press.

Jaeggi, R. 2005. "'No Individual Can Resist': *Minima Moralia* as Critique of Forms of Life", J. Ingram (trans.). *Constellations* **12**(1): 65–82.

Jameson, F. 1990. *Late Marxism: Adorno, or, the Persistence of the Dialectic*. New York: Verso.

Jarvis, S. 1998. *Adorno: A Critical Introduction*. New York: Routledge.

Jarvis, S. 2004. "What is Speculative Thinking?" *Revue internationale de Philosophie* **1**(227): 69–84.

Jay, M. 1984. *Adorno*. London: Fontana.

Kant, I. 1929. *Critique of Pure Reason*, N. Kemp Smith (trans.). New York: St Martin's Press.

Kant, I. 1971. "Idea for a Universal History with a Cosmopolitan Purpose". In *Kant's Political Writings*, H. Reiss (ed.), H. B. Nisbet (trans.), 41–53. Cambridge: Cambridge University Press.

Kaufmann, D. 2004. "Correlations, Constellations and the Truth: Adorno's Ontology of Redemption". In *Theodor W. Adorno*, vol. 1, *Philosophy, Ethics and Critical Theory*, G. Delanty (ed.), 163–81. London: Sage.

Leiss, W. 1994. *The Domination of Nature*. Montreal: McGill-Queen's University Press.

Lukács, G. 1971. *History and Class Consciousness: Studies in Marxist Dialectics*. R. Livingstone (trans.). Cambridge, MA: MIT Press.

Marcuse, H. 1964. *One-Dimensional Man: Studies in the Ideology of Advanced Industrial Society*. Boston, MA: Beacon Press.

Marcuse, H. 1999. *Reason and Revolution: Hegel and the Rise of Social Theory*. New York: Humanity Books.

Marx, K. 1957. *Grundrisse der Kritik der politischen Ökonomie*. Berlin: Dietz.

Marx, K. 1964. *Economic and Philosophic Manuscripts of 1844*, M. Mulligan (trans.). New York: International Publishers.

Marx, K. 1973. *Grundrisse: Foundations of the Critique of Political Economy*. M. Nicolaus (trans.). New York: Vintage Books.

Marx, K. 1976a. *Capital*, vol. 1, *A Critique of Political Economy*, B. Fowkes (trans.). New York: Vintage Books.

Marx, K. 1976b. *Capital*, vol. 3, *The Process of Capitalist Production as a Whole*, B. Fowkes (trans.). Harmondsworth: Penguin.

Marx, K. & F. Engels 1932. *Die Deutsche Ideologie*. In *Marx–Engels Gesamtausgabe*, vol. 5. Berlin: Marx–Engels Verlag.

Marx, K. & F. Engels 1970. *The German Ideology, Part One with Selections from Parts Two and Three, together with Marx's "Introduction to a Critique of Political Economy"*, W. Lough, C. Dutt & C. P. Magill (trans.). New York: International Publishers.

Marx, K. & F. Engels 1976. *Collected Works*, vol. 5, W. Lough, C. Dutt & C. P. Magill (trans.). London: Lawrence & Wishart.

McDowell, J. 1994. *Mind and World*. Cambridge, MA: Harvard University Press.

McLaughlin, A. 1995. "The Heart of Deep Ecology". See Sessions (1995), 85–93.

Merchant, C. 1980. *The Death of Nature: Women, Ecology, and the Scientific Revolution*. San Francisco, CA: Harper & Row.

Merchant, C. 1989. *Ecological Revolutions: Nature, Gender, and Science in New England*. Chapel Hill, NC: University of North Carolina Press.

Merchant, C. 1992. *Radical Ecology: The Search for a Livable World*. London: Routledge.

Merchant, C. 1995. *Earthcare: Women and the Environment*. New York: Routledge.

Merchant, C. 2003. *Reinventing Eden: The Fate of Nature in Western Culture*. London: Routledge.

Moss, L. 2010. "Science, Normativity, and Skill: Reviewing and Renewing the Anthropological Basis of Critical Theory". Unpublished paper presented at Loyola University, Rome campus, July.

Müller-Doohm S. 2005 *Adorno: A Biography*, R. Livingstone (trans.). Cambridge: Polity.

Naess, A. 1986. "Intrinsic Value: Will the Defenders of Nature Please Rise?" In *Conservation Biology: The Science of Scarcity and Diversity*, M. E. Soulé (ed.), 504–15. Sunderland, MA: Sinauer Associates.

Naess, A. 1988a. "Deep Ecology and Ultimate Premises". *Ecologist* **18**(4–5): 128–31.

Naess, A. 1988b. "Identification as a Source of Deep Ecological Attitudes". In *Deep Ecology*, M. Tobias (ed.), rev. edn, 256–70. San Marcos, CA: Avant Books.

Naess, A. 1989. *Ecology, Community and Lifestyle: Outline of an Ecosophy*, D. Rothenberg (trans.). Cambridge: Cambridge University Press.

Naess, A. 1993. "Beautiful Action: Its Function in the Ecological Crisis". *Environmental Values* **2**(1): 67–71.

Naess, A. 1995a. "The Deep Ecology 'Eight Points' Revisited". See Sessions (1995), 213–21.

Naess, A. 1995b. "The Deep Ecological Movement". See Sessions (1995), 64–84.

Naess, A. 1995c. "Deepness of Questions and the Deep Ecology Movement". See Sessions (1995), 204–12.

Naess, A. 1995d. "The Place of Joy in a World of Fact". See Sessions (1995), 249–58.

Naess, A. 1995e. "Politics and the Ecological Crisis". See Sessions (1995), 445–53.

Naess, A. 1995f. "Self-Realization". See Sessions (1995), 225–39.

Naess, A. 1999a. "The Deep Ecology Platform". See Witoszek & Brennan (1999), 8–9.

Naess, A. 1999b. "'Man Apart' and Deep Ecology: A Reply to Reed". See Witoszek & Brennan (1999), 198–205.

Naess, A. 1999c. "Response to Jon Wetlesen". See Witoszek & Brennan (1999), 418–19.

Naess, A. 1999d. "Response to Peder Anker". See Witoszek & Brennan (1999), 444–50.

Naess, A. & S. Bodian 1995. "Simple in Means, Rich in Ends: An Interview with Arne Naess". See Sessions (1995), 26–36.

Naess, A., A. Ayer & F. Elder 1999. "The Glass is on the Table: The Empiricist versus Total View". See Witoszek & Brennan (1999), 10–28.

Nietzsche, F. 1982a. *Thus Spoke Zarathustra*. In *The Portable Nietzsche*, W. Kaufmann (trans.), 121–439. New York: Penguin.

Nietzsche, F. 1982b. *Twilight of the Idols*. In *The Portable Nietzsche*, W. Kaufmann (trans.), 466–563. New York: Penguin.

O'Connor, B. 2004. *Adorno's Negative Dialectic: Philosophy and the Possibility of Critical Rationality*. Cambridge, MA: MIT Press.

Plumwood, V. 1999. "Comment: Self-Realization or Man Apart? The Reed–Naess Debate". See Witoszek & Brennan (1999), 206–10.

Postone, M. 1993. *Time, Labor, and Social Domination: A Reinterpretation of Marx's Critical Theory*. Cambridge: Cambridge University Press.

Pritchard, E. A. 2004. "*Bilderverbot* meets Body in Adorno's Inverse Theology". *Theodor W. Adorno*, vol. 1, *Philosophy, Ethics and Critical Theory*, G. Delanty (ed.), 184–211. London: Sage.

Rose, G. 1978. *The Melancholy Science: An Introduction to the Thought of Theodor W. Adorno*. New York: Columbia University Press.

Rosiek, J. 2000. *Maintaining the Sublime: Heidegger and Adorno*. New York: Peter Lang.

Russon, J. 2004. *Reading Hegel's Phenomenology*. Bloomington, IN: Indiana University Press.

Schmidt, A. 1971. *The Concept of Nature in Marx*, B. Fowkes (trans.). London: New Left Books.

Schmidt, J. 1998. "Language, Mythology, and Enlightenment: Historical Notes on Horkheimer's and Adorno's *Dialectic of Enlightenment*". *Social Research* **65**(4): 807–38.

Schnädelbach, H. 2007. "The Dialectical Critique of Reason: Adorno's Reconstruction of Rationality". In *Theodor Adorno: Critical Evaluations in Cultural Theory*, vol. 4, S. Jarvis (ed.), N. Walker (trans.), 155–77. New York: Routledge.

Schweppenhäuser, G. 2003. *Theodor W. Adorno zur Einführung*, rev. edn. Hamburg: Junius Verlag.

Schweppenhäuser, G. 2009. *Theodor W. Adorno: An Introduction*, J. Rolleston (trans.). Durham, NC: Duke University Press.

Searle, J. 1992. *The Rediscovery of the Mind*. Cambridge, MA: MIT Press.

Searle, J. 2007. *Freedom and Neurobiology: Reflections on Free Will, Language, and Political Power*. New York: Columbia University Press.

Sessions, G. (ed.) 1995. *Deep Ecology for the Twenty-First Century*. London: Shambhala Publications.

Sherratt, Y. 2002. *Adorno's Positive Dialectic*. Cambridge: Cambridge University Press.

Short, J. 2007. "Experience and Aura: Adorno, McDowell, and 'Second Nature'". In *Adorno and the Need in Thinking: New Critical Essays*, D. A. Burke, C. J. Campbell, K. Kiloh, M. K. Palamarek & J. Short (eds), 181–200. Toronto: University of Toronto Press.

Sloterdijk, P. 1987. *Critique of Cynical Reason*, M. Eldred (trans.). Minneapolis, MN: University of Minnesota Press.

Smith, N. H. (ed.) 2002. *Reading McDowell on Mind and World*. London: Routledge.

Soper, K. 1979. "Marxism, Materialism and Biology". In *Issues in Marxist Philosophy*, vol. 2, *Materialism*, J. Mepham & D.-H. Ruben (eds), 61–100. New York: Humanities Press.

Soper, K. 1995. *What is Nature? Culture, Politics and the Nonhuman*. Oxford: Blackwell.

Stewart, I. 1989. *Does God Play Dice? The Mathematics of Chaos*. Oxford: Blackwell.

Stone, A. 2006. "Adorno and the Disenchantment of Nature". *Philosophy and Social Criticism* **32**(2): 231–53.

Stone, A. 2008. "Adorno and Logic". In *Theodor Adorno: Key Concepts*, D. Cook (ed.), 47–62. Stocksfield: Acumen.

Testa, I. 2007. "Criticism from within Nature: The Dialectic between First and Second Nature from McDowell to Adorno". *Philosophy and Social Criticism* **33**(4): 473–97.

Theunissen, M. 1983. "Negativität bei Adorno" [Negativity in Adorno]. In *Adorno-Konferenz, 1983*, 41–65. Frankfurt: Suhrkamp. Published in English as "Negativity in Adorno", N. Walker (trans.). In *Theodor Adorno: Critical Evaluations in Cultural Theory*, 178–98, S. Jarvis (ed.) (London: Routledge, 2007).

Thyen, A. 1989. *Negative Dialektik und Erfahrung: Zur Rationalität des Nichtidentischen bei Adorno* [Negative dialectics and experience: On the rationality of the nonidentical in Adorno]. Frankfurt: Suhrkamp.

Thyen, A. 2007. "Dimensions of the Nonidentical", N. Walker (trans.). In *Theodor Adorno: Critical Evaluations in Cultural Theory*, vol. 4. S. Jarvis (ed.), 199–220. New York: Routledge.

Timpanaro, S. 1975. *On Materialism*, L. Garner (trans). London: New Left Books.

Tucker, R. 1967. *Philosophy and Myth in Karl Marx*. Cambridge: Cambridge University Press.

Vaki, F. 2005. "Adorno *contra* Habermas and the Claims of Critical Theory as Immanent Critique". *Historical Materialism* **13**(4): 79–120.

Vogel, S. 1996. *Against Nature: The Concept of Nature in Critical Theory*. Albany, NY: SUNY Press.

Weber, M. 1930. *The Protestant Ethic and the Spirit of Capitalism*, T. Parsons (trans.). London: Unwin Hyman.

Weber, M. 1949. "Objectivity in Social Science and Social Policy". In *Max Weber on the Methodology of the Social Sciences*, E. A. Shils & H. A. Finch (trans.), 49–112. Glencoe, IL: Free Press.

Wetlesen, J. 1999. "Value in Nature: Intrinsic or Inherent?" See Witoszek & Brennan (1999), 405–17.

Whitebook, J. 1995. *Perversion and Utopia: A Study in Psychoanalysis and Critical Theory*. Cambridge, MA: MIT Press.

Whitebook, J. 2004a. "The Marriage of Marx and Freud: Critical Theory and Psychoanalysis". In *The Cambridge Companion to Critical Theory*, F. Rush (ed.), 74–102. Cambridge: Cambridge University Press.

Whitebook, J. 2004b. "The *Urgeschichte* of Subjectivity Reconsidered". In *Theodor W. Adorno*, vol. 3, *Social Theory and the Critique of Modernity*, G. Delanty (ed.), 91–105. London: Sage.

Whitebook, J. 2004c. "Weighty Objects: On Adorno's Kant–Freud Interpretation". See Huhn (2004a), 51–78.

Witoszek, N. & A. Brennan (eds) 1999. *Philosophical Dialogues: Arne Naess and the Progress of Ecophilosophy*. Lanham, MD: Rowman & Littlefield.

Zuidervaart, L. 1991. *Adorno's Aesthetic Theory: The Redemption of Illusion*. Cambridge, MA: MIT Press.

Zuidervaart, L. 2007. *Social Philosophy after Adorno*. Cambridge: Cambridge University Press.

INDEX